EASTERN EUROPE

OPPOSING VIEWPOINTS®

EASTERN EUROPE

OPPOSING VIEWPOINTS®

David Bender & Bruno Leone, *Series Editors*

Janelle Rohr, *Book Editor*

OPPOSING VIEWPOINTS SERIES ®

Greenhaven Press, Inc.   PO Box 289009   San Diego, CA 92198-0009

Library of Congress Cataloging-in-Publication Data

Eastern Europe : opposing viewpoints / Janelle Rohr, book editor.
    p. cm. — (Opposing viewpoints series)
  Includes bibliographical references and index.
  Summary: Presents opposing viewpoints on the division of Europe, the effects of recent revolutions in Eastern Europe, economic policies Eastern Europe should adopt, the impact of German unification, and the possibility of a united Europe.
  ISBN 0-89908-480-X (lib.). — ISBN 0-89908-455-9 (pap.)
  1. Europe, Eastern—Politics and government—1989- 2. Europe, Eastern—Economic policy. 3. German reunification question (1949-   ) 4. European federation. [1. Europe, Eastern. 2. German reunification question (1949-   ) 3. European federation.]
  I. Rohr, Janelle, 1963-   . II. Series: Opposing viewpoints series (Unnumbered)
  DJK51.E27 1990
  947—dc20   90-44330
                                                                   CIP
                                                                    AC

"Congress shall make no law . . .
abridging the freedom of speech,
or of the press."

First Amendment to the U.S. Constitution

The basic foundation of our democracy is the first amendment
guarantee of freedom of expression. The Opposing Viewpoints
Series is dedicated to the concept of this basic freedom and the
idea that it is more important to practice it than to enshrine it.

Contents

Why Consider Opposing Viewpoints?

The Importance of Examining Opposing Viewpoints

The purpose of the Opposing Viewpoints Series, and this book in particular, is to present balanced, and often difficult to find, opposing points of view on complex and sensitive issues.

Probably the best way to become informed is to analyze the positions of those who are regarded as experts and well studied on issues. It is important to consider every variety of opinion in an attempt to determine the truth. Opinions from the mainstream of society should be examined. But also important are opinions that are considered radical, reactionary, or minority as well as those stigmatized by some other uncomplimentary label. An important lesson of history is the eventual acceptance of many unpopular and even despised opinions. The ideas of Socrates, Jesus, and Galileo are good examples of this.

Readers will approach this book with their own opinions on the issues debated within it. However, to have a good grasp of one's own viewpoint, it is necessary to understand the arguments of those with whom one disagrees. It can be said that those who do not completely understand their adversary's point of view do not fully understand their own.

A persuasive case for considering opposing viewpoints has been presented by John Stuart Mill in his work *On Liberty*. When examining controversial issues it may be helpful to reflect on this suggestion:

9

The only way in which a human being can make some approach to knowing the whole of a subject, is by hearing what can be said about it by persons of every variety of opinion, and studying all modes in which it can be looked at by every character of mind. No wise man ever acquired his wisdom in any mode but this.

Analyzing Sources of Information

The Opposing Viewpoints Series includes diverse materials taken from magazines, journals, books, and newspapers, as well as statements and position papers from a wide range of individuals, organizations, and governments. This broad spectrum of sources helps to develop patterns of thinking which are open to the consideration of a variety of opinions.

Pitfalls to Avoid

A pitfall to avoid in considering opposing points of view is that of regarding one's own opinion as being common sense and the most rational stance, and the point of view of others as being only opinion and naturally wrong. It may be that another's opinion is correct and one's own is in error.

Another pitfall to avoid is that of closing one's mind to the opinions of those with whom one disagrees. The best way to approach a dialogue is to make one's primary purpose that of understanding the mind and arguments of the other person and not that of enlightening him or her with one's own solutions. More can be learned by listening than speaking.

It is my hope that after reading this book the reader will have a deeper understanding of the issues debated and will appreciate the complexity of even seemingly simple issues on which good and honest people disagree. This awareness is particularly important in a democratic society such as ours where people enter into public debate to determine the common good. Those with whom one disagrees should not necessarily be regarded as enemies, but perhaps simply as people who suggest different paths to a common goal.

Developing Basic Reading and Thinking Skills

In this book, carefully edited opposing viewpoints are purposely placed back to back to create a running debate; each viewpoint is preceded by a short quotation that best expresses the author's main argument. This format instantly plunges the reader into the midst of a controversial issue and greatly aids that reader in mastering the basic skill of recognizing an author's point of view.

A number of basic skills for critical thinking are practiced in the activities that appear throughout the books in the series. Some of the skills are:

Evaluating Sources of Information. The ability to choose from among alternative sources the most reliable and accurate source in relation to a given subject.

Separating Fact from Opinion. The ability to make the basic distinction between factual statements (those that can be demonstrated or verified empirically) and statements of opinion (those that are beliefs or attitudes that cannot be proved).

Identifying Stereotypes. The ability to identify oversimplified, exaggerated descriptions (favorable or unfavorable) about people and insulting statements about racial, religious, or national groups, based upon misinformation or lack of information.

Recognizing Ethnocentrism. The ability to recognize attitudes or opinions that express the view that one's own race, culture, or group is inherently superior, or those attitudes that judge another culture or group in terms of one's own.

It is important to consider opposing viewpoints and equally important to be able to critically analyze those viewpoints. The activities in this book are designed to help the reader master these thinking skills. Statements are taken from the book's viewpoints and the reader is asked to analyze them. This technique aids the reader in developing skills that not only can be applied to the viewpoints in this book, but also to situations where opinionated spokespersons comment on controversial issues. Although the activities are helpful to the solitary reader, they are most useful when the reader can benefit from the interaction of group discussion.

Using this book and others in the series should help readers develop basic reading and thinking skills. These skills should improve the reader's ability to understand what is read. Readers should be better able to separate fact from opinion, substance from rhetoric, and become better consumers of information in our media-centered culture.

This volume of the Opposing Viewpoints Series does not advocate a particular point of view. Quite the contrary! The very nature of the book leaves it to the reader to formulate the opinions he or she finds most suitable. My purpose as publisher is to see that this is made possible by offering a wide range of viewpoints that are fairly presented.

David L. Bender
Publisher

Introduction

"The most difficult questions, the great unknowns, lie in the eastern rather than the western half of the old continent."

Timothy Garton Ash, *The Spectator,* January 6, 1990.

In 1989, when first the Poles, then the Hungarians, the East Germans, the Czechs, the Bulgarians, and finally the Romanians deposed Communist rulers in their countries, many people around the world rejoiced. Five of the six revolutions were peacefully accomplished with little or no bloodshed. The peoples of Eastern Europe, long subjugated by mightier nations, at last seemed to be seizing the right to determine their own futures. One of the lessons many drew from these revolutions was the power of nationalism—the yearning for national independence among peoples ruled by foreign powers.

Nationalism has more often been a force for conflict than for peace and stability. Nationalism, for example, was a prime catalyst sparking World War I. Some observers have now begun to suggest that the same tensions which at the century's beginning embroiled Europe in that long and destructive war are again present at century's end in Eastern Europe.

At the beginning of the century, much of Eastern Europe was dominated by the Austro-Hungarian Empire, a sprawling territory that included the present-day nations of Austria, Hungary, Czechoslovakia, and parts of Poland, the Soviet Union, Romania, Yugoslavia, and Italy. There were over fifty million people in the Austro-Hungarian Empire, less than half of whom were either Austrian or Hungarian. The others, representing a variety of ethnic backgrounds, had one thing in common: They resented and resisted Austro-Hungarian control. World War I began when a Serbian nationalist assassinated the heir to the throne of Austria-Hungary.

When World War I ended, the Austro-Hungarian Empire was dissolved. Diplomats met at the French palace of Versailles to agree on a peace treaty. The goal of some diplomats was to grant self-determination to ethnic groups when possible. The Versailles participants redrew the map of Europe. They joined the Czechs and Slovaks into one nation; granted the Poles self-rule; and joined several ethnic groups, including the Serbians, to form the new country of Yugoslavia. In some regions, however, a settle-

13

ment satisfactory to most people was impossible. Transylvania, for example, had long been populated and contested by both ethnic Hungarians and Romanians. It was impossible to definitively answer who had the greater claim to the land, according to author Robert R. King. In this situation, Transylvania was given to the Romanians, rather than the Hungarians, because Romania had been on the winning side of the war.

Robert D. Kaplan, an author and journalist, argues that now, at century's end, Europe is haunted by historic nationalist conflicts never effectively addressed. During the 1980s, Kaplan states, ethnic Hungarians fled Transylvania, complaining that the Romanians mistreated them. Yugoslavia suffers from frequent ethnic riots, often between Serbians and the Albanian minority in the region of Kosovo. And for several years, Bulgaria has forced its Turkish minority to either drop their Turkish identity and take Bulgarian names or be deported. American Enterprise Institute researcher Benjamin Frankel fears that Europe may become "a continent again awash in conflict, populated by mistrustful nations, long on memories, short on forgiving and forgetting." He and other observers argue that Eastern Europe lacks a tradition of tolerating others, thus making future nationalist struggles likely.

Historian Gaddis Smith is one of many, however, who points to important differences between Eastern Europe at the turn of the century and Eastern Europe today. First, at the turn of the century there was no Poland, Czechoslovakia, independent Hungary, or Yugoslavia, and the borders of Romania and Bulgaria were in flux. "Conditions now are less volatile," Smith argues, because the borders have been stable for decades. This makes it less likely that any of these countries would fight over regional borders. Second, the statements of Eastern European leaders such as Czech president Vaclav Havel offer reason for optimism. Havel hopes that Europe will become "a community of many different but equal people who will . . . show empathy and tolerance to all other communities." Such statements have led many people to believe that Eastern Europe has at last transcended the legacy of its violent past.

While many argue that it is pivotal, nationalism is just one issue that makes the study of Eastern Europe important. The viewpoints in *Eastern Europe: Opposing Viewpoints* address many significant topics. The questions debated are Historical Chapter: What Led to the Division of Europe? Do Eastern European Revolutions Signal the Demise of Communism? What Economic Policies Should Eastern Europe Adopt? How Will a United Germany Affect Europe? Is European Unification Possible? Whether the national yearnings of Eastern Europeans can at last be satisfied without the bitterness and discord of earlier decades in this century is a topic that will inspire continued debate and reflection.

CHAPTER 1

Historical Debate: What Led to the Division of Europe?

EASTERN EUROPE

Chapter Preface

Although the nations of Eastern Europe contain diverse peoples and traditions, these countries share a common experience: they have often been subject to the will of larger, more powerful countries.

World War II had a devastating impact on Eastern Europe because this region was directly in the path of two ambitious countries—Nazi Germany and the Soviet Union. Nazi ruler Adolf Hitler began to encroach on Eastern Europe in 1938 when he demanded and got the Sudetenland region of Czechoslovakia. He later established control of the country as a whole. In 1939, Hitler's troops overran Poland, thus beginning World War II. Hitler continued to pressure other Eastern European countries until they signed alliances with him. His troops invaded those that resisted. By the spring of 1941, Eastern Europe was completely subject to German rule—Hitler's troops controlled all the land between Germany and the Soviet border. At this point, Hitler invaded the Soviet Union. Although German armies advanced deep into the Soviet Union, the invasion was ultimately repulsed. By 1945, Eastern Europe had been liberated from Nazi control but was now subject to Soviet control.

Eastern Europe's fate was discussed at the February 1945 Yalta conference. U.S. president Franklin Roosevelt, British prime minister Winston Churchill, and Soviet ruler Josef Stalin agreed upon "the right of all peoples to choose the form of government under which they will live." These leaders jointly declared that they would help "the peoples liberated from the domination of Nazi Germany, and the peoples of the former Axis satellite States of Europe to solve by democratic means their pressing political and economic problems." But this declaration set up no specific plan to ensure self-determination for Eastern Europe. The presence of Stalin's troops, not the vague Yalta agreement, determined the region's future.

The viewpoints in the following chapter address events occurring shortly after the end of World War II. They help to explain why, after suffering six brutal years of war, Eastern Europe once again was subject to the control of a powerful nation.

"From Stettin in the Baltic to Trieste in the Adriatic, an iron curtain has descended across the Continent."

Soviet Tyranny Divides Europe (1946)

Winston Churchill

Winston Churchill (1874-1965) was a prominent English journalist before becoming a member of Parliament in 1900. He became Britain's prime minister in 1940, months after war had broken out with Nazi Germany. In 1953 he won the Nobel Prize for Literature both for his writing and for his stirring orations. The following viewpoint is an excerpt from one of Churchill's most famous speeches. Addressing an audience at Westminster College in Fulton, Missouri in 1946, he warns that the Soviet Union is interfering in the countries of Eastern Europe, strengthening the Communist parties there, and preventing democracy.

As you read, consider the following questions:

1. Now that America is preeminent in world power and influence, according to Churchill, what are its duties?
2. What events are behind the author's alarm about Soviet intentions?
3. How can the Soviet Union's expansionist tendencies be curbed, in the author's view?

Winston Churchill, "Alliance of English-Speaking People," speech given at Westminster College, Fulton, Missouri, March 15, 1946.

The United States stands at this time at the pinnacle of world power. It is a solemn moment for the American Democracy. For with primacy in power is also joined an awe-inspiring accountability to the future. If you look around you, you must feel not only the sense of duty done but also you must feel anxiety lest you fall below the level of achievement. Opportunity is here now, clear and shining for both our countries. To reject it or ignore it or fritter it away will bring upon us all the long reproaches of the after-time. It is necessary that constancy of mind, persistency of purpose and the grand simplicity of decision shall guide and rule the conduct of the English-speaking peoples in peace as they did in war. We must, and I believe we shall, prove ourselves equal to this severe requirement.

Guaranteeing Safety for All

When American military men approach some serious situation they are wont to write at the head of their directive the words 'overall strategic concept'. There is wisdom in this, as it leads to clarity of thought. What then is the overall strategic concept which we should inscribe today? It is nothing less than the safety and welfare, the freedom and progress, of all the homes and families of all the men and women in all the lands. And here I speak particularly of the myriad cottage or apartment homes where the wage-earner strives amid the accidents and difficulties of life to guard his wife and children from privation and bring the family up in the fear of the Lord, or upon ethical conceptions which often play their potent part.

To give security to these countless homes, they must be shielded from the two giant marauders, war and tyranny. We all know the frightful disturbances in which the ordinary family is plunged when the curse of war swoops down upon the breadwinner and those for whom he works and contrives. The awful ruin of Europe, with all its vanished glories, and of large parts of Asia glares us in the eyes. When the designs of wicked men or the aggressive urge of mighty States dissolve over large areas the frame of civilized society, humble folk are confronted with difficulties with which they cannot cope. For them all is distorted, all is broken, even ground to pulp.

When I stand here this quiet afternoon I shudder to visualize what is actually happening to millions now and what is going to happen in this period when famine stalks the earth. None can compute what has been called 'the unestimated sum of human pain'. Our supreme task and duty is to guard the homes of the common people from the horrors and miseries of another war. We are all agreed on that. . . .

Changes in Europe After World War II

Territorial Changes After World War II

Notes: — The United States, British, and French Zones of Germany merged in 1949 as the Federal Republic of Germany.
— The Russian Zone of Germany became the German Democratic Republic in 1949.
— The four zones of Austria merged in 1955 to become the Federal Republic of Austria.

Reprinted by permission of the publisher, from *American Foreign Policy*, edited by Thomas G. Paterson, J. Garry Clifford, and Kenneth J. Hagan. Lexington, Mass.: D.C. Heath and Company, © 1983, D.C. Heath and Company.

Now I come to the second danger of these two marauders which threatens the cottage, the home, and the ordinary people—namely, tyranny. We cannot be blind to the fact that the liberties enjoyed by individual citizens throughout the British Empire are not valid in a considerable number of countries, some of which are very powerful. In these States control is enforced upon the common people by various kinds of all-embracing police governments. The power of the State is exercised without restraint, either by dictators or by compact oligarchies operating through a privileged party and a political police. It is not our duty at this time when difficulties are so numerous to interfere forcibly in the internal affairs of countries which we have not conquered in war. But we must never cease to proclaim in fearless tones the great principles of freedom and the rights of man which are the joint inheritance of the English-speaking world and which through Magna Carta, the Bill of Rights, the Habeas Corpus, trial by jury, and the English common law find their most famous expression in the American Declaration of Independence.

All this means that the people of any country have the right, and should have the power by constitutional action, by free unfettered elections, with secret ballot, to choose or change the character or form of government under which they dwell; that freedom of speech and thought should reign; that courts of justice, independent of the executive, unbiased by any party, should administer laws which have received the broad assent of large majorities or are consecrated by time and custom. Here are the title deeds of freedom which should lie in every cottage home. Here is the message of the British and American peoples to mankind. Let us preach what we practise—let us practise what we preach. . . .

A Shadow Has Fallen

A shadow has fallen upon the scenes so lately lighted by the Allied victory. Nobody knows what Soviet Russia and its Communist international organization intends to do in the immediate future, or what are the limits, if any, to their expansive and proselytizing tendencies. I have a strong admiration and regard for the valiant Russian people and for my wartime comrade, Marshal Stalin. There is deep sympathy and goodwill in Britain—and I doubt not here also—towards the peoples of all the Russias and a resolve to persevere through many differences and rebuffs in establishing lasting friendships. We understand the Russian need to be secure on her western frontiers by the removal of all possibility of German aggression. We welcome Russia to her rightful place among the leading nations of the world. We welcome her flag upon the seas. Above all, we welcome constant, frequent and growing contacts between the Russian people and our own people on both sides of the Atlantic. It is my duty, however, for I am sure you would wish me to state the facts as I see them to you, to place before you certain facts about the present position in Europe.

An Iron Curtain Has Descended

From Stettin in the Baltic to Trieste in the Adriatic, an iron curtain has descended across the Continent. Behind that line lie all the capitals of the ancient states of Central and Eastern Europe. Warsaw, Berlin, Prague, Vienna, Budapest, Belgrade, Bucharest and Sofia, all these famous cities and the populations around them lie in what I must call the Soviet sphere, and all are subject in one form or another, not only to Soviet influence but to a very high and, in many cases, increasing measure of control from Moscow. Athens alone—Greece with its immortal glories—is free to decide its future at an election under British, American and French observation. The Russian-dominated Polish Government has been encouraged to make enormous and wrongful inroads upon Germany, and mass expulsions of millions of Germans on a scale grievous and undreamed-of are now taking place. The Communist parties, which were very small in all these Eastern States of Europe, have been raised to pre-eminence and power far beyond their numbers and are seeking everywhere to obtain totalitarian control. Police governments are prevailing in nearly every case, and so far, except in Czechoslovakia, there is no true democracy.

Coercion and Subterfuge

The peoples of a number of countries of the world have recently had totalitarian regimes forced upon them against their will. The Government of the United States has made frequent protests against coercion and intimidation, in violation of the Yalta agreement, in Poland, Rumania, and Bulgaria. . . .

The world is not static, and the *status quo* is not sacred. But we cannot allow changes in the *status quo* in violation of the Charter of the United Nations by such methods as coercion, or by such subterfuges as political infiltration.

Harry Truman, Special Message to the Congress, March 12, 1947.

Turkey and Persia [Iran] are both profoundly alarmed and disturbed at the claims which are being made upon them and at the pressure being exerted by the Moscow Government. An attempt is being made by the Russians in Berlin to build up a quasi-Communist party in their zone of Occupied Germany by showing special favours to groups of left-wing German leaders. At the end of the fighting in June 1945, the American and British Armies withdrew westwards, in accordance with an earlier agreement, to a depth at some points of 150 miles upon a front of nearly four hundred miles, in order to allow our Russian allies to occupy this vast expanse of territory which the Western Democracies had conquered.

If now the Soviet Government tries, by separate action, to build up a pro-Communist Germany in their areas, this will cause new serious difficulties in the British and American zones, and will give the defeated Germans the power of putting themselves up to auction between the Soviets and the Western Democracies. Whatever conclusions may be drawn from these facts—and facts they are—this is certainly not the Liberated Europe we fought to build up. Nor is it one which contains the essentials of permanent peace.

Unity in Europe Is Needed

The safety of the world requires a new unity in Europe, from which no nation should be permanently outcast. It is from the quarrels of the strong parent races in Europe that the world wars we have witnessed, or which occurred in former times, have sprung. Twice in our own lifetime we have seen the United States, against their wishes and their traditions, against arguments, the force of which it is impossible not to comprehend, drawn by irresistible forces, into these wars in time to secure the victory of the good cause, but only after frightful slaughter and devastation had occurred. Twice the United States has had to send several millions of its young men across the Atlantic to find the war; but now war can find any nation, wherever it may dwell between dusk and dawn. Surely we should work with conscious purpose for a grand pacification of Europe, within the structure of the United Nations and in accordance with its Charter. That I feel is an open cause of policy of very great importance. . . .

I have felt bound to portray the shadow which, alike in the west and in the east, falls upon the world. I was a high minister at the time of the Versailles Treaty and a close friend of Mr Lloyd George, who was the head of the British delegation at Versailles. I did not myself agree with many things that were done, but I have a very strong impression in my mind of that situation, and I find it painful to contrast it with that which prevails now. In those days there were high hopes and unbounded confidence that the wars were over, and that the League of Nations would become all-powerful. I do not see or feel that same confidence or even the same hopes in the haggard world at the present time.

On the other hand I repulse the idea that a new war is inevitable; still more that it is imminent. It is because I am sure that our fortunes are still in our own hands and that we hold the power to save the future, that I feel the duty to speak out now that I have the occasion and the opportunity to do so. I do not believe that Soviet Russia desires war. What they desire is the fruits of war and the indefinite expansion of their power and doctrines. But what we have to consider here today while time remains, is the permanent prevention of war and the establishment of conditions of freedom and democracy as rapidly as possible in all countries. Our difficulties and dangers will not be removed by closing our eyes to them. They will not be removed by mere waiting to see what happens; nor will they be removed by a policy of appeasement. What is needed is a settlement, and the longer this is delayed, the more difficult it will be and the greater our dangers will become.

America Must Be Firm

America ought to understand that the only way to treat the Russians is to be firm with them. America gives in too easily. If America is firm with Russia, I think the East and West can get together again some time. But I don't know when.

Jan Masaryk, quoted in *The Reader's Digest*, September 1948.

From what I have seen of our Russian friends and Allies during the war, I am convinced that there is nothing they admire so much as strength, and there is nothing for which they have less respect than for weakness, especially military weakness. For that reason the old doctrine of a balance of power is unsound. We cannot afford, if we can help it, to work on narrow margins, offering temptations to a trial of strength. If the Western Democracies stand together in strict adherence to the principles of the United Nations Charter, their influence for furthering those principles will be immense and no one is likely to molest them. If, however, they become divided or falter in their duty and if these all-important years are allowed to slip away, then indeed catastrophe may overwhelm us all.

Last time I saw it all coming and cried aloud to my own fellow-countrymen and to the world, but no one paid any attention. Up till the year 1933 or even 1935, Germany might have been saved from the awful fate which has overtaken her and we might all have been spared the miseries Hitler let loose upon mankind. There never was a war in all history easier to prevent by timely action than the one which has just desolated such great areas of the globe. It could have been prevented in my belief without the firing of a single shot, and Germany might be powerful, prosperous and honoured today; but no one would listen and one by one we were all sucked into the awful whirlpool. We surely must not let that happen again. This can only be achieved by reaching now, in 1946, a good understanding on all points with Russia under the general authority of the United Nations Organization and by the maintenance of that good understanding through many peaceful years, by the world instrument, supported by the whole strength of the English-speaking world and all its connections. There is the solution which I respectfully offer to you in this Address to which I have given the title 'The Sinews of Peace'.

United to Defend Our Traditions

Let no man underrate the abiding power of the British Empire and Commonwealth. Because you see the forty-six millions in our island harassed about their food supply, of which they only grow one-half, even in wartime, or because we have difficulty in restarting our industries and export trade after six years of passionate war effort, do not suppose that we shall not come through these dark years of privation as we have come through the glorious years of agony, or that half a century from now, you will not see seventy or eighty millions of Britons spread about the world and united in defence of our traditions, our way of life, and of the world causes which you and we espouse. If the population of the English-speaking Commonwealths be added to that of the United States with all that such co-operation implies in the air, on the sea, all over the globe and in science and in industry, and in moral force, there will be no quivering, precarious balance of power to offer its temptation to ambition or adventure. On the contrary, there will be an overwhelming assurance of security. If we adhere faithfully to the Charter of the United Nations and walk forward in sedate and sober strength seeking no one's land or treasure, seeking to lay no arbitrary control upon the thoughts of men; if all British moral and material forces and convictions are joined with your own in fraternal association, the highroads of the future will be clear, not only for us but for all, not only for our time, but for a century to come.

"Millions of . . . common people, having tried the Communists in the fire of struggle and resistance to fascism, . . . decided that the Communists deserve completely the confidence of the people."

The Soviets Are Not Dividing Europe (1946)

Josef Stalin, interviewed by *Pravda*

In the latter years of World War II, Soviet troops recaptured the Eastern European lands that Nazi Germany had conquered. Soon after the war ended, Communist governments came to power in Eastern Europe. In the following viewpoint, Soviet ruler Josef Stalin (1879-1953) reacts to Winston Churchill's claim that the Soviets are thwarting the establishment of democracy in Eastern Europe. He argues that the Eastern European people have freely chosen communism. Stalin became a Communist in 1903. Before the Russian Revolution in 1917, he worked underground to overthrow Czar Nicholas II and edited the revolutionary Communist newspaper, *Pravda*. He became the ruler of the Soviet Union in 1924 and led the country until his death in 1953.

As you read, consider the following questions:

1. How does the author compare Adolf Hitler and Winston Churchill?
2. How does Stalin dispute the contention that Soviet policy in Eastern Europe is expansionist?
3. Why does the author defend the governments of Eastern Europe?

Josef Stalin, interviewed by *Pravda;* translated text of a Moscow radio broadcast appearing in the March 14, 1946 edition of *The New York Times,* © United Press International. Reprinted with permission.

A few days ago a *Pravda* correspondent approached Stalin with a request to clarify a series of questions connected with the speech of Mr. Churchill. Comrade Stalin gave clarifications, which are set out below in the form of answers to the correspondent's questions.

Q. How do you assess the last speech of Mr. Churchill which was made in the United States?

A. I assess it as a dangerous act calculated to sow the seed of discord among the Allied governments and hamper their cooperation.

Q. Can one consider that the speech of Mr. Churchill is damaging to the cause of peace and security?

A. Undoubtedly, yes. In substance, Mr. Churchill now stands in the position of a firebrand of war. And Mr. Churchill is not alone here. He has friends not only in England but also in the United States of America.

Reminded of Hitler

In this respect, one is reminded remarkably of Hitler and his friends. Hitler began to set war loose by announcing his racial theory, declaring that only people speaking the German language represent a fully valuable nation. Mr. Churchill begins to set war loose also by a racial theory, maintaining that only nations speaking the English language are fully valuable nations, called upon to decide the destinies of the entire world.

The German racial theory brought Hitler and his friends to the conclusion that the Germans, as the only fully valuable nation, must rule over other nations. The English racial theory brings Mr. Churchill and his friends to the conclusion that nations speaking the English language, being the only fully valuable nations, should rule over the remaining nations of the world.

In substance, Mr. Churchill and his friends in England and the United States present nations not speaking the English language with something like an ultimatum: "Recognize our lordship voluntarily and then all will be well. In the contrary case, war is inevitable."

But the nations have shed their blood during five years of cruel war for the sake of liberty and the independence of their countries, and not for the sake of exchanging the lordship of Hitler for the lordship of Churchill.

It is, therefore, highly probable that the nations not speaking English and which, however, make up an enormous majority of the world's population, will not consent to go into a new slavery. The tragedy of Mr. Churchill lies in the fact that he, as a deep-rooted Tory, cannot understand this simple and obvious truth.

26

There is no doubt that the set-up of Mr. Churchill is a set-up for war, a call to war with the Soviet Union. It is also clear that such a set-up as that of Mr. Churchill is incompatible with the existing treaty of alliance between England and the U.S.S.R. It is true that Mr. Churchill, in order to confuse his readers, declares in passing that the length of the Anglo-Soviet treaty for mutual aid and cooperation could easily be extended to fifty years.

But how can one reconcile such a statement by Mr. Churchill with his set-up for war against the Soviet Union, his preaching of war against the Soviet Union? It is clear that these things can in no way be compatible.

If Mr. Churchill, calling for war against the Soviet Union, still considers it possible to extend the duration of the Anglo-Soviet treaty to fifty years, then it means that he considers this treaty as an empty piece of paper, to be used in order to conceal and disguise his anti-Soviet set-up.

Our Most Important Duty

The Soviet Union has always given first place to promoting peace and collaboration with other countries for universal peace and the development of international business relations.

As long as we live in a system of States, and roots of fascism and imperialistic aggression have not been finally pulled up, our vigilance as regards possible new breakers of peace must not be slackened and efforts to consolidate collaboration among peaceful powers will remain, as before, our most important duty.

V. Molotoff, Broadcast from Moscow, November 6, 1945.

On this account, one cannot consider seriously the declaration of Mr. Churchill's friends in England about the extension of the Soviet-English treaty to fifty years or more. Problems of the duration of a treaty have no sense if one of the parties violates the treaty and turns it into an empty scrap of paper.

Q. How do you assess that part of Mr. Churchill's speech in which he attacks the democratic regime of the European countries which are our neighbors and in which he criticizes the good neighborly relations established between these countries and the Soviet Union?

A. This part of Mr. Churchill's speech is a mixture of the elements of the libel with the elements of rudeness and lack of tact. Mr. Churchill maintains that Warsaw, Berlin, Prague, Vienna, Budapest, Belgrade, Bucharest and Sofia, all these famous cities and the populations of those areas, are within the Soviet sphere and are all subjected to Soviet influence and to the increasing control of Moscow.

Mr. Churchill qualifies this as the "boundless expansionist tendencies of the Soviet Union." It requires no special effort to show that Mr. Churchill rudely and shamelessly libels not only Moscow but also the above-mentioned States neighborly to the U.S.S.R.

To begin with, it is quite absurd to speak of the exclusive control of the U.S.S.R. in Vienna and Berlin, where there are Allied control councils with representatives of four States, where the U.S.S.R. has only one-fourth of the voices.

It happens sometimes that some people are unable to refrain from libel, but still they should know a limit.

Secondly, one cannot forget the following fact: the Germans carried out an invasion of the U.S.S.R. through Finland, Poland, Rumania, Bulgaria and Hungary. The Germans were able to carry out the invasion through these countries by reason of the fact that these countries had governments inimical to the Soviet Union.

As a result of the German invasion, the Soviet Union has irrevocably lost in battles with the Germans, and also during the German occupation and through the expulsion of Soviet citizens to German slave labor camps, about 7,000,000 people. In other words, the Soviet Union has lost in men several times more than Britain and the United States together.

It may be that some quarters are trying to push into oblivion these sacrifices of the Soviet people which insured the liberation of Europe from the Hitlerite yoke.

But the Soviet Union cannot forget them. One can ask, therefore, what can be surprising in the fact that the Soviet Union, in a desire to ensure its security for the future, tries to achieve that these countries should have governments whose relations to the Soviet Union are loyal? How can one, without having lost one's reason, qualify these peaceful aspirations of the Soviet Union as "expansionist tendencies" of our Government?

"Rude, Offensive Libel"

Mr. Churchill further maintains that the Polish Government under Russian lordship has been spurred to an unjust and criminal spoliation against Germany. Here, every word is a rude and offensive libel. Contemporary, democratic Poland is led by outstanding men. They have shown in deeds that they know how to defend the interests and worth of their homeland, as their predecessors failed to do.

What reason has Mr. Churchill to maintain that the leaders of contemporary Poland can submit their country to a lordship by representatives of any country whatever? Does Mr. Churchill here libel the Russians because he has intentions of sowing the seeds of discord between Poland and the Soviet Union?

Mr. Churchill is not pleased that Poland should have turned her policy toward friendship and alliance with the U.S.S.R. There was a time when in the mutual relations between Poland and the U.S.S.R. there prevailed an element of conflict and contradiction. This gave a possibility to statesmen, of the kind of Mr. Churchill, to play on these contradictions, to take Poland in hand under the guise of protection from the Russians, to frighten Russia by specters of a war between Poland and herself, and to take for themselves the role of arbiters.

But this time is past. For enmity between Poland and Russia has given place to friendship between them, and Poland, present democratic Poland, does not wish any longer to be a playing-ball in the hands of foreigners. It seems to be that this is just what annoys Mr. Churchill and urges him to rude, tactless outbursts against Poland. After all, it is no laughing matter for him. He is not allowed to play for other people's stakes.

In the Vanguard

In the vanguard of the struggle for peace and security marches the Soviet Union, which played an outstanding part in smashing Fascism and fulfilled its great mission of liberation. The nations liberated by the Soviet Union from the fascist yoke received an opportunity of building their state rule on democratic foundations, of realizing their historic aspirations. On this road they find fraternal assistance on the part of the Soviet Union.

Josef Stalin, Statement broadcast on Moscow Radio, May 1, 1946.

As for Mr. Churchill's attack on the Soviet Union in connection with the extending of the western boundaries of Poland, as compensation for the territories seized by the Germans in the past, it seems to me that he quite blatantly distorts the facts.

As is known, the western frontiers of Poland were decided upon at the Berlin conference of the three powers, on the basis of Poland's demands.

The Soviet Union repeatedly declared that it considered Poland's demands just and correct. It may well be that Mr. Churchill is not pleased with this decision. But why does Mr. Churchill, not sparing his darts against the Russians in the matter, conceal from his readers the fact that the decision was taken at the Berlin conference unanimously, that not only the Russians voted for this decision but also the English and Americans?

Why did Mr. Churchill have to delude people? Mr. Churchill

further maintains that the Communist parties were very insignificant in all these Eastern European countries but reached exceptional strength, exceeding their numbers by far, and are attempting to establish totalitarian control everywhere; that police-government prevailed in almost all these countries, even up to now, with the exception of Czechoslovakia, and that there exists in them no real democracy.

As is known in Britain at present there is one party which rules the country—the Labor party. The rest of the parties are barred from the Government of the country. This is called by Churchill a true democracy, meanwhile Poland, Rumania, Yugoslavia, Bulgaria and Hungary are governed by several parties—from four to six parties. And besides, the opposition, if it is loyal, is guaranteed the right to participate in the Government. This, Churchill calls totalitarian and the Government of police.

On what grounds? Do you expect an answer from Churchill? Does he not understand the ridiculous situation he is putting himself in by such speeches on the basis of totalitarianism and police rule. Churchill would have liked Poland to be ruled by Soankowski and Anders, Yugoslavia by Mikhailovitch, Rumania by Prince Stirbey and Radescu, Hungary and Austria by some king from the House of Habsburg, and so on.

Mr. Churchill wants to assure us that these gentlemen from the Fascist servants' hall can ensure true democracy. Such is the Democracy of Mr. Churchill. Mr. Churchill wanders around the truth when he speaks of the growth of the influence of the Communist parties in Eastern Europe. It should, however, be noted that he is not quite accurate. The influence of Communist parties grew not only in Eastern Europe but in almost every country of Europe where fascism has ruled before: Italy, Germany, Hungary, Bulgaria, Rumania, Finland, and in countries which have suffered German, Italian or Hungarian occupation: France, Belgium, Holland, Norway, Denmark, Poland, Czechoslovakia, Yugoslavia, Greece, the Soviet Union and so on.

Reliable and Self-Sacrificing Communists

The growth of the influence of communism cannot be considered accidental. It is a normal function. The influence of the Communists grew because during the hard years of the mastery of fascism in Europe, Communists showed themselves to be reliable, daring and self-sacrificing fighters against fascist regimes for the liberty of peoples.

Mr. Churchill sometimes recalls in his speeches the common people from small houses, patting them on the shoulder in a lordly manner and pretending to be their friend. But these people are not so simple-minded as it might appear at first sight. Common people, too, have their opinions and their own politics. And they know how to stand up for themselves.

It is they, millions of these common people, who voted Mr. Churchill and his party out in England, giving their votes to the Labor party. It is they, millions of these common people, who isolated reactionaries in Europe, collaborators with fascism, and gave preference to Left democratic parties.

Progressive Reforms

A number of European countries have carried out such fundamental social reforms as the abolition of the obsolete system of landed estates, turning land over to the poor peasants. This undermines the former strength of the reactionary Fascist forces and stimulates the development of the democratic and Socialist movements in these countries. . . .

Certain reactionary publications are trying to make out that these bold democratic reforms are largely due to the increased influence of the Soviet Union; such arguments, however, are patently unfounded. In a sense it is common knowledge that problems of this kind have been successfully solved in the progressive countries of Europe before now.

V. Molotoff, Broadcast from Moscow, November 6, 1945.

It is they, millions of these common people, having tried the Communists in the fire of struggle and resistance to fascism, who decided that the Communists deserve completely the confidence of the people. Thus grew the Communists' influence in Europe. Such is the law of historical development.

Of course, Mr. Churchill does not like such a development of events. And he raised the alarm, appealing to force. But he also did not like the appearance of the Soviet regime in Russia after the First World War. Then, too, he raised the alarm and organized an armed expedition of fourteen states against Russia with the aim of turning back the wheel of history.

But history turned out to be stronger than Churchill's intervention and the quixotic antics of Churchill resulted in his complete defeat. I do not know whether Mr. Churchill and his friends will succeed in organizing after the Second World War a new military expedition against Eastern Europe. But if they succeed in this, which is not very probable, since millions of common people stand on guard over the peace, then one man confidently says that they will be beaten, just as they were beaten twenty-six years ago.

"Communism has flooded half Europe. . . . It has subjugated millions of men and women who could not or did not know how to fight back."

The West Must Oppose Soviet Aims in Eastern Europe (1950)

Jan Stransky

The following viewpoint is written by Jan Stransky, a Czech who returned from exile when his country was liberated by the Soviet Army after World War II. Unlike Poland, Hungary, Romania, and Yugoslavia, Czechoslovakia managed to establish a democratic government after the war. But in February 1948, the democratic government resigned, bowing to Soviet intimidation and the growing influence of the Communists in Czechoslovakia. Stransky was a member of that democratic government and witnessed the tactics the Communists used to intimidate people and gain power. He argues that the West must stand firm against Soviet communism, because the Soviets threaten everyone's freedom, not just the Eastern European's.

As you read, consider the following questions:

1. Why did the Red Army have such an impact on Eastern Europe, in Stransky's view?
2. Why does the author believe Eastern Europeans gave up resisting the Germans and then were too weak to resist the Soviets?

From *East Wind over Prague* by Jan Stransky. Copyright © 1950 by Jan Stransky. Reprinted by permission of Random House, Inc.

The Red Army is the largest military force in the world. It is an enormous and truly indescribable compound of men, nationalities, material, colours, ideas and traditions. It has to be seen to be believed, and it has to be seen from near and while on the move: its tank divisions, which clear the way, well disciplined, well armed and trained and composed of picked soldiers; the columns of guns and lorries, the parachute divisions, motor cyclists, technical units. . . . But this is not the real Red Army, it is only its vanguard and the nucleus of its striking force. More than anything else the Red Army is a mass—and again one feels like thinking of a mass of water which bursts its dam and goes on spreading in width and depth: columns of marching soldiers, dirty, tired, clad in ragged uniforms. Tens and hundreds of thousands of columns moving on the dusty roads of central and eastern Europe. They march slowly in close rank with a long even step. Sometimes a song bursts from the marching column, usually something slow and poignantly sad. So they march, men young and old, men from Russian towns and villages, from the Ukraine and the Tartar republics, the Ural mountains and the Caucasus, the Baltic countries, Siberia, Mongolia. . . .

Fearing the Red Army

[Eastern Europeans] felt great respect towards the liberating army, but they also felt fear. At first they realized the Russian Army's strength, and soon they began to realize how small was the value of a human life in that enormous mass and how little it cared, educated in a different way of thought and feeling, for the fate of the individual, his personality, his interests and feelings. . . .

In the formerly occupied countries, people were accustomed to Nazi looting. Yet they did not expect that the looting would continue, perpetrated by the Russians, their idealized Liberators. Besides, the Germans while looting were accustomed to giving some sort of legal form to their thefts. A citizen who under pressure from the Gestapo had to "sell" his jewels, pictures, furniture or house, at least received a written receipt. He knew that he had suffered a cruel injustice, but he had a feeling that it had happened, so to say, through official channels, impersonally, and outwardly in a conventional way. Therefore he was upset the more when he saw the Russian soldier looting: his ideals fell down with a crash. . . .

All illusions were gone, and the experience—the terrific moral shock—proved to be one of the most important factors in the subsequent political development of the Russian-liberated countries: the Russian St George came, killed the dragon and liberated the imprisoned princess, but then he got drunk, looted the castle and raped the princess. No wonder the liberated ones longed for him to leave as soon as possible and, especially, prayed that he should never, never come back again. . . .

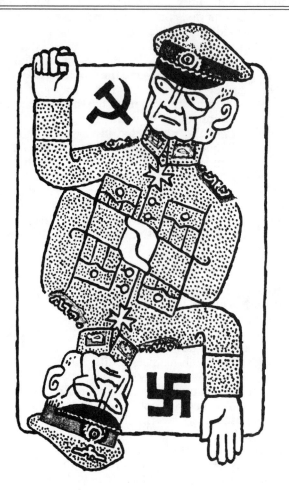

The Reporter, 1950. Copyright 1950 by Fortnightly Publishing Co. Inc.

Take a village; any village that had to billet a unit of Russian soldiers. The peasant, who day after day had to give them his milk and butter, feed their horses, lodge them, resign himself to their stealings and be constantly on the alert on behalf of his wife and daughter, was at first very annoyed and deeply hurt. But he was also frightened, and so he looked for protection. He looked for it from those who, according to his opinion, were nearest to the Russians, who might have some influence with them and therefore a possibility of helping: the local Communists. If I am in the Party, he thought, my wife and daughter might be safer: if I am in the Party, maybe the requisitioning might stop and they would not steal my chickens any more—they would not steal from a Comrade.

A shopkeeper who wanted to save his textile material from the trophy-hunters followed the same line of thought; the civil servant hoped that, once he entered the Party, he would not have to billet Soviet officers in his flat any longer. To hundreds of thousands of people the Communist Party appeared a potential safeguard against the brutality of military government and the economic consequences of Soviet administration. Thus the Communists realized that after having lost one advantage, they had struck another much more precious: a large field of new and unexpected possibilities for propaganda had been opened to them. The Red Army failed as an effective enticement; it still could and would serve even better as a very effective threat.

They did not trouble therefore to apologise for the army's behaviour. They just pretended to ignore the matter and concentrated instead on extolling Soviet power, Soviet invincibility and, indeed, Soviet ruthlessness. They depicted the Union as the only real military power in the world, the only real victor over Germany. It no longer mattered if the Soviet system was the best: it was the strongest anyway, and woe to those who tried to cross its path!

It was a shameful game on the Communists' part, because it played on human weakness. It was an effective and successful game, though, as there was plenty of weakness on which to play. The European nations survived the German occupation, but they emerged with broken backs, crushed will-power and weakened resistance. That is a fact; and this fact was one of the crucial elements in the history of post-war Communist growth. . . .

Morally Broken

At the beginning people did resist the Germans, both mentally and physically. They refused to accept force, and, as far as possible, tried to hit back. But then they witnessed how might was overcoming right in one country after the other, and more and more they felt their own weakness. They were being arrested, tortured, executed. Nearly every family was mourning some member and all were terrified for each other's safety. To revolt meant not only to lay down one's life but also the lives of one's wife and children, parents and other relations. When "Butcher" Reinhard Heydrich was killed in Prague, over ten thousand Czechs had to die in reprisal. It was a lesson which the Czechs were bound not to forget in a hurry; just as the Poles who witnessed the slaughtering of millions of European Jews have not forgotten a similar lesson; or the Serbians, decimated first by war and then by guerrilla fighting, or the French, the Belgians, the Dutch. The fight was far too uneven, because all weapons and all material power were on the side of the occupants. It was not an empty phrase to say that the European nations lived in serfdom—it was stern reality. Who went through such a reality did not become really—which means inwardly—free immediately the chains were broken, just as a tree which has been kept tied down for a long time does not straighten up at once if you remove the pole to which it is bound.

A Warning to the Democracies

The fate of Czechoslovakia after the Second World War is the story of a futile attempt to arrive at good relations with the Soviets, of the vain struggle of a little democracy against the active force of totalitarian Communism, of an abuse of trust and of a betrayed friendship. It is also, and above all, a story which can and should serve as a warning to all the democracies, large and small, which are carrying on the fight for freedom against the new totalitarian drive.

Hubert Ripka, *Czechoslovakia Enslaved*, 1950.

Thus the subjugated nations, even if they never accepted the occupation, could not avoid its physical and moral results. Gradually they lost faith in their own strength and in the possibility of their own independent resistance. Daily they were confirmed in the sense of their own helplessness, daily they had to endure new humiliations and thus they became accustomed to them. They knew well that right was on their side, but on the side of the enemy was the brutal power which held them immobilized. The power repelled them, but at the same time they were impressed by it. Gradually they had to give up all outward symbols of their independence, their civil rights and human dignity. Finally they kept only what is strongest in every living being: the instinct of self-preservation.

The Communists grasped the psychological position and directed their propaganda accordingly. At the beginning, before we understood the deep moral changes brought about by occupation, we laughed at their methods. We saw how, by stupid imitation, they substituted the symbols of Soviet rule for the symbols of German domination, and we were sure this would bring a healthy reaction. It seemed absurd to remove German street inscriptions only to replace them with Russian ones; to re-christen every "Adolf Hitlerstrasse" as "Marshal Stalin Street"; to hang the Soviet dictator's portrait on the very spot where, a week before, the portrait of the German dictator had still been hanging; to order where and how Soviet flags should be hung out; to force school children to learn Russian instead of German; to billet the [Soviet secret police, the] N.K.V.D. right in the former Gestapo quarters; to begin and end every public speech with Stalin and his glorious Red Army. We expected that people would be even quicker in realizing the spiritual relationship between Nazism and Communism and the similarity of their methods. In fact they realized it well enough—but that is not the point.

The point is that their reaction was different from what we expected: they might have been disgusted, but mainly they were frightened and inclined to accept this situation as inevitable. So it appears that we were probably good democrats but bad psychologists. We relied on elements which are the indivisible part of a democratic state of mind; the feeling of inner freedom and an unquenchable will to be free. Unfortunately these elements in occupied Europe had become badly weakened. The Communists knew better; instead they took into account human weakness, weariness, cowardice, and, as time has shown and still shows, they were right—at least temporarily. . . .

Soviet Invincibility

Far too many people in Europe thought that they were too weak and that they could not spit against the wind. The Communist agitator came to offer them Party membership, and behind him stood the Communist Minister of the Interior, the Communist Police, the Red Army and all the strength of the Soviet Union. "What can we do?" people were asking. "We are too weak; we do not want to go through all of it once more: to be thrown out of jobs again, to be arrested, tortured." So they turned the way the wind was blowing. Thus in the areas liberated or occupied—never mind which we call it—by the Red Army, in a few months the local Communist Party already had a good start towards becoming the largest party in the country. . . .

After Czechoslovakia was occupied by the Germans, I succeeded in escaping to Poland and in the summer of 1939 I arrived in England. Our British friends were exceedingly kind to me and to all my exiled compatriots. Munich lay heavy on their consciences and they went to infinite pains to show us how sorry they were for our misfortune: in fact, amongst ourselves, we used to have a name for the parties which they gave for us: we used to call them "sorry-parties." Yet I remember

37

how unpopular it was, even at that time, to say that Hitler would go on with his policy of expansion and that, sooner or later, he would precipitate a war upon the world. "He would not dare!" they argued. "We must not even admit such a possibility. Can you imagine what disaster war would bring with bombing and gas and all that? There would be no civilization left—it is a question if humanity would survive a modern war. . . . Of course we understand how you feel about what happened to your country, but even you must feel what tragedy war would bring to everybody, to your people at home more than anyone else—"

The Extent of Soviet Domination

I think it is very useful for us to look more closely at this planet which we inhabit and observe how far the Soviet Union has gone toward domination of this globe. Spin the globe in front of your eyes and stop it at Western Europe and ask yourselves, "How far has the Soviet Union gone so far?" It is really surprising to realize, and not many of us have stopped to add it up. The Soviet Union has taken over *eleven* European countries, not counting Eastern Germany. Since 1939 the Soviet Union has brought under effective control Finland, Estonia, Latvia, Lithuania, Poland, Czechoslovakia, Austria, Hungary, Romania, Bulgaria, and Yugoslavia. These countries are effectively a part of the Soviet Union. These countries have a population of 120,000,000 people.

H.R. Knickerbocker, Speech before the Economic Club of Chicago, March 15, 1946.

It was bad taste then to mention war and it is even worse taste now. There is an etiquette which an exile should observe. It is bad enough that he is an exile, a walking reminder of the world's instability, a disturbing sight in a fool's paradise. He should keep quiet and take things as he finds them. His hosts may ask him, after a good dinner, when the butler brings in the black coffee and liqueurs, to tell his escape story: how he dodged the police on guard around his house, how he had to hide in a hay stack, how he made his way to the frontier in a cattle truck, how he had to swim a river while the frontier guards were shooting at him. . . .

But it is quite a different matter to give some thought to his unpleasant and disturbing experiences with the Communists and his ideas of their methods, aims and preparations. It might spoil the party. Anyway, who wants to listen to that sort of war-mongering? . . .

It is no good saying that detailed plans for Communist world domination written by Lenin, Stalin and others, can be bought in any bookshop, and that up to now Communist practice has not deviated from those plans by one inch. What is the good? Was not Hitler's *Mein Kampf* written and translated for every-body to read and was not the ideology it contained applied step by step for everybody to see—yet how many profited from it? Millions of lives could have been saved if Hitler had been ren-dered inoffensive in '33 or '34 or even later—at any time except the one which he chose because it suited him best. Yet the les-son is lost. . . .

Encouragement for the Subjugated Millions

Communism has flooded half Europe, using a ground well fertilized by war and German occupation. It has subjugated millions of men and women who could not or did not know how to fight back because they were too frightened, too tired or morally infected or confused. Today they are Soviet tools, once more slaves working for the gang of some far distant Führers. Their masters know that they can make them toil in factories, in mines, in steel and iron works, in fields and offices. But they know just as well that they can never use them as reliable sol-diers. A Czech or Rumanian or Polish army can be a hundred times purged and re-purged, the officers' corps can go through the most minute political schooling, but still it will be an army of deserters—an army which must not be allowed anywhere near the front line because it would cross to the side of the western enemy, and which must not be armed because it would turn its arms against the great Soviet ally. The same ap-plies to the civilians. They will work in silence, they will march on May Day under red flags and banners, they will vote Communist and apply for membership of the Party, but all the time—and the ruling gang knows it well—they will be waiting for their hour. If they are given a chance, they will take it. Some heroically, going into open battle, but most rather unas-sumingly and undemonstratively in the shrewd, rather passive way which they learned under German occupation and which helped so much to speed up Hitler's defeat. They will not take unnecessary risks—both Nazi and Soviet ruthlessness has taught them to think twice before endangering their own lives and the lives of their families. But they will try to keep their faith and save their breath for the time when it will be needed. All they want is some encouragement: to be told, now and then, that they have not been forgotten.

"We should recognize that we have no . . . business in the political *affairs of Eastern Europe."*

The West Must Not Oppose Soviet Aims in Eastern Europe (1946)

Henry A. Wallace

Henry A. Wallace (1888–1965) was the U.S. secretary of agriculture during the first two terms of Franklin D. Roosevelt. He was the nation's vice president from 1941 to 1944. In 1945 he was appointed U.S. secretary of commerce by President Harry Truman. In the following viewpoint, excerpted from a speech, Wallace argues that the U.S. should strive for good relations with the Soviet Union. He contends that Americans must recognize that the Soviets have security concerns in Eastern Europe just as the U.S. has security concerns in Latin America, thus Soviet domination of Eastern Europe is not unreasonable. As a result of this speech, Truman asked Wallace to resign his position in the Commerce Department. Although Wallace renounced his pro-Soviet views in 1952, this 1946 speech remains an important document in the history of the debate about U.S. policy toward the Soviet Union.

As you read, consider the following questions:

1. Why does the author caution against the U.S. allying too closely with Great Britain?
2. What must the U.S. understand about the Soviets in order to form a wise policy toward them, in Wallace's view?

Henry A. Wallace, speech delivered to a joint meeting of the National Citizens Political Action Committee and the Independent Citizens Committee of the Arts, Sciences, and Professions, New York City, September 12, 1946.

Never have the common people of all lands so longed for peace. Yet, never in a time of comparative peace have they feared war so much. Up till now peace has been negative and unexciting. War has been positive and exciting. Far too often, hatred and fear, intolerance and deceit have had the upper hand over love and confidence, trust and joy. Far too often, the law of nations has been the law of the jungle; and the constructive spiritual forces of the Lord have bowed to the destructive forces of Satan.

The significance of peace has been increased immeasurably by the atom bomb, guided missiles and airplanes which soon will travel as fast as sound. Make no mistake about it—another war would hurt the United States many times as much as the last war. We cannot rest in the assurance that we invented the atom bomb—and therefore that this agent of destruction will work best for us. He who trusts in the atom bomb will sooner or later perish by the atom bomb—or something worse.

I say this as one who steadfastly backed preparedness throughout the Thirties. We have no use for namby-pamby pacifism. But we must realize that modern inventions have now made peace the most the exciting thing in the world—and we should be willing to pay a just price for peace. If modern war can cost us $400 billion, we should be willing and happy to pay much more for peace. But certainly, the cost of peace is to be measured not in dollars but in the hearts and minds of men.

The Price of Peace

The price of peace—for us and for every nation in the world—is the price of giving up prejudice, hatred, fear, and ignorance.

Let's get down to cases here at home.

First we have prejudice, hatred, fear and ignorance of certain races. The mass lynching in Georgia was not merely the most unwarranted, brutal act of mob violence in the United States in recent years; it was also an illustration of the kind of prejudice that makes war inevitable.

Hatred breeds hatred. The doctrine of racial superiority produces a desire to get even on the part of its victims. If we are to work for peace in the rest of the world, we here in the United States must eliminate racism from our unions, our business organizations, our educational institutions, and our employment practices. Merit alone must be the measure of man.

Second, in payment for peace, we must give up prejudice, hatred, fear and ignorance in the economic world. This means working earnestly, day after day, for a larger volume of world trade. It means helping undeveloped areas of the world to industrialize themselves with the help of American technical assistance and loans.

Governor Thomas Dewey has expressed himself as favoring an alliance of mutual defense with Great Britain as the key to our foreign policy. This may sound attractive because we both speak the same language and many of our customs and traditions have the same historical background. Moreover, to the military men, the British Isles are our advanced air base against Europe.

Certainly we like the British people as individuals. But to make Britain the key to our foreign policy would be, in my opinion, the height of folly. We must not let the reactionary leadership of the Republican party force us into that position. We must not let British balance-of-power manipulations determine whether and when the United States gets into war.

A Succession of Good Deeds

I think the Russians are appreciative of all the fine words that we give them, all the promises of cooperation, and all the rest of that. But I am convinced they have got to be shown a succession of good deeds, that we do not intend to enter any combination against them, before they are going to drop this mistrust that they hold towards us.

Russell Barnes, Speech before the Economic Club of Detroit, November 12, 1945.

Make no mistake about it—the British imperialistic policy in the Near East alone, combined with Russian retaliation, would lead the United States straight to war unless we have a clearly-defined and realistic policy of our own.

Neither of these two great powers wants war now, but the danger is that whatever their intentions may be, their current policies may eventually lead to war. To prevent war and insure our survival in a stable world, it is essential that we look abroad through our own American eyes and not through the eyes of either the British Foreign Office or a pro-British or anti-Russian press.

In this connection, I want one thing clearly understood. I am neither anti-British nor pro-British—neither anti-Russian nor pro-Russian. And when President Truman read these words, he said that they represented the policy of his administration.

I plead for an America vigorously dedicated to peace—just as I plead for opportunities for the next generation throughout the world to enjoy the abundance which now, more than ever before, is the birthright of man.

To achieve lasting peace, we must study in detail just how the Russian character was formed—by invasions of Tartars, Mongols, Germans, Poles, Swedes, and French; by the czarist rule based on ignorance, fear and force; by the intervention of the British, French and Americans in Russian affairs from 1919 to 1921; by the geography of the huge Russian land mass situated strategically between Europe and Asia; and by the vitality derived from the rich Russian soil and the strenuous Russian climate. Add to all this the tremendous emotional power which Marxism and Leninism gives to the Russian leaders—and then we can realize that we are reckoning with a force which cannot be handled successfully by a "Get tough with Russia" policy. "Getting tough" never bought anything real and lasting—whether for schoolyard bullies or businessmen or world powers. The tougher we get, the tougher the Russians will get.

False Friends Provoke War

Throughout the world there are numerous reactionary elements which had hoped for Axis victory—and now profess great friendship for the United States. Yet, these enemies of yesterday and false friends of today continually try to provoke war between the United States and Russia. They have no real love of the United States. They only long for the day when the United States and Russia will destroy each other.

We must not let our Russian policy be guided or influenced by those inside or outside the United States who want war with Russia. This does not mean appeasement.

We most earnestly want peace with Russia—but we want to be met half way. We want cooperation. And I believe that we can get cooperation once Russia understands that our primary objective is neither saving the British Empire nor purchasing oil in the Near East with the lives of American soldiers. We cannot allow national oil rivalries to force us into war. All of the nations producing oil, whether inside or outside of their own boundaries, must fulfill the provisions of the United Nations Charter and encourage the development of world petroleum reserves so as to make the maximum amount of oil available to all nations of the world on an equitable peaceful basis—and not on the basis of fighting the next war.

For her part, Russia can retain our respect by cooperating with the United Nations in a spirit of openminded and flexible give-and-take.

Spheres of Influence

The real peace treaty we now need is between the United States and Russia. On our part, we should recognize that we have no more business in the *political* affairs of Eastern Europe than Russia has in the *political* affairs of Latin America, Western Europe and the United States. We may not like what Russia does in Eastern Europe. Her type of land reform, industrial expropriation, and suppression of basic liberties offends the great majority of the people of the United States. But whether we like it or not the Russians will try to socialize their sphere of influence just as we try to democratize our sphere of influence. This applies also to Germany and Japan. We are striving to democratize Japan and our area of control in Germany, while Russia strives to socialize eastern Germany.

The Russian Buffer

What is behind the Russian's desire, of course, to set up this buffer zone stretching from the Baltic down to the Black Sea and the Mediterranean, is a desire to get a buffer which will give them defense in depth, and give them the help of the armies of those countries, in case we should attack Russia in order to smash Communism.

Now, I personally do not blame the Russians too much for that. In the face of the record we have established of hostility towards Russia, I feel we, in their position, would do the very same thing.

Russell Barnes, Speech before the Economic Club of Detroit, November 12, 1945.

As for Germany, we all must recognize that an equitable settlement, based on a unified German nation, is absolutely essential to any lasting European settlement. This means that Russia must be assured that never again can German industry be converted into military might to be used against her—and Britain, Western Europe and the United States must be certain that Russia's Germany policy will not become a tool of Russian design against Western Europe.

The Russians have no more business in stirring up native communists to political activity in Western Europe, Latin America and the United States than we have in interfering in the politics of Eastern Europe and Russia. We know what Russia is up to in Eastern Europe, for example, and Russia knows what we are up to. We cannot permit the door to be closed against our trade in Eastern Europe any more than we can in China. But at the same time we have to recognize that the Balkans are closer to Russia than to us—and that Russia cannot permit either England or the United States to dominate the politics of that area.

China is a special case and although she holds the longest frontier in the world with Russia, the interests of world peace demand that China remain free from any sphere of influence, either politically or economically. We insist that the door to trade and economic development opportunities be left wide open in China as in all the world. However, the open door to trade and opportunities for economic development in China are meaningless unless there is a unified and peaceful China—built on the cooperation of the various groups in that country and based on a hands-off policy of the outside powers.

We are still arming to the hilt. Our excessive expenses for military purposes are the chief cause for our unbalanced budget. If taxes are to be lightened we must have the basis of a real peace with Russia—a peace that cannot be broken by extremist propagandists.We do not want our course determined for us by master minds operating out of London, Moscow or Nanking.

Friendly Competition

Russian ideas of social-economic justice are going to govern nearly a third of the world. Our ideas of free enterprise democracy will govern much of the rest. The two ideas will endeavor to prove which can deliver the most satisfaction to the common man in their respective areas of political dominance. But by mutual agreement, this competition should be put on a friendly basis and the Russians should stop conniving against us in certain areas of the world just as we should stop scheming against them in other parts of the world. Let the results of the two systems speak for themselves.

Meanwhile, the Russians should stop teaching that their form of communism must, by force if necessary, ultimately triumph over democratic capitalism—while we should close our ears to those among us who would have us believe that Russian communism and our free enterprise system cannot live, one with another, in a profitable and productive peace.

Under friendly peaceful competition the Russian world and the American world will gradually become more alike. The Russians will be forced to grant more and more of the personal freedoms; and we shall become more and more absorbed with the problems of social-economic justice.

Russia must be convinced that we are not planning for war against her and we must be certain that Russia is not carrying on territorial expansion or world domination through native communists faithfully following every twist and turn in the Moscow party line. But in this competition, we must insist on an open door for trade throughout the world. There will always be an ideological conflict—but that is no reason why diplomats cannot work out a basis for both systems to live safely in the world side by side. . . .

In brief, as I see it today, the World Order is bankrupt—and the United States, Russia and England are the receivers. These are the hard facts of power politics on which we have to build a functioning, powerful United Nations and a body of international law. And as we build, we must develop fully the doctrine of the rights of small peoples as contained in the United Nations Charter. This law should ideally apply as much to Indonesians and Greeks as to Bulgarians and Poles—but practically, the application may be delayed until both British and Russians discover the futility of their methods. . . .

Entirely Justified

I think that in the light of our own behavior, the Russians are entirely justified in telling us to stay out of that part of the world. We have told European nations to stay out of the Western Hemisphere, because we don't want them over here as a threat to our own security. We have gone almost as far in the Pacific in telling the Russians that we are going to run Japan; that we are going to take those bases in the Pacific, and the Russians should stay out. So, I think the Russians are entirely within their rights, from their point of view in insisting that they have governments under their own control in such countries as Poland, Roumania, Hungary, Yugoslavia, and Bulgaria.

Russell Barnes, Speech before the Economic Club of Detroit, November 12, 1945.

In the United States an informed public opinion will be all-powerful. Our people are peace-minded. But they often express themselves too late—for events today move much faster than public opinion. The people here, as everywhere in the world, must be convinced that another war is not inevitable. And through mass meetings, and through persistent pamphleteering, the people can be organized for peace—even though a large segment of our press is propagandizing our people for war in the hope of scaring Russia. And we who look on this war-with-Russia talk as criminal foolishness must carry our message direct to the people—even though we may be called communists because we dare to speak out.

I believe that peace—the kind of peace I have outlined—is the basic issue, both in the Congressional campaign this fall and right on through the Presidential election in 1948. How we meet this issue will determine whether we live not in "one world" or "two worlds"—but whether we live at all.

"The imperialists have turned the German question into an abiding source of international tension."

Western Interference in Berlin Promotes Conflict (1958)

Nikita Khrushchev

Nikita Khrushchev (1894-1971) became the first secretary of the Soviet Communist Party in 1953. He became the Soviet Premier in 1958, and held both posts until he was removed from power in 1964. The following viewpoint is an excerpt from a speech he gave to members of the Soviet and Polish Communist parties. At that time, Germany was divided into a Communist-led East Germany allied with the USSR, and a capitalist, democratic West Germany allied with the U.S. and other Western powers. The city of Berlin was likewise divided, and Western troops were stationed in the city. In his speech, Khrushchev argues that the Western powers use West Berlin to destabilize the East German government. He demands that the West leave Berlin.

As you read, consider the following questions:

1. What are the obligations of the Potsdam Agreement, in the author's view? How has the West violated them?
2. Which obligation has the West not violated, according to Khrushchev? Why does he believe the West has upheld this part of the Agreement?

Excerpted, with permission, from *Khrushchev Speaks*, edited by Thomas P. Whitney. Ann Arbor: University of Michigan Press, 1963.

Comrades, a new balance of forces has developed in the world today. The mighty socialist camp is growing and gaining in strength and nothing can arrest the peoples' advance toward socialism and communism. Therefore, the attempts of the forces of reaction to prevent the building of socialism in the People's Democracies are doomed to failure.

It is high time for Messrs. Imperialists to realize that the remnants of the reactionary forces in the People's Democracies have no genuine support among the people. In all the People's Democracies the leading role of the working class has become more prominent. The labouring peasantry is in close alliance with it. The intelligentsia is working for the welfare of the people and serves them honestly.

Imperialist Ambitions

The fact that the balance of forces in the world today is in favour of socialism reduces to hopelessness the imperialist ambitions of restoring the old order of things in the socialist countries. Only incorrigible adventurists can dream of this today. The social gains of the working people in every socialist country are guarded by the might of the entire socialist camp.

Fortunately for mankind, the course of international developments today does not depend entirely on the will of the ruling circles of the imperialist Powers. Experience shows that the international prestige of the countries of the socialist camp, and its influence on the entire flow of world history and the destinies of mankind are growing year by year. In recent years the world has time and again been spared from catastrophic explosions that threatened to touch off a new world conflagration. This has been made possible primarily by the solidarity of the socialist countries, the consistency of their peace policy, and the determination of all the peoples to uphold world peace.

Why are the political and military leaders of certain Western Powers subject to paroxysms of war hysteria? It is because big capital, the monopoly owners, need a tense international situation constantly to intensify the arms race and to enrich themselves at the expense of the working people. Therein lies the main reason for the ever new gambles which the imperialist circles, disregarding realities, undertake. They are hoping thereby to keep mankind constantly on the brink of war, to receive huge super-profits, to subjugate countries which have committed themselves to aggressive military blocs.

The imperialists have turned the German question into an abiding source of international tension. The ruling circles of West Germany are doing everything to whip up military passions against the German Democratic Republic, against the Polish People's Republic, against all the socialist countries.

48

Speeches by Chancellor Konrad Adenauer and Defence Minister Franz Josef Strauss, the arming of the Bundeswehr with nuclear weapons and various military manoeuvres all bespeak a definite trend in the policy of the ruling circles of West Germany.

A Dangerous Road

We wish to warn the leaders of the Federal Republic of Germany: The road followed by West Germany today is a road dangerous to peace in Europe and fatal to West Germany herself. Indeed, can realistic politicians today hope for success in a new "march to the East"? Hitler in his time also did everything to fan war hysteria, in order to prepare the ground for an attack on the Soviet Union. However, it is well known how this all ended. It is not hard to imagine the fate of those who would try to unleash new aggression against the socialist states. No speeches by Chancellor Adenauer or his Minister Strauss can change the balance of forces in favour of imperialism. To march against the East would mean marching to death for West Germany.

Illegal Occupation

The three Western powers forfeited their right to take part in the occupation and administration of Berlin when they began systematically to violate the decisions of Yalta and Potsdam in the parts of Germany which they occupied. . . .

The Western powers themselves acknowledged this by setting up a Three-Power Occupation Statute for West Berlin. This illegal unilateral action on the part of the Western powers constitutes formal legal confirmation that the Western powers themselves terminated the Four-Power status, thus depriving the presence of their troops and military authorities in West Berlin of its legal basis.

East German Ministry of Foreign Affairs, *Documentation on the Question of West Berlin*, 1964.

It is high time to realize that the times when imperialists could act from "positions of strength" with impunity have gone, never to return, and try as they may, the imperialists will not be able to change the balance of forces in their favour. Nor should they forget the geographical position of West Germany which—with means of warfare what they are today—would not survive a single day of modern warfare.

We do not desire another military conflict. It would be fatal to West Germany and would bring untold disaster to the peoples of other countries. The Soviet Union and the other socialist countries are doing everything to keep the adventurists who are dreaming of new wars from making a fatal step. The West

German policy-makers would do well to appraise the existing situation more soberly and desist from whipping up war passions. . . .

The German question, in the sense of reunification of the two German states now in existence, can only be settled by the German people themselves along the lines of *rapprochement* between these states. The conclusion of a peace treaty with Germany is an entirely different matter which, indeed, should be settled primarily by the Four Powers which formed the anti-Hitler coalition, in co-operation with representatives of Germany. The signing of a peace treaty with Germany would help to normalize the entire situation in Germany and in Europe generally. The Soviet Union has proposed, and is proposing, that this measure should be tackled without delay.

The Potsdam Agreement

If one is to discuss the Four Powers' undertakings with regard to Germany, one must consider the obligations springing from the Potsdam Agreement.

Let us recall the main obligations assumed by the parties to the Potsdam Agreement with regard to their policy in Germany, what course of development for Germany was determined in Potsdam.

At that time, the members of the anti-Hitler coalition assumed clear-cut and definite obligations: to extirpate German militarism, to prevent its resurgence once and for all, to do everything to prevent Germany from ever again threatening her neighbours or world peace.

The parties to the Potsdam Agreement also recognized the necessity for putting an end to German fascism, blocking its revival in Germany, and curbing all fascist activities and propaganda.

Another important integral part of the Potsdam Agreement was the commitment to liquidate the rule of the cartels, syndicates and other monopolies in the German economy, that is, forces that had brought Hitler to power and had encouraged and financed his military ventures. Such is the substance of the agreements concluded in Potsdam in 1945.

And what do we have today, more than 13 years after the Potsdam Conference?

No one can deny that the Soviet Union, on its part, has scrupulously observed all these agreements and that they have been carried out in full in the eastern part of Germany, the German Democratic Republic. Let us see how the Potsdam Agreement is being carried out in the western part of Germany, in the Federal Republic of Germany, the responsibility for whose development rests with the three Western Powers—the United States, Britain and France.

It should be openly said that militarism, far from having been eradicated, is rearing its head ever higher in West Germany. The Powers which should have fought against the resurgence of German militarism have drawn West Germany into the aggressive military bloc of NATO [North Atlantic Treaty Organization] that they have created. They are doing everything to promote the growth of German militarism and the establishment in West Germany of a mass army equipped with the latest weapons.

By decision of the Government of the Federal Republic of Germany, and, of course, with the approval of the NATO Powers, West Germany is building an army which the German militarists envisage as stronger than the armies of Britain and France. It is, perhaps, already stronger than the French army, in view of the fact that a substantial part of the French army is maintained outside the country in the colonies, where the liberation movement against the French colonialists is at the boiling point.

An Untenable Situation

The Soviet Union has come to the conclusion that the present situation in Berlin is untenable and must be changed, a situation where part of the city is practically split from the GDR [German Democratic Republic], is occupied by the USA, Great Britain and France and serves as basis for subversive activities against the GDR, the Soviet Union and other socialist states, that means activities which—to use the words of leading US politicians—may be called with full right an "indirect aggression".

For a proper approach to the Berlin question it is necessary to recall the historic development of Germany in the post-war period. This development has led to the creation of two separate independent states which are internationally recognised and which for years have acted as independent sovereign states in international life. All this makes the maintenance of any form of occupation in Germany by the victor nations of the past war an anachronism, which in the present situation is neither sensible nor justified any longer.

Soviet Government, Note to the East German Government, November 27, 1958.

The armed forces that are being re-created in West Germany are again headed by Nazi generals and admirals. The West German army is being trained in the predatory spirit of the Nazi Wehrmacht, in the spirit of *revanche* and hatred for the Soviet Union and other peaceful states.

Moreover, the German militarists—with the blessing of the Western Powers, and primarily the United States—are receiving

51

nuclear weapons. The Federal Republic already has American rockets which can be fitted with nuclear war-heads.

Economically, West Germany is literally grasping her West European allies by the throat. It is enough to note, for the sake of comparison, that in 1957, for instance, the Federal Republic produced 24,500,000 tons of steel as against 22,000,000 in Britain and little more than 14,000,000 in France.

West Germany is today also financially stronger than either Britain or France. Consider their gold and currency reserves, for instance. According to official figures, West Germany's reserves amounted to over $5,600 million at the end of 1957, as compared with Britain's $2,370 million and France's $775 million. All these economic resources of West Germany are being placed at the service of reviving German imperialism.

No matter which basic provisions of the Potsdam Agreement concerning the demilitarization of Germany and prevention of the resurgence of fascism we may consider, we shall inevitably arrive at the conclusion that these provisions, bearing the signatures of the United States, Britain and France, have been violated by them.

What then is left of the Potsdam Agreement?

One thing, in effect: The so-called Four-Power status of Berlin, that is, a position providing the three Western Powers—the United States, Britain and France—with the possibility of lording it in West Berlin, turning that part of the city, which is the capital of the German Democratic Republic, into a kind of state within a state and profiting by this to conduct subversive activities from West Berlin against the German Democratic Republic, the Soviet Union and the other Warsaw Treaty countries. On top of all this, they make use of the right of unrestricted communication between West Berlin and West Germany via the air space, railways, highways and waterways of the German Democratic Republic, a state which they do not even deign to recognize.

Western Interests in Divided Berlin

The question arises: Who stands to benefit from this situation and why have the United States, France and Britain not violated this part of the quadripartite agreement as well? The answer is clear: They have no intention of violating this part of the Potsdam Agreement. On the contrary, they cling to it, for the agreement on Berlin is advantageous to the Western Powers, and only them. The Western Powers, of course, would not be averse to perpetuating such "interallied" privileges for ever, even though they have long destroyed the legal basis for their presence in Berlin.

Is it not time for us to draw appropriate conclusions from the

52

fact that the key items of the Potsdam Agreement concerning the maintenance of peace in Europe and, consequently, throughout the world, have been violated and that certain forces continue to nurture German militarism, strongly encouraging it in the direction in which it was pushed before the Second World War, that is, towards the East? Is it not time for us to reconsider our attitude to this part of the Potsdam Agreement and to repudiate it?

Ending the Occupation of Berlin

The time has obviously arrived for the signatories of the Potsdam Agreement to discard the remnants of the occupation régime in Berlin and thereby make it possible to create a normal situation in the capital of the German Democratic Republic. The Soviet Union, on its part, would hand over to the sovereign German Democratic Republic the functions in Berlin that are still exercised by Soviet agencies. This, I think, would be the correct thing to do.

The West Has Revived Nazism

Under the rule of the Western powers the monopolists responsible for war and fascism, and the activity of their militarist and nazi associates, were once more admitted and supported. This was contrary to the decisions passed by the joint Municipal Assembly of Berlin, to the Potsdam Agreement and to the other agreements which formed the basis of the participation of the Western powers in the occupation and administration of Berlin. All the old trusts have been revived; not only fascist and militarist organisations have come back in large numbers, but the entire machinery of state is honeycombed with active nazis, thus resuming its former function as an instrument of reactionary and revanchist policy. As the Western powers destroyed the unity of Germany and Berlin by the segregation of the western zone and the formation of a West German state with a view to carrying out their plans to re-establish German monopoly capitalism, to remilitarise and incorporate Germany in the western pact system, they have forfeited their right of presence in Berlin; they have thus also lost all claims, all moral and political justification, for continuing the occupation of West Berlin.

Walter Ulbricht, Speech, October 27, 1958.

Let the United States, France and Britain themselves build their relations with the German Democratic Republic, let them reach agreement with it themselves if they are interested in any questions concerning Berlin. As for the Soviet Union, we shall sacredly honour our obligations as an ally of the German

Democratic Republic—obligations which stem from the Warsaw Treaty and which we have repeatedly reaffirmed to the German Democratic Republic.

If any forces of aggression attack the German Democratic Republic, which is a full-fledged member of the Warsaw Treaty, we shall regard this as an attack on the Soviet Union, on all the Warsaw Treaty countries. We shall then rise to the defence of the German Democratic Republic, and this will signify the defence of the vital security interests of the Soviet Union, of the entire socialist camp, and of the cause of world peace. . . .

West Germany and the Soviet Union

The leaders of West Germany say that good relations between the Soviet Union and the Federal Republic of Germany can only be established if the Soviet Union ceases to support the German Democratic Republic and if it brings pressure to bear on it along lines required by the West. Bonn does not, apparently, desire good relations with the Soviet Union if it entertains such absurd hopes. If the Government of the Federal Republic really wants to have good relations with the Soviet Union it should abandon, once and for all, the hope that we shall cease to support the German Democratic Republic.

VIEWPOINT

"A police state regime has been imposed on the Eastern sector of this city and country."

Soviet Attempts to Dominate Berlin Promote Conflict (1963)

John F. Kennedy

After serving in Congress for several years, John F. Kennedy (1917–1963) became the U.S. president in 1961. Soon after taking office, Kennedy went to Vienna to meet with Soviet Premier Nikita Khrushchev. Khrushchev threatened to conclude a peace treaty with East Germany, thus cutting off the West's access to West Berlin. Soon after, the East German government built the Berlin Wall. The following viewpoint is taken from an address Kennedy gave in 1963 at the Free University of West Berlin. Kennedy contends that Soviet and East German tyranny prevent a peaceful settlement of the Berlin crisis. He argues that Soviet efforts to expand the East German police state into West Berlin will fail.

As you read, consider the following questions:

1. According to Kennedy, what are the duties of the citizens of West Berlin?
2. Why does Kennedy believe it is important that citizens of East Berlin be kept in contact with citizens of West Berlin?
3. Why does the author conclude that "dogmatic police states are an anachronism"?

John F. Kennedy, speech given at the Free University, Berlin, Germany, June 26, 1963.

Sir, Mr. Mayor, Chancellor, distinguished Ministers, members of the faculty, and Fellows of this university, fellow students: I am honored to become an instant graduate of this distinguished university. The fact of the matter is, of course, that any university, if it is a university, is free. So one might think that the words "Free University" are redundant. But not in West Berlin. So I am proud to be here today, and I am proud to have this association, on behalf of my fellow countrymen, with this great center of learning.

Universities' Role in a Free Society

Prince Bismarck once said that one-third of the students of German universities broke down from overwork, another third broke down from dissipation, and the other third ruled Germany. I do not know which third of the student body is here today, but I am confident that I am talking to the future rulers of this country, and also of other free countries, stretching around the world, who have sent their sons and daughters to this center of freedom in order to understand what the world struggle is all about. I know that when you leave this school you will not imagine that this institution was founded by citizens of the world, including my own country, and was developed by citizens of West Berlin—that you will not imagine that these men who teach you have dedicated their life to your knowledge—in order to give this school's graduates an economic advantage in the life struggle. This school is not interested in turning out merely corporation lawyers or skilled accountants. What it is interested in—and this must be true of every university—is it must be interested in turning out citizens of the world, men who comprehend the difficult, sensitive tasks that lie before us as free men and women, and men who are willing to commit their energies to the advancement of a free society. That is why you are here, and that is why this school was founded, and all of us benefit from it. . . .

Goethe believed that education and culture were the answer to international strife. "With sufficient learning," he wrote, "a scholar forgets national hatreds, stands above nations, and feels the well-being or troubles of a neighboring people as if they happened to his own." That is the kind of scholar that this university is training. In the 15 turbulent years since this institution was founded, dedicated to the motto "Truth, Justice, and Liberty," much has changed. The university enrollment has increased sevenfold, and related colleges have been founded. West Berlin has been blockaded, threatened, harassed, but it continues to grow in industry and culture and size, and in the

56

hearts of free men. Germany has changed. Western Europe and, indeed, the entire world has changed, but this university has maintained its fidelity to these three ideals—truth, justice, and liberty. I choose, therefore, to discuss the future of this city briefly in the context of these three obligations.

Let Them Come to Berlin

Two thousand years ago the proudest boast was "civis Romanus sum." Today, in the world of freedom, the proudest boast is "Ich bin ein Berliner.". . .

There are many people in the world who really don't understand, or say they don't, what is the great issue between the Free World and the Communist world. Let them come to Berlin. There are some who say that communism is the wave of the future. Let them come to Berlin. And there are some who say in Europe and elsewhere we can work with the Communists. Let them come to Berlin. And there are even a few who say that it is true that communism is an evil system, but it permits us to make economic progress. "Lass' sie nach Berlin kommen." Let them come to Berlin!

John F. Kennedy, Speech at the West Berlin City Hall, June 26, 1963.

Speaking a short time ago in the center of the city, I reaffirmed my country's commitment to West Berlin's freedom and restated our confidence in its people and their courage. The shield of the military commitment with which we, in association with two other great powers, guard the freedom of West Berlin will not be lowered or put aside so long as its presence is needed. Behind that shield it is not enough to mark time, to adhere to a *status quo*, while awaiting a change for the better in a situation fraught with challenge. The last 4 years in the world have seen the most extraordinary challenges, the significance of which we cannot even grasp today. Only when history and time have passed can we realize the significant events that happened at the end of the fifties and the beginning of the sixties. In a situation fraught with change and challenge, in an era of this kind, every resident of West Berlin has a duty to consider where he is, where his city is going, and how best it can get there. The scholar, the teacher, the intellectual, have a higher duty than any of the others, for society has trained you to think as well as do. This community has committed itself to that objective, and you have a special obligation to think and to help forge the future of this city in terms of truth and justice and liberty.

First, what does truth require? It requires us to face the facts as they are, not to involve ourselves in self-deception—to refuse to think merely in slogans. If we are to work for the future of the city, let us deal with the realities as they actually are, not as they might have been and not as we wish they were. Reunification, I believe, will someday be a reality. The lessons of history support that belief, especially the history in the world of the last 18 years. The strongest force in the world today has been the strength of the state, of the idea of nationalism of a people; and in Africa and in Latin America and in Asia, all around the globe, new countries have sprung into existence determined to maintain their freedom. This has been one of the strongest forces on the side of freedom. And it is a source of satisfaction to me that so many countries of Western Europe recognized this and chose to move with this great tide, and, therefore, that tide has served us and not our adversaries.

But we all know that a police state regime has been imposed on the Eastern sector of this city and country. The peaceful reunification of Berlin and Germany will, therefore, not be either quick or easy. We must first bring others to see their own true interests better than they do today. What will count in the long run are the realities of Western strength, the realities of Western commitment, the realities of Germany as a nation and a people, without regard to artificial boundaries of barbed wire. Those are the realities upon which we rely and on which history will move, and others too would do well to recognize them.

The Requirements of Justice

Secondly, what does justice require? In the end, it requires liberty. And I will come to that. But in the meantime justice requires us to do what we can do in this transition period to improve the lot and maintain the hopes of those on the other side. It is important that the people on the quiet streets in the East be kept in touch with Western society. Through all the contacts and communication that can be established, through all the trade that Western security permits, above all whether they see much or little of the West, what they see must be so bright as to contradict the daily drumbeat of distortion from the East. You have no higher opportunity, therefore, than to stay here in West Berlin, to contribute your talents and skills to its life, to show your neighbors democracy at work, a growing and productive city offering freedom and a better life for all. You are helping now by your studies and by your devotion to freedom, and you, therefore, earn the admiration of your fellow students from wherever they come.

Today I have had a chance to see all of this myself. I have

seen housing and factories and office buildings and commerce and a vigorous academic and scientific life here in this community. I have seen the people of this city, and I think that all of us who have come here know that the morale of this city is high, that the standard of living is high, the faith in the future is high, and that this is not merely an isolated outpost cut off from the world, cut off from the West. Students come here from many countries, and I hope more will come, especially from Africa and Asia. Those of you who may return from study here to other parts of Western Europe will still be helping to forge a society which most of those across the wall yearn to join. The Federal Republic of Germany, as all of us know from our visit better than ever, has created a free and dynamic economy from the disasters of defeat and a bulwark of freedom from the ruins of tyranny.

Dismembering Germany

The Soviet demand to "liquidate" what they describe as the "remnants of World War II" calls for a "peace treaty" which amounts to a dismemberment of Germany by decree—with two or, if a "free City of West Berlin" is included, two and a half German states. There is only one way for the West to counter such a demand, and that is to insist that the right of self-determination be granted to the whole German people. No other Western response can be meaningful.

Willy Brandt, *The Ordeal of Coexistence,* 1963.

West Berlin and West Germany have dedicated and demonstrated their commitment to the liberty of the human mind, the welfare of the community, and to peace among nations. They offer social and economic security and progress for their citizens, and all this has been accomplished—and this is the important point—not only because of their economic plant and capacity but because of their commitment to democracy, because economic well-being and democracy must go hand in hand.

The Requirements of Liberty

And finally, what does liberty require? The answer is clear. A united Berlin in a united Germany, united by self-determination and living in peace. This right of free choice is no special privilege claimed by the Germans alone. It is an elemental requirement of human justice. So this is our goal, and it is a goal which may be attainable most readily in the context of the reconstitution of the larger Europe on both sides of the harsh line which now divides it. This idea is not new in the postwar West. Secretary George C. Marshall, soon after he delivered his famous speech at Harvard University urging aid to the reconstruction of Europe, was asked what areas his proposal might cover, and he replied that he was "taking the commonly accepted geography of Europe—west of Asia." His offer of help and friendship was rejected, but it is not too early to think once again in terms of all of Europe, for the winds of change are blowing across the Curtain as well as the rest of the world.

The cause of human rights and dignity, some two centuries after its birth in Europe and the United States, is still moving men and nations with ever-increasing momentum. The Negro citizens of my own country have strengthened their demand for equality and opportunity. And the American people and the American Government are going to respond. The pace of decolonization has quickened in Africa. The people of the developing nations have intensified their pursuit of economic and social justice. The people of Eastern Europe, even after 18 years of oppression, are not immune to change. The truth doesn't die. The desire for liberty cannot be fully suppressed. The people of the Soviet Union, even after 45 years of party dictatorship, feel the forces of historical evolution. The harsh precepts of Stalinism are officially recognized as bankrupt. Economic and political variation and dissent are appearing, for example, in Poland, Rumania, and the Soviet Union itself. The growing emphasis on scientific and industrial achievement has been accompanied by increased education and by intellectual ferment. Indeed, the very nature of the modern technological society requires human initiative and the diversity of free minds. So history itself runs against the Marxist dogma, not toward it.

Police States Are an Anachronism

Nor are such systems equipped to deal with the organization of modern agriculture and the diverse energy of the modern consumer in a developed society. In short, these dogmatic police states are an anachronism. Like the division of Germany and of Europe, it is against the tide of history. The new Europe of the West, dynamic, diverse, and democratic, must exert an ever-increasing attraction to the people of the East, and when the possibilities of reconciliation appear we in the West will make it clear that we are not hostile to any people or system providing they choose their own destiny without interfering with the free choice of others.

There will be wounds to heal and suspicions to be eased on both sides. The difference in living standards will have to be reduced by leveling up, not down. Fair and effective agreements to end the arms race must be reached. These changes will not come today or tomorrow. But our efforts for a real settlement must continue undiminished.

I am not impressed by the opportunities open to popular fronts throughout the world. I do not believe that any democrat can successfully ride that tiger. But I do believe in the necessity of great powers working together to preserve the human race, or otherwise we can be destroyed. This process can only be helped by the growing unity of the West, and we must all work toward that unity, for in unity there is strength, and that is why I travel to this continent—the unity of this continent—and any division or weakness only makes our task more difficult. Nor can the West ever negotiate a peaceful reunification of Germany from a divided and uncertain and competitive base. In short, only if they see over a period of time that we are strong and united, that we are vigilant and determined, are others likely to abandon their course of armed aggression or subversion. Only then will genuine, mutually acceptable proposals to reduce hostility have a chance to succeed.

This is not an easy course. There is no easy course to the reunification of Germany, the reconstitution of Europe. But life is never easy. There is work to be done, and obligations to be met, obligations to truth, to justice, and to liberty.

The Bettmann Archive. Reprinted with permission.

Distinguishing Between Fact and Opinion

This activity is designed to help develop the basic reading and thinking skill of distinguishing between fact and opinion. Consider the following statement: "By 1948, the majority of the nations in Eastern Europe were ruled by Communist governments." This statement is a fact which could be verified by checking encyclopedias, almanacs, or other sources which describe the governments of various countries. But the statement, "Soviet Russia brutally forced Eastern Europeans to submit to barbaric Communist rule" is clearly an opinion. The role the Soviets played in Eastern Europe after the war is a subject of debate and not everyone would agree that communism is barbaric.

When investigating controversial issues it is important that one be able to distinguish between statements of fact and statements of opinion. It is also important to recognize that not all statements of fact are true. They may appear to be true, but some are based on inaccurate or false information. For this activity, however, we are concerned with understanding the difference between those statements which appear to be factual and those which appear to be based primarily on opinion.

Most of the following statements are taken from the viewpoints in this chapter. Consider each statement carefully. *Mark O for any statement you believe is an opinion or interpretation of facts. Mark F for any statement you believe is a fact. Mark I for any statement you believe is impossible to judge.*

If you are doing this activity as a member of a class or group, compare your answers with those of other class or group members. Be able to defend your answers. You may discover that others come to different conclusions than you do. Listening to the reasons others present for their answers may give you valuable insights in distinguishing between fact and opinion.

O = opinion
F = fact
I = impossible to judge

1. In some countries civil liberties are not respected.

2. In both world wars, the United States sent millions of soldiers to Europe.

3. The American Declaration of Independence contains elements of English law such as the Bill of Rights and trial by jury.

4. Only English-speaking nations should decide the fate of Europe.

5. The Soviets lost about seven million people in World War II because of the German invasion.

6. In 1946 the United States stood at the pinnacle of world power.

7. The Red Army was the largest military force in the world in 1950.

8. The Red Army was a threat to people unless they were members of the Communist Party.

9. Because of the previous German occupation, the Eastern European peoples were used to a lack of freedom and they accepted Soviet domination.

10. Governor Thomas Dewey is in favor of an alliance with Great Britain in order to assure U.S. security.

11. The British are too imperialistic to stay out of another war for long.

12. The British, French, and Americans intervened in Russian affairs from 1919 to 1921.

13. Under friendly peaceful competition the Russian world and the American world will gradually become more alike.

14. The Communist countries have repeatedly brought the world back from the brink of World War III.

15. Capitalists need a tense international situation to intensify the arms race and enrich themselves.

16. West Germany is financially stronger than Britain; it has $5,600 million in reserves compared to Britain's $2,370 million in 1957.

17. West Germany's leaders want a new war with the East and are arming themselves accordingly.

18. All students who graduate from universities should be willing to dedicate themselves to the advancement of a free society.

CHAPTER 2

Do Eastern European Revolutions Signal the Demise of Communism?

Chapter Preface

One of the most distinctive aspects of communist ideology is its view of history. Karl Marx and other nineteenth-century communists believed that society would naturally progress from an unfair social system, capitalism, with great disparities between rich and poor people, to a fair social system, communism, where private property would be abolished and all wealth would be shared. They believed that this historical progression was inevitable and that communist ideas would triumph.

As the first nation to establish a Communist government, the Soviet Union implemented policies consistent with the goal of advancing communism. After World War II, the Soviets took advantage of turmoil in Eastern Europe and helped Communist groups take control of governments there. This advance for communism was important—it seemed proof that the world was moving toward this ideology. It also led to the conclusion that any revolt that threatened Soviet dominance had to be suppressed. A definitive statement of this idea was the 1968 Brezhnev Doctrine. That year, Soviet troops invaded Czechoslovakia to depose a government that Soviet leaders considered threatening because it was adopting radical reforms. In a speech defending the invasion, Soviet ruler Leonid Brezhnev said, "The establishment and defense of the sovereignty of states which have embarked upon the road of building socialism is of particular significance for Communists." Brezhnev warned the West against encroaching on the borders of any socialist country: "These frontiers are defended by the entire armed might of the socialist community." Thus the Soviet Union ensured that Eastern Europe remained on the communist path.

All of this changed abruptly in the autumn of 1989 when another Soviet leader, Mikhail Gorbachev, reversed the Brezhnev Doctrine. At that time, protests in Eastern Europe against communism were increasing and the rule of some hard-line Communist leaders was already shaky. Rather than calling for socialist unity against the opponents of communism, Gorbachev said, "The events that are now taking place in the countries of Eastern Europe concern the countries and peoples of that region. We have no moral or political right to interfere in events happening there." This and other statements made by Gorbachev suggest that the Soviet Union will no longer use force to ensure that the world progresses toward communism.

This startling reversal raises many questions about communism's future. The following chapter considers these questions.

"Liberty is an idea whose time has come in Eastern Europe."

Eastern Europeans Are Rejecting Communism

George Bush

George Bush has been active in politics for several years. He was a congressman before he became the nation's vice president in 1981 at the start of the Reagan administration. Bush became the U.S. president in 1989. The following viewpoint is an excerpt from one of the first and most significant speeches he gave on Eastern Europe. Delivered before the fall of 1989, when several revolutions swept Eastern Europe, Bush points to democratization in Poland and predicts that Eastern Europeans will reject communism. He states that the U.S. will help the Eastern Europeans overcome the economic damage communism inflicted on them.

As you read, consider the following questions:

1. What events does the author point to which make him believe the Cold War is ending?
2. What conditions does Bush attach to his proposal to aid Poland?
3. Who is responsible for Poland's new freedom, in Bush's view?

George Bush, "Encouraging Political and Economic Reform in Poland," speech given at Hamtramck, Michigan, April 17, 1989.

Americans are not mildly sympathetic spectators of events in Poland. We are bound to Poland by a very special bond—a bond of blood, of culture, and shared values. So it is only natural that, as dramatic change comes to Poland, we share the aspirations and excitement of the Polish people.

In my inaugural address, I spoke of the new breeze of freedom gaining strength around the world. "In man's heart," I said, "if not in fact, the day of the dictator is over. The totalitarian era is passing, its old ideas blown away like leaves from an ancient lifeless tree." I spoke of the spreading recognition that prosperity can only come from a free market and the creative genius of the individual. I spoke of the new potency of democratic ideas—of free speech, free elections, and the exercise of free will.

Democracy's Resurgence in Europe

We should not be surprised that the ideas of democracy are returning with renewed force in Europe—the homeland of philosophers of freedom whose ideals have been so fully realized in America. Victor Hugo said: "An invasion of armies can be resisted, but not an idea whose time has come." Liberty is an idea whose time has come in Eastern Europe.

For almost half a century, the suppression of freedom in Eastern Europe, sustained by the military power of the Soviet Union, has kept nation from nation, neighbor from neighbor. As East and West seek to reduce arms, it must not be forgotten that arms are a symptom, not a source, of tension. The true source of tension is the imposed and unnatural division of Europe.

How can there be stability and security in Europe and the world as long as nations and people are denied the right to determine their future—a right explicitly promised them by agreements among the victorious powers at the end of World War II? How can there be stability and security in Europe as long as nations, which once stood proudly at the front rank of industrial powers, are impoverished by a discredited ideology and stifling authoritarianism? The United States has never accepted the legitimacy of Europe's division. We accept no spheres of influence that deny the sovereign rights of nations.

Yet the winds of change are shaping a new European destiny. Western Europe is resurgent. Eastern Europe is awakening to yearnings for democracy, independence, and prosperity. In the Soviet Union itself, we are encouraged by the sound of voices long silent and the sight of the rulers consulting the ruled. We see "new thinking" in some aspects of Soviet foreign policy. We are hopeful that these stirrings presage meaningful, lasting, and more far-reaching change.

Let no one doubt the sincerity of the American people and their government in our desire to see reform succeed in the Soviet Union. We welcome the changes that have taken place, and we will continue to encourage greater recognition of human rights, market incentives, and elections.

East and West are negotiating on a broad range of issues, from arms reductions to the environment. But the Cold War began in Eastern Europe; if it is to end, it will end in this crucible of world conflict—and it must end. The American people want to see East and Central Europe free, prosperous, and at peace. With prudence, realism, and patience, we seek to promote the evolution of freedom—the opportunities sparked by the Helsinki accords and deepening East-West contact. . . .

© Kirk/Rothco. Reprinted with permission.

In Poland, on April 5, 1989, Solidarity leader Lech Walesa and Interior Minister Czeslaw Kiszczak signed agreements that will be a watershed in the postwar history of Eastern Europe.

Under the auspices of the roundtable agreements, the free trade union, Solidarity, will be formally restored; a free opposition press will be legalized; independent political and other free associations will be permitted; and elections for a new Polish senate will be held. These agreements testify to the realism of Gen. [Wojciech] Jaruzelski and his colleagues. And they are inspiring testimony to the spiritual guidance of the Catholic

Church, the indomitable spirit of the Polish people, and the strength and wisdom of Lech Walesa.

Poland faces, and will continue to face for some time, severe economic problems. A modern French writer observed that communism is not another form of economics; it is the death of economics. In Poland, an economic system crippled by the inefficiencies of central planning almost proved to be the death of initiative and enterprise. Almost—but economic reforms can still give free rein to the enterprising impulse and creative spirit of the Polish people.

Reviewing U.S. Policies

The Polish people understand the magnitude of this challenge. Democratic forces in Poland have asked for the moral, political, and economic support of the West. And the West will respond. My Administration is completing a thorough review of our policies toward Poland and all of Eastern Europe. I have carefully considered ways the United States can help Poland. We will not act unconditionally. We will not offer unsound credits. We will not offer aid without requiring sound economic practices in return. We must remember that Poland is still a member of the Warsaw Pact. We must take no steps that compromise the security of the West.

The Congress, the Polish-American community, the American labor movement, our allies, and international financial institutions must work in concert if Polish democracy is to take root anew and sustain itself. We can and must answer this call to freedom. . . .

The Poles are taking concrete steps that deserve our active support. I have decided on specific steps by the United States, carefully chosen to recognize reforms underway, and to encourage reforms yet to come once Solidarity is legal.

• I will ask Congress to join me in providing Poland access to our Generalized System of Preferences, which offers selective tariff relief to beneficiary countries.

• We will work with our allies and friends in the Paris Club to develop sustainable new schedules for Poland to repay its debt, easing a heavy burden so that a free market can grow.

• I will also ask Congress to join me in authorizing the Overseas Private Investment Corporation to operate in Poland, to the benefit of both Polish and U.S. investors.

• We will propose negotiations for a private business agreement with Poland to encourage cooperation between U.S. firms and Poland's private businesses. Both sides can benefit.

• The United States will continue to consider supporting, on their merits, viable loans to the private sector by the International Finance Corporation.

- We believe that the roundtable agreements clear the way for Poland to be able to work with the International Monetary Fund on programs that support sound, new, market-oriented economic policies.
- We will encourage business and private nonprofit groups to develop innovative programs to swap Polish debt for equity in Polish enterprises and for charitable, humanitarian, and environmental projects.
- We will support imaginative educational, cultural, and training programs to help liberate the creative energies of the Polish people. . . .

Great Promise

The historic, democratic movements that we are witnessing across Europe—here in Prague and in Bratislava, in Warsaw and Budapest, in Berlin, Sofia, Belgrade, and Bucharest—hold great promise for all of us. They hold the promise that Europe can achieve what President Vaclav Havel has called "the era of freedom;" what President Bush has called a "Europe whole and Free."

James A. Baker III, Prepared Address at Charles University in Prague, February 7, 1990.

If Poland's experiment succeeds, other countries may follow. While we must still differentiate among the nations of Eastern Europe, Poland offers two lessons for all. First, there can be no progress without significant political and economic liberalization. Second, help from the West will come in concert with liberalization. Our friends and European allies share this philosophy. . . .

What has brought us to this opening? The unity and strength of the democracies, and something else—the bold new thinking in the Soviet Union; the innate desire for freedom in the hearts of all men. We will not waver in our dedication to freedom now. If we are wise, united, and ready to seize the moment, we will be remembered as the generation that helped all of Europe find its destiny in freedom.

Two centuries ago, a Polish patriot named Thaddeus Kosciuszko came to these American shores to stand for freedom. Let us honor and remember this hero of our own struggle for freedom by extending our hand to those who work the shipyards of Gdansk, and walk the cobbled streets of Warsaw. Let us recall the words of the Poles who struggled for independence: "For your freedom and ours." Let us support the peaceful evolution of democracy in Poland. The cause of liberty knows no limits; the friends of freedom, no borders.

"Far from crumbling as some Western 'experts' would have it, Communism has simply adopted a new strategy in dealing with its Western enemies."

Eastern Europeans Are Not Rejecting Communism

Cardinal Mindszenty Foundation

Founded in 1958, the Cardinal Mindszenty Foundation has long worked to educate people about the dangers of communism. In the following viewpoint, the editors of the Foundation's newsletter, *The Mindszenty Report*, argue that communism is still active in Eastern Europe. They believe that the changes in that region are part of the Soviet plan to establish world communism. By allowing Eastern Europeans to liberalize and take apparent steps toward democracy, Moscow will fool the United States into disarming, the editors warn. They predict that with no one to oppose the Communists, they will take over all of Europe.

As you read, consider the following questions:

1. What point do the authors make by quoting Communist leaders?
2. What was behind the "Prague Spring" of 1968, in the authors' opinion?
3. Why are so many Americans unaware of the Soviets' new plot, according to the Mindszenty Foundation's editors?

Cardinal Mindszenty Foundation, "A Continuation of Red October," *The Mindszenty Report*, March 1990.

Reading the Communist press, which often features excerpts or entire transcripts of speeches and declarations by top international CP (Communist Party) leaders, including Mikhail Gorbachev, might well throw cold water on Western enthusiasm over "changes" now going on in the Communist world. Perhaps that is the reason the media never refer to these official documents where the Communists themselves go on in great lengthy essays explaining, for example, that in Eastern Europe "it is a socialist renewal and not capitalist revival that is taking place." (*People's Daily World*, Dec. 1, 1989.)

Surely something is taking place in the Iron Curtain countries, but is it what the media and some "experts" on Communism tell us? Is there evidence that Communism is crumbling like the Berlin Wall, its most infamous symbol of repression, oppression and suppression? . . .

Socialism's New Face

"The new image of socialism is its human face, which is in complete harmony with Marx's idea of socialism as a society of the future, ruled by humanism. The construction of such a society is the goal of perestroika," declares Communist Party General Secretary Mikhail Gorbachev (*Pravda*, Nov. 26, 1989.) "The idea of socialism as we understand it today," Gorbachev goes on, "is above all the idea of freedom. . . . Socialism is the bearer and upholder of the universally accepted democratic and human ideals and values."

Pravda, on Nov. 5, 1989, featured other thoughts of Chairman Gorbachev addressing a national student forum on the meaning of perestroika to wit:

> We are carrying forth a Marxism-Leninism freed from layers of dogmatism, staleness and short-sighted considerations. We are returning to its roots and creatively developing it in order to move ahead. In a word, we don't want an idealized Lenin, but a living Lenin. Lenin could not answer all questions of subsequent social development, and we must search for these answers ourselves, guided by the spirit of Leninism, the style of Leninist thinking, the method of dialectical knowledge. . . .

From these and countless other proclamations by Communist leaders and the Party press, far from crumbling as some Western "experts" would have it, Communism has simply adopted a new strategy in dealing with its Western enemies. As the *People's Daily World* explained: ". . . changes do not mean an end of the struggle between socialism and Western imperialism, between workers and monopoly capitalism. Only the form of that struggle will change. Now, instead of an emphasis of military confrontation between two military blocs—Warsaw Treaty and NATO [North Atlantic Treaty Organization]—the struggle will be centered more in the economic and political spheres."

This same point was made in a remarkable book published in 1984 by Anatoliy Golitsyn, a former Soviet KGB officer and expert on Communist disinformation who defected to the U.S. in 1961. Golitsyn's *New Lies For Old* predicted many of the events that captured headlines in 1989 as a result of what the *People's Daily World* referred to as "the process now known as perestroika." Ironically, *New Lies for Old* appeared a year before the April 1985 meeting of the Soviet Communist Party Central Committee where the world first heard the word perestroika put forth as official Communist strategy.

A Facade of Reform

Gorbachev's general program for Eastern Europe includes the erection of a facade of reform or internal perestroika (restructuring) as a means to get American troops out of Western Europe and to get a massive infusion of U.S. and western financial aid, capitalistic expertise, and technology. . . .

One of Gorbachev's double standards is his encouragement of "reform" in places like Poland and Hungary in order to get U.S. and western aid, while not allowing such changes in the USSR itself. Gorbachev has amassed more titles and personal power than any Soviet leader since Stalin, and is so sure of his position that he can threaten to resign knowing he would be persuaded to stay on by communist supporters. . . .

Soviet "reforms" have been presented to the West before in the guise of detente and peaceful coexistence, to say nothing of Lenin's own New Economic Policy (NEP). And the Soviet "reforms" have been consistently followed by greater repression and control internally, and military expansionism and aggression externally. . . .

The long arm and shadow of Gorbachev can be seen behind the musical chair changes of government leaders in Eastern Europe.

David B. Funderburk, *The New American*, January 29, 1990.

"Communist strategists are now poised to enter into the final, offensive phase of the long-range policy, entailing a joint struggle for the complete triumph of communism," Golitsyn wrote in the 1984 book. These Communist strategists, he added, "are equipped, in pursuing their policy, to engage in maneuvers and strategems beyond the imagination of Marx or the practical reach of Lenin and unthinkable to Stalin. Among previously unthinkable strategies are the introduction of false liberalization in

Eastern Europe and, probably, in the Soviet Union, and the exhibition of spurious independence on the part of the regimes in Romania, Czechoslovakia and Poland."

False Reforms

As an expert on Soviet strategy and disinformation, Golitsyn suggested, *in pre-perestroika 1984*—what other surprises might be in the making. At the time he was writing his book Leonid Brezhnev was still alive and in power. Brezhnev's successor, Golitsyn said, "may well appear to be a kind of Soviet Dubcek," the Czech "reform Communist" president to whom Brezhnev's successor, Gorbachev, is often compared to today in the media.

> The succession will be important only in a presentational sense. The reality of collective leadership and the leaders' common commitment to the long-range policy will continue unaffected. Conceivably an announcement will be made to the effect that the economic and political foundations of communism in the Soviet Union have been laid and that democratization is therefore possible. This would provide the framework for the introduction of a new set of "reforms."

> The picture being deliberately painted now of stagnation and deficiencies in the Soviet economy, should be seen as part of the preparation for deceptive innovations; it is intended to give the innovations greater impact on the West when they are introduced. . . .

"'Liberalization' in Eastern Europe," Golitsyn noted in his 1984 book, "would probably involve the return to power in Czechoslovakia of Dubcek and his associates. If it should be extended to East Germany, demolition of the Berlin Wall might even be contemplated. Western acceptance of the new 'liberalization' as genuine would create favorable conditions for the fulfillment of communist strategy for the United States, Western Europe, and even, perhaps, Japan."

A Dress Rehearsal

Noting that Alexander Dubcek's "Prague Spring" of 1968 "was accepted by the West. . . as the spontaneous and genuine evolution of a communist regime into a form of democratic, humanistic socialism despite the fact that basically the regime, the structure of the party and its objectives remained the same," Golitsyn pointed out that the "Prague Spring" was only a dress rehearsal of things that might come to pass:

> A broad-scale "liberalization" in the Soviet Union and elsewhere would have an even more profound effect. Euro-communism could be revived. The pressure for united fronts between communist and socialist parties and trade unions at national and international levels would be intensified. This time, the socialists might finally fall into the trap. United

74

front governments under strong communist influence might well come to power in France, Italy and possibly other countries. Elsewhere the fortunes and influence of communist parties would be much revived. The bulk of Europe might well turn to left-wing socialism, leaving only a few pockets of conservative resistance.

Most importantly, Golitsyn predicted in 1984, "NATO could hardly survive this process," with increasing Communist pressure for "dissolution of the Warsaw Pact in return for the dissolution of NATO." Today, says the *People's Daily World*, "changes in the Eastern European socialist countries, coupled with the USSR's many disarmament proposals and unilateral arms cuts, are in fact making NATO itself an anachronism." In fact, on Nov. 14, 1989, the same Communist paper declared: "Socialist countries, including the GDR (East Germany) . . . have offered to dissolve the Warsaw Pact if NATO is simultaneously disbanded." Golitsyn explained what that would portend:

"The disappearance of the (Communist) Warsaw Pact would have little effect on the coordination of the communist bloc, but the dissolution of NATO could well mean the departure of American forces from the European continent and a closer alignment with a 'liberalized' Soviet bloc." In other words, Golitsyn predicted the possibility of "a neutral, socialist Europe" with Soviet representation in an "all-European socialist parliament" under the slogan "Europe from the Atlantic to the Urals." A "common European home" is indeed one of the themes of Communist "liberalization." Here is how Gorbachev explained it on Feb. 5, 1990 at the Soviet Communist Party Central Committee meeting to discuss the 28th Party Congress platform:

> We remain committed to the choice made in October 1917, the socialist idea. But we move away from its dogmatic interpretation . . . the all-important thing for us now is to push forward the process of negotiating disarmament, deepen dialogue and mutual understanding on crucial sections of international development, and facilitate in every way efforts to expand and strengthen the ground which was covered in building a common European home.

With a "neutral, socialist Europe," Golitsyn went on, the only choice for the United States "betrayed by her former European allies" would be "to withdraw into fortress America" or seek an alliance with Communist China "as the only counterweight to Soviet power." The "greater the fear of a Soviet-socialist European coalition, the stronger the argument for 'playing the China card'—on the false assumption that China is a true enemy of the Soviet Union," he added. The U.S.'s refusal to take any strong action against Peking over the brutal repression of

75

students in Tian'anmen Square in 1989 is strong evidence that a U.S.-Communist China alliance is not unthinkable in the future. China, however, is no enemy of the Soviets, Golitsyn insisted, but will be used as a Trojan horse against the U.S. as Communist strategists have been planning for years.

No one, "not the CIA [Central Intelligence Agency]" or any other U.S. experts on Communism would have predicted what startling changes have taken place in the Soviet bloc a few months ago, U.S. Secretary of Defense Dick Cheney declared on national television on March 4, 1990. *No one?*

Anatoliy Golitsyn predicted many of these changes in the first draft of *New Lies for Old* in 1968. After his defection he shared much of its contents with British and U.S. officials who, with few exceptions, rejected his analysis of what changes in Soviet strategy could be expected in the future. The book, finally published in 1984, was ignored or criticized as too controversial. Golitsyn insisted, much to the consternation of some "experts" that, for example, the Polish Solidarity movement was being used by the Communists to soften-up Western public opinion on the long-range objectives of international Communism.

Meek Dictators?

The national press gleefully reports the events in Eastern Europe, where Communist dictators, after forty years of iron-fisted rule and the slaughter of millions of their own citizens, are now alleged to be meekly allowing a sudden disintegration of their empire. But the media tell us little about the backgrounds of these new leaders, neglecting to supply their anti-communist credentials.

Thomas R. Eddlem, *The New American*, January 29, 1990.

The Communists' major strategy "has been in preparation by the bloc for the past twenty years," Golitsyn pointed out in his book. This strategy was explained by the late Italian Communist Party leader Palmiro Togliatti, said Golitsyn, as "the consistent effort to bring about a political and economic consolidation of individual communist regimes, the construction of so-called mature communist societies, and the preparation of a semblance of democratization in order to provide support for the communists outside the bloc in realization of the major strategies.". . .

How do Communist leaders view what has happened in the Soviet bloc? What are the "Long-range Perspectives for Socialism," the title of U.S. Communist Party Chairman Gus

Hall's article in the *People's Daily World* of Feb. 9, 1990?

Recent developments, says Hall, "are short-term setbacks that are preparing the soil for long-term gains, creating the basis for a new and higher level of a more democratic socialism. . . . Socialism is inevitable because the decay of capitalism is an inevitable process. . . . Socialism will go through a painful transition to a higher stage of socialism. . . . A new kind of democracy, but a socialist democracy, will emerge. . . . At such times a positive outlook can be sustained more by understanding the long-range direction of human events—the progressive, inevitable direction of history itself."

Poised to Triumph

Far from seeing themselves "cast upon the dustbin of history," Communists—from Gorbachev to Gus Hall—are predicting a bright future of "democratic" Marxism-Leninism. As Anatoliy Golitsyn put it in *pre-perestroika* 1984—ironically the title of George Orwell's apocalyptic novel depicting the ultimate triumph of totalitarianism—"Communist strategists are now poised to enter into the final, offensive phase of the long-range policy, entailing a joint struggle for the complete triumph of Communism."

"The newly democratizing governments in Eastern Europe will not opt for some kind of democratic socialism, but will move quickly to relatively unrestricted market economies."

Eastern Europeans Will Adopt Western Liberal Values

Francis Fukuyama

Shortly before the 1989 revolutions in Eastern Europe, Francis Fukuyama wrote an essay arguing that communism was dead. In his controversial essay, Fukuyama stated that the Western liberal ideas of liberty and equality had triumphed. The following viewpoint is an excerpt from an essay he wrote after the revolutions in Eastern Europe. In it, he argues that Eastern Europeans have rejected the ideology of Marx and Lenin, and are adopting the economic and political values which guide many Western countries. Fukuyama is the deputy director of the U.S. State Department's policy planning staff.

As you read, consider the following questions:

1. What does the author mean when he uses the phrase, "the end of history"?
2. The author believes that Marxism-Leninism has been defeated. What trends in world politics does he predict now that communism is no longer influential?
3. Why does Fukuyama contend that economic concerns are now more important in world politics than in the past?

While the suddenness of Communism's collapse in Eastern Europe in 1989 surprised many of us, the fact that it occurred in the first place should not have. The fall of the regimes in Poland, Hungary, East Germany, and Czechoslovakia was the direct result of the death of Marxism-Leninism in the original homeland of the world proletariat, the Soviet Union. That death was not one of concrete institutions, but of an *idea*, and it is in turn part of a larger phenomenon—the remarkable consensus that has developed in the past couple of centuries over the viability and desirability of economic and political liberalism. It is this consensus around liberal democracy as the final form of government that I have called "the end of history."

History as a Process

The notion of the end of history is not an original one. Its best known propagator was of course Karl Marx, who believed that historical development was purposeful and would come to an end only with the achievement of a Communist utopia. But Marx borrowed from his great German predecessor, Georg Wilhelm Friedrich Hegel, the concept of history as a dialectical process with a beginning, a middle, and an end. We owe to Hegel the notion that history is propelled forward through the overcoming of contradictions between thesis and antithesis.

"History," for Hegel, can be understood in the narrower sense of the "history of ideology," or the history of thought about first principles, including those governing political and social organization. The end of history, then, means not the end of worldly events but the end of the evolution of thought about such first principles. That evolution comes to rest in the liberal-democratic states descended from the French and American revolutions and based on the principles of liberty and equality.

In the past century, there have been two major challenges to liberalism: fascism and Communism. Fascism was destroyed as a living ideology by World War II. Communism's challenge was far more severe. Marx asserted that liberal society contained a fundamental and unresolved contradiction, that between capital and labor. This has been the chief accusation against liberalism ever since. But surely the class issue has been successfully resolved in the West. The egalitarianism of modern America represents essentially the attainment of the classless society envisioned by Marx. The economic inequalities that persist and in some cases have grown worse in recent years are not an outgrowth of the legal and social structure of our society but the legacy of a preliberal past that includes slavery. . . .

It is the developments in the Soviet Union under Mikhail Gorbachev that have driven the final nail into the coffin of

Marxism-Leninism. Although formal institutions are changing only now, what has happened in the realm of ideas is a revolutionary assault on the most fundamental principles of Stalinism. The Soviet Union could not be described as a liberal or democratic country at present, though it made important strides in 1989. But at the end of history it is not necessary that all societies become successful liberal democracies, merely that they end their ideological pretensions to represent different and higher forms of human society. Despite his tactical invocations of Lenin, Gorbachev has permitted people to say what they have privately understood for years: that the magical incantations of Marxism-Leninism were nonsense, that Soviet socialism was not superior to the West in any respect but was in fact a monumental failure.

Jim Morin. Reprinted with special permission of King Features Syndicate, Inc.

What are the implications of the end of history for international relations? Suppose for a moment that Marxism-Leninism ceases to be a factor driving the foreign policies of Russia and China—a prospect that the past few years have made a real possibility. How will a de-ideologized world change at such a hypothetical juncture?

The most common answer is—not very much. Many observers of international relations believe that under the skin of ideology is a hard core of great-power national interest that guarantees a fairly high level of competition and conflict between nations. Believers in this line of thought take the 19th-century European balance of power as a model for what a de-ideologized contemporary world would look like. For example, the syndicated columnist Charles Krauthammer recently contended that if the U.S.S.R. is shorn of Marxist-Leninist ideology, its behavior will revert to that of 19th-century imperial Russia.

Waning Nationalism

In fact, the notion that ideology is a superstructure imposed on a substratum of permanent great-power interest is a highly questionable proposition. Since Hitler's fiery defeat, the legitimacy of any kind of territorial aggrandizement has been thoroughly discredited. European nationalism has been defanged and shorn of any real relevance to foreign policy, so the 19th-century model of great power behavior has become a serious anachronism. The most extreme form of nationalism that any Western European state has mustered since 1945 has been Gaullism, whose self-assertion has been confined largely to the realms of nuisance politics and culture. International life for the part of the world that has reached the end of history is far more preoccupied with economics than with politics or strategy.

To take the "neo-realist" theory seriously, one would have to believe that "natural" competitive behavior would reassert itself were Russia and China to disappear from the face of the earth. For example, West Germany and France would arm themselves against each other as they did in the 1930s, and the U.S.-Canadian border would become fortified. Such a prospect is, of course, ludicrous: Minus Marxist-Leninist ideology, we are far more likely to see the "common marketization" of world politics than the disintegration of the European Community into 19th-century competitiveness. Indeed, as our experience in dealing with Western Europe on matters such as terrorism or Libya proves, it is much farther than we down the road that denies the legitimacy of the use of force in international politics, even in self-defense. . . .

Soviet New Thinking

The real question for the future, however, is the degree to which Soviet elites have assimilated the consciousness of the universal homogeneous state that is post-Hitler Europe. From their writings and from my personal encounters with them, the liberal Soviet intelligentsia rallying around Gorbachev have undoubtedly arrived at the end-of-history view in a remarkably short time, owing in no small measure to contacts since the Brezhnev era with the larger European civilization around them. "New political thinking," the general rubric for their views, describes a world where economic concerns are dominant, where no ideological grounds exist for major conflict between nations, and where, consequently, the use of military force becomes less legitimate.

This post-historical consciousness represents only one possible future for the Soviet Union, however. The strong and persistent current of Russian chauvinism has found freer expression since the advent of glasnost. Unlike the propagators of traditional Marxism-Leninism, ultranationalists in the U.S.S.R. believe in the Slavophile cause passionately, and one senses that the fascist alternative has not played itself out entirely there. The Soviet Union, then, is at a fork in the road: It can start down the path that was staked out by Western Europe 45 years ago, a path that most of Asia has followed, or it can insist on its own uniqueness and remain stuck in history.

Adopting Western Values

The dramatic changes that have been taking place in Eastern Europe are a signal not only of political liberalization. They indicate that the nations of the region, completely disillusioned with socialist ideology, are in the process of filling their post-socialist ideological vacuum with values similar to values of American conservatism or European liberalism: a strong belief in individual rights, a governing system composed of checks and balances, and an economy shaped not by state planning but by the "invisible hand" of the free market.

Rafal H. Krawczyk, Speech at The Heritage Foundation, May 3, 1989.

The passing of Marxism-Leninism first from China and then from the Soviet Union will mean its death as a living ideology of world historical significance. For while there may be some isolated true believers left in places like Managua, Pyongyang, or Cambridge, Massachusetts, the fact that there is not a single large state in which it is a going concern undermines completely its pretensions to occupy the vanguard of history. The death of this ideology means a lessened likelihood of large-scale conflict between states.

This in no way implies the end of international conflict per se. For the world at that point would be divided between a part that was historical and a part that was post-historical. Conflict would remain possible between states still in history, and between those states and the others at the end of history. There would still be a high and perhaps rising level of ethnic and nationalist violence, since those impulses are incompletely played out, even in parts of the post-historical world. Palestinians and Kurds, Sikhs and Tamils, Irish Catholics and Walloons, Armenians and Azerbaijanis, will continue to have unresolved grievances. This implies that terrorism and wars of national liberation will continue to be important. But large-scale conflict must involve large states still in the grip of history, and they appear to be passing from the scene.

The Importance of Economic Concerns

The victory of political and economic liberalism suggests the vastly greater importance of economics to world politics. Indeed, the meaning of "great power" will be based increasingly on economic rather than military, territorial, or other more traditional measures of might. But the consensus that has formed around economic liberalism and market principles is only in part a victory of producers. Consumers, not producers, have the upper hand in the definition of national political goals; it is certainly consumers (or more correctly, potential consumers) who are driving the democratic revolution in Eastern Europe.

Producers in the developed world have been deregulated, taxed at lower rates, and generally liberated to operate more efficiently—not because their interests are regarded as paramount, but only because such a course seemed the best way to satisfy the demands of consumers. Consumers do not always want what can be measured in GNP [gross national product]: They also demand things like clean air and a safe environment for their children, and it is this broader set of goals that will shape the political agendas, both domestic and international, of the post-historical world.

For the moment, however, the potential consumers of Eastern Europe seem to want to liberate producers to create the prosperity they see in the West. Even Gorbachev redefined the essence of socialism to mean that the weak should get out of the way of the strong and efficient. The reforms announced in Poland suggest that the newly democratizing governments in Eastern Europe will not opt for some kind of democratic socialism, but will move quickly to relatively unrestricted market economies.

We are not quite yet on the other side of history. The spread of liberal democracy does not happen automatically or in a linear fashion. Individuals and governments will have to intervene actively to bring it about. The interdependence of politics and economics has never been more evident than in the delicate process of rebuilding liberal political institutions and market economies in the countries of Eastern Europe.

"What is absurd is the notion that the only available alternative to 'Stalinism,' or Communist centralized statism, is Fukuyama's 'Western liberal democracy.'"

Eastern Europeans Will Not Adopt Western Liberal Values

E.P. Thompson

E.P. Thompson is a prominent British historian. His books include *The Making of the English Working Class, The Poverty of Theory, The Heavy Dancers, European Nuclear Disarmament,* and *Beyond the Cold War.* He has also long been active in European peace movements. Thompson is the Raoul Wallenberg Visiting Professor at Rutgers University in New Brunswick, New Jersey. In the following viewpoint, he disputes the notion that Eastern Europeans will adopt capitalist democracy now that they have rejected Soviet-style communism. Thompson argues that there are many alternative socialist political ideas that may prevail in Eastern Europe.

As you read, consider the following questions:

1. For what reasons does the author disagree with the argument that the West won the Cold War because of its superior political ideas?
2. Why does Thompson believe that the Cold War ended with the Soviets making more effort than the Americans?
3. Why does the author object to the phrase, "the end of history"?

E.P. Thompson, "History Turns on a New Hinge," *The Nation,* January 29, 1990, © 1990 by The Nation Company. Reprinted with permission.

We have witnessed astonishing events, coming pell-mell one after another, rising in a surreal crescendo in the final two months of 1989.

The first signals were ideological, with the overthrow of forty-year-old taboos, with the publication of nonauthors and the rehabilitation of nonpersons. Then, in the Soviet Union, the curbing of the K.G.B., the surge forward in *glasnost,* the assertion of some forms of law. Then the astonishing televised theater of the Soviet Parliament and the defeat and humiliation of party officials in elections, followed by waves of strikes, especially of the miners, and the outburst of nationalisms. Then the rapid loosening of controls in Eastern and Central Europe and the virtual dissolution of the Hungarian Communist Party (I never thought I would see the sacrosanct Leninist dogma, the "leading role" of the C.P., withdrawn by the party itself). Power sharing in Poland. Then the spectacle of thousands upon thousands of East Germans crossing to the West, at first through Hungary and Czechoslovakia and later through the peaceful "revolution" in the G.D.R. [German Democratic Republic] and the opening of the Berlin wall. Then even the cautious Bulgarians joining democracy's chorus; the exciting days that transformed Czechoslovakia.

As a fearsome counterpoint to all this, the terrible theater of Tiananmen Square, the tank assault on students. And, as a climax to the year, compressing all the lessons of Stalinism into one horrendous week of bloodshed, the partly nineteenth-century and partly TV-inspired revolution in Rumania, with the Christmas Day execution of the Ceausescus.

Communism's Future

How, it must seem, could it be possible for any system to be more discredited than communism or any set of ideas to be exposed as more bankrupt than Marxism-Leninism? The question is enforced by the total loss of self-confidence in the ruling Communist circles in Eastern Europe and, very widely, in the Soviet Union.

No wonder Western cold warriors are sounding off their triumphal notes. It would be strange if they did not. Francis Fukuyama wrote "The End of History?" as a contribution to a symposium in *The National Interest*. He celebrates the "unabashed victory of economic and political liberalism," whose consequence will be "the universalization of Western liberal democracy as the final form of human government." Another contributor to the symposium, Professor Allan Bloom, is even more ecstatic:

This glorious victory . . . is the noblest achievement of democracy, a miracle of steadfastness on the part of an alliance of popular governments . . . over a fifty year period. . . . This victory is the victory of justice, of freedom over tyranny, the rallying of all good and reasonable men and women. . . . It is the *ideas* of freedom and equality that have animated the West and have won.

I must thank Professor Bloom for voicing with such naïveté the thoughts of so many others, and for giving me a text to interrogate. This text says that "we have won" the cold war and that this is due to the ideas and steadfastness of "the West."

The West Did Not Win

But hold on! It does not seem to be "the West" but the Soviet, Polish, Hungarian, East German, Czechoslovak, Bulgarian and Rumanian peoples who have started to settle their own accounts. The ideas of the "free West" have never, I think, been greatly at risk in the West from Communist tyranny—indeed that tyranny has often been a foil to set off Western freedoms to greater advantage. Certainly, notions of human rights have been strongly endorsed in some Western codes and institutions, although imperfectly practiced. But the peoples on "The other side" are not being dispensed these rights by some Western charity; they are obtaining them by their own efforts.

Indeed, one might call into question the whole triumphalist

Matt Wuerker. Reprinted with permission.

script, on several grounds:

• Far from hastening these changes, it can be argued that the NATO [North Atlantic Treaty Organization] posture delayed them. Nothing is more obvious than that the changes were long overdue, and that we are seeing the release of pent-up pressures. Leonid Brezhnev and his clique derived their only legitimacy precisely from the Western "threat" and from the need to "defend" against a heavily armed nuclear adversary. No human rights were ever introduced by the threat of nukes.

• One is also perplexed by the smug notion that over there they are adopting "our" values. I wish that I knew what "our" values are. (Medicare, or cutting the capital gains tax?) Some of these people, it seems, are guided by their own values.

In fact, the "free West" has had rather little influence, apart from the negative one of delay, upon these changes. In terms of challenge to Stalinism and Communist orthodoxy, one major stream has always been that of Communist self-reform, from Nikita Khrushchev, from Laszlo Rajk, Imre Nagy and Pal Maleter, from Alexander Dubcek to Mikhail Gorbachev. Another has certainly been human rights dissidents, but anyone familiar with Charter 77 in Czechoslovakia or with the Hungarian opposition over the past few years will know what a wide spectrum of ideas and values is involved: There is no simple transfer to the ideas of the "free West."

A Ludicrous Notion

• There is a ludicrous notion that the whole of Eastern and Central Europe is now intent upon hurling itself helter-skelter into a market economy, the restoration of capitalism in a Thatcherite form. Certainly the absurdities and the absolute failures of a command economy are making many in Poland and Hungary look in that direction. And the Poles, who will never listen to anyone and who must always learn everything for themselves the hard way, are just now on a "free market" high. (There is also a perceptible widening of the gap between a new political class, *Solidarnosc's nomenklatura,* and the proletarian founding members of the union who are falling out of the national discourse.)

But we are in times of great political plasticity, of rapid swings in trends and fashions. After Hungarians and Poles have swallowed the remedies of U.S. advisers and are suffering the consequences of steep price rises and unemployment, one can expect a more balanced reflection upon public and private priorities.

• In any case, what is absurd is the notion that the only available alternative to "Stalinism," or Communist centralized statism, is Fukuyama's "Western liberal democracy" (with the free market). Leninism and Stalinism have been subjected to dozens of other critiques. There have been critiques that shared some Communist premises—by Rosa Luxemburg, Victor Serge, Alexandra Kollontai, and thence to Nicolae Bukharin, Trotsky and so on. There has been the major social democratic critique and alternative, in all its variety. There are now the green environmentalist critique, the models of workers' control and smaller-scale autonomous and cooperative units, and many more.

The Revival of Radical Ideas

With Bolshevism disintegrating, capitalism long abandoned and state capitalist democracy in decline, there are prospects for the revival of libertarian socialist and radical democratic ideals that had languished, including popular control of the workplace and investment decisions, and, correspondingly, the entrenchment of political democracy as constraints imposed by private power are reduced. These and other emerging possibilities are still remote, but are no less exciting than the dramatic events unfolding in Eastern Europe.

Noam Chomsky, *The Nation*, January 29, 1990.

So we must watch and listen before predicting the outcome. And the outcome may well be different in different nations. New forms and improvisations may be discovered, drawing upon social democratic, cooperative and private initiatives. One can also envision a bleaker outcome, in which Central Europe becomes a dumping ground and a cheap labor manufactory for West German and Japanese capitalists.

Predictions of the Peace Movement

In all this we are told repeatedly that everything that is now happening is extraordinary, unprecedented, quite unpredictable. And yet the very substantial confederation of political forces gathered around the European Nuclear Disarmament movement (E.N.D.) not only predicted some of it but has been actively working toward it for a decade. From 1980 on, we put the causes of peace and freedom together. We repeatedly crossed East-West frontiers, entered into dialogue with official and unofficial voices and prized open the doors through which the events of 1989 have come. To our surprise, after 1985 our own words started to come back to us—from Moscow. It was Gorbachev who took our lines, who spoke of ridding Europe of nuclear weapons "from the Atlantic to the Urals," who proposed a practical agenda for the dissolution of both blocs, who advocated the withdrawal of Soviet and U.S. troops behind their own borders by the year 2000. . . .

The events on the "other side" have utterly destroyed the credibility of cold war military scenarios. As West German Foreign Minister Hans-Dietrich Genscher has asked, "Do we really want to acquire new nuclear rockets that can reach the Poland of Lech Walesa . . . or the Hungary of humaneness and democratization?" He said this before the Berlin wall was opened, which (to everyone except British Prime Minister Margaret Thatcher) terminated any possible notion of modernizing short-range nuclear weapons in Europe.

Ending U.S. Intervention

All this has fulfilled a good half of E.N.D.'s agenda. But not the whole of it. We had always proposed a mutual and reciprocal process of disengagement and withdrawal. We are still waiting for the other shoe to drop.

What do I mean by the "other shoe"? It is not just Western economic aid. It is certainly something more than Western applause and human rights rhetoric. Let me give examples. The Brezhnev Doctrine has been explicitly renounced. But as yet there has been no sign whatsoever of the renunciation of the Truman Doctrine of 1947, by which the United States asserted not only a right to intervene in Greece and Turkey but also to intervene when *any* nation was threatened by Communist "subversion." Nor is there any repudiation of the Eisenhower Doctrine of 1957, which extended the U.S. sphere of direct intervention to the Middle East (further extended by Jimmy Carter to the Persian Gulf).

The Truman Doctrine was nothing less than the direct passing-on of ugly British imperialist and royalist strategies to the United States during Clement Attlee's bankrupt second Labour Party administration. These doctrines license the perpetual presence in the Mediterranean and Persian Gulf of the Sixth and Seventh Fleets. I often wonder what on earth Americans suppose their fleet is doing raging up and down this European and African sea, from time to time shelling Lebanon or sending bombers over Libya. If Gorbachev can take his nuclear submarines out of Baltic waters, which lap against Soviet shores, it is surely time to withdraw some elements of the U.S. Navy from the Mediterranean. (The question may provide its own answer: The cold war with the Soviet Union is not the true reason for the deployment of the fleet but the pretext or plausible excuse for a wider exercise in imperialist control, an excuse made less plausible every day.)

The Soviet withdrawal from Afghanistan and self-criticism of its military adventure there have been matched by no such self-criticism by the United States of its sponsorship of civil war in Nicaragua. Gorbachev now speaks of his willingness to withdraw Soviet troops and bases from Central and Eastern Europe as part of a reciprocal agreement with NATO. But the United States has not responded by offering to remove bases from Italy, Turkey, Greece, Spain, Britain, Belgium or West Germany.

One could give further examples that show that the cold war is ending, but with one-sided concessions. If the Soviet leadership is, for the time being, satisfied with this, the peace movement in the West cannot be. There is work enough for us to do.

Strong Socialist Traditions

"Back to the market," has as many meanings as it has advocates. For some, "a mixed economy" is the answer to the overplanned, command economy that has all but collapsed in Eastern Europe and the Soviet Union. Others are hoping for a return to some kind of "free market" liberal capitalism combined with a strong welfare state. Many others favor "socialist renovation." A recent survey of 600 randomly chosen East Berliners found that 55 percent were still for a more equitable, democratically controlled socialism, and 30 percent favored free market solutions. It appears that the major demand in this more economically developed country focuses on political democratization, and the end of Communist Party rule rather than a return to capitalism. Amid the gloating by Western media that socialism has "failed," few seem to remember that strong socialist traditions among the working class and intelligentsia predate Communist and fascist rule by decades in Germany and Czechoslovakia. Far from a return to capitalist social relations, the revolutionary upheavals in these countries may produce the first genuine democratic socialist regimes in world history.

Stanley Aronowitz, *New Politics,* Winter 1990.

How on earth can these prestigious persons in Washington ramble on in their sub-intellectual way about the "end of history"? As I look forward into the twenty-first century I sometimes agonize about the times in which my grandchildren and their children will live. It is not so much the rise in population as the rise in universal material expectations of the globe's huge population that will be straining its resources to the very limits. North-South antagonisms will certainly sharpen, and religious and nationalist fundamentalisms will become more intransigent. The struggle to bring consumer greed within moderate control, to find a level of low growth and satisfaction that is not at the expense of the disadvantaged and poor, to defend the environment and to prevent ecological disasters, to share more equitably the world's resources and to insure their renewal—all this is agenda enough for the continuation of "history."

It is an agenda that will not find all the answers in an unrestrained market economy. On the contrary, we are going to need the fullest repertory of forms—cooperative, individual enterprise, social democratic, the centralized planning of some resources, autonomous units—as well as new forms and ways based on families, communities and neighborhoods, and new forms of self-government and simplified styles of living.

In all this, socialism has not been discredited, although command economy communism has; socialism is part of the inheritance we shall need, although drawn upon critically and selectively. The most viable future may well be a kind of socialism, although of a green and individualistic kind, with strong anti-state resistances.

A Wasteful, Destructive Dead End

It is profoundly moving to see the forms of the old cold war dissolving before one's eyes, but they are dissolving primarily on the other side. The cold war has not been a heroic episode, an occasion for triumph, but the most futile, wasteful, humanly destructive dead end in history. It has led to an inconceivable investment in weapons with inconceivable destructive powers that threaten the very survival of the human species and of other species perhaps more worthy of survival. It has nourished and reproduced reciprocal paranoias. It has enlarged authoritarian powers and the license of over-mighty security services. It has deadened imagination with a language of worst-case analysis and a definition of half the human race as an Enemy Other. Its refraction into internal ideological and political life has been malign for both sides. I need not document the offenses against human rights on the other side. On this side we have had absurd spy games, McCarthyism and redbaiting, the purging of trade unions and academies and the inhibition or closure of many intellectual areas.

"The events in Eastern Europe are not a crisis for socialism."

The Revolutions Pave the Way for True Socialism

George Fish

When Karl Marx and Friedrich Engels wrote *The Communist Manifesto* in 1848, they deliberately chose the term "communist" to distinguish their ideas from the utopian socialist ideas that had been developed by such thinkers as Pierre Joseph Proudhon and Robert Owen. The split between socialists and communists has persisted, and in fact, there are many factions within communism and socialism. Thus many socialists and communists object to the contention that the dismantling of communism in Eastern Europe proves that socialist ideas have failed. Many agree with George Fish, the author of the following viewpoint, who argues that what failed in Eastern Europe was Stalinism, a brutal distortion of socialist ideas. Now that Stalinism has been defeated, Fish believes the path has been cleared for the eventual triumph of true socialism. He is a freelance writer in Minnesota whose articles have appeared in many radical periodicals.

As you read, consider the following questions:

1. How does Fish describe Stalinism?
2. What does Fish mean by the term "socialist bourgeoisie"? How did the Soviet Communists become a socialist bourgeoisie?
3. Why does the author believe that "reality is Marxist"?

George Fish, "Marx Vindicated by East European Crisis," *Guardian,* November 15, 1989. Reprinted with permission.

Events in Poland, East Germany and Hungary seem like the realization of an orthodox Marxist's worst nightmare. But what are we actually witnessing in these developments in Eastern Europe, not to mention those occurring in the Soviet Union as well? Is Zbigniew Brzezinski right, that communism has failed, and is showing its living failure daily? Are Ronald Reagan and George Bush (not to mention Donald Trump) correct in asserting that capitalism is the wave of the future? Must we Marxists put aside our copies of *Capital, State and Revolution* and *Critique of the Gotha Program* and pick up Adam Smith and Milton Friedman instead?

A Crisis for Stalinism

Hardly. For the events in Eastern Europe are not a crisis for socialism, a socialism properly conceived, i.e., one humane and democratic. They are, however, a crisis for Stalinism. They are a crisis for a "socialism" conceived of as top-down collectivization, authoritarian, bureaucratic rule and management and dominance over all areas of life—economic, political, social, cultural, religious—by a rigid, self-proclaimed vanguard party. Under attack are these self-perpetuating elites, whose principal means of coming to terms with the recalcitrant masses is to make sure that the ministries of internal security and prisons are operating at full efficiency. This is the crisis of Eastern Europe, this is the crisis of "already existing socialism."

What was it that brought "already existing socialism" to this state? Was there an alternative, and what can now be realized in this tatterdemalion state of affairs?

To understand and assess this situation we must go back to the theoretical roots and reexamine the real possibilities inherent in anticapitalist societies. Real, not fanciful, possibilities.

For a funny thing happened on the way to the socialist millennium: several cherished shibboleths of Marxism were refuted by events. One of the casualties was Trotsky's theory of permanent revolution, which was shown to be a half-truth. A vital and enlightening half-truth, to be sure; but a half-truth nonetheless.

Still, a half-truth is half right. And Trotsky was certainly correct in asserting that there was no halfway house of a "bourgeois democratic" revolution between a moribund capitalism and seizure of power by the proletariat. This has been borne out by history since the Bolshevik Revolution. In 1917 only the Bolsheviks were capable of reconstructing a Russia on the verge of collapse and organizing an effective government. So it was with the Communist Parties put into power on the bayonets of the Red Army after World War 2—they alone had

Turner © 1990 Cartoonists & Writers Syndicate. Reprinted with permission.

the organization and the discipline to govern. The old, traditional bourgeoisies and their supporters were in doddering disarray, with not a few of them discredited as Nazi collaborators. And the social democrats were impotent. Only the Communists, in most places having the support of the working classes, at least initially, could shoulder the burdens of postwar reconstruction and the building of a social order not based on capitalist wealth and traditional privilege.

So anticapitalist measures were on the agenda, if by "capitalism" we mean the traditional capitalism of a market-oriented economy and a bourgeoisie of industrialists and financiers. But contrary to Trotsky, these anticapitalist measures do not mean the taking up of a socialist agenda, especially in states with underdeveloped economies, such as existed in Russia in 1917 and in Eastern Europe after World War 2. In most cases the essential economic task was accumulation—and even primitive accumulation. Accumulation and primitive accumulation can occur in only one way, the way delineated by Marx in "Capital" in his analysis of capitalist reproduction: by the extraction and appropriation of surplus value from the working class.

And this law is just as true in a collectivized developing economy as it is in an advanced capitalist one—collectivization by itself creates no new wealth. The new wealth for industrial development must be squeezed from every pore of the collectivized society—and the most porous sectors are the working class and the peasantry. They must literally be squeezed. Hence, the ruling Communists must use their power to squeeze the working class and peasantry in the name of, and even against the will of, the working class and peasantry.

Establishing a Socialist Bourgeoisie

The Communists then become the "socialist bourgeoisie," a ruling strata whose social role is to extract surplus value from the existing working class and peasantry in order to purchase the society of Communist plenty sometime in the indefinite future.

This hard logic of accumulation was discerned by a few perspicacious Bolsheviks, most notably Evgeny Preobrazhensky. Trotsky understood it too. In *The Revolution Betrayed* he compares the social role of the Stalinist bureaucracy to that of a police officer: in an economy of scarcity, where everything must be rationed, the police officer is there to keep order in the food lines, to dole out to each person his or her share, to make sure no one gets more than their due, and to keep the grumbling malcontents in line and prevent them from being unruly.

But where Preobrazhensky, Trotsky and the others erred was in surmising that there was something socialistic in all this just because the economy was collectivized. There was not. The collectivized economy was only pursuing capitalist tasks in a collectivist manner.

And the "socialist Bourgeoisie" was *forced* to play this role despite any subjective intentions or statements in party platforms. There was no alternative.

But that is only part of it. Our "socialist bourgeoisie" in the Soviet Union and Eastern Europe might have been relatively benign, governing the accumulation process firmly but not brutally, were it not for their being caught up in, and acquiescing to, the particular legacies, methods and insanities of historically developed Stalinism. This meant the pell-mell rush to industrialization, the madness of Soviet-style collectivization of agriculture, the fratricide of the purges, the omnipresence throughout society of the gulag and its threat, the Byzantine and obscurantist policies and pronouncements in culture, the arts, science and Marxism. Also part of this Stalinist model was the deliberate promotion of social inequities through the privileges and prerogatives awarded the party and state bureaucracies, the grotesque leadership cults and the steady rule of terror, by either barbarian or Kafkaesque means.

Socialism Has Not Failed

As Socialists who have always held, like Marx, that socialism and democracy are inseparable and who denounced Lenin's distortion of Marxism right from 1917, we vehemently deny that it is socialism that has failed in eastern Europe. What has failed there is totalitarian state capitalism falsely masquerading as socialism. Socialism, as a worldwide society based on the common ownership and democratic control of productive resources and the abolition of the wages system and the market with goods and services being produced and distributed instead to meet needs, has yet to be tried and more than ever remains the only way forward for humanity.

The Executive Committee of the Socialist Party of Great Britain, *Socialist Standard*, January 1990.

And now our "socialist bourgeoisies" with Stalinist faces find themselves vulnerable, pushed to the wall, by economic shortcomings, invidious comparisons with the West and a more educated and sophisticated populace. The "socialist bourgeoisies" can, in response, choose the vain course of trying to hold the centrifugal forces together, as in East Germany and Czechoslovakia; or can roll with the tide and try to reform, as in the USSR. And then there is a third option: to abjure any pretense to Marxism and communism whatsoever and abdicate in favor of bourgeois democracy, as in Poland and Hungary.

For 40 years in Eastern Europe, and for over 60 years in the Soviet Union, the iron rule of the Stalinist "socialist bourgeoisies" has been trumpeted to the masses as the building of socialism, the road to the realization of communism. They have paraded themselves as communists and as Communists—members of the vanguard party of the working class.

But the working classes know bosses when they see them, and they see these Communist "socialist bourgeoisies" clearly as bosses. What they don't see, however, is that these leaders could not have undertaken truly socialist tasks under the economic conditions that existed, and that their professed communism was hopelessly contaminated with Stalinism.

The working classes see only that they were denied freedom and self-determination by people who called themselves communists, and who justified unfreedom in the name of Marxism. From this experience comes the simple-minded political equations that currently rage through the societies of Eastern Europe: unfreedom equals communism equals Marxism; freedom equals capitalism equals democracy.

Reality Is Marxist

But as Che Guevara said, "I can't help it if reality is Marxist." And the reality of the Marxist dialectic dictates this: just as Stalin was a distorted version of Marx and Lenin, and just as Stalinism is the negation of Marxism, so the workers' anticommunism in Eastern Europe is negation of Stalinism, a necessary step in purging Marxism of the Stalinist incubus.

But the dialectic will not stop there, and new negations and new syntheses must inevitably follow, for the situation is too unstable to remain as it is. The workers will find out that rule by a traditional bourgeoisie is no better than rule by a "socialist bourgeoisie," that private capitalism is no better than collectivized "capitalism." And then the opening will be there for the rediscovery of Marx, for the proper understanding of the economic tasks of a society at a given stage of development and for mastery by the masses of the means to tame the "socialist bourgeoisie."

I believe the East European workers, peasants and intellectuals will find this out for themselves through experiences and political struggles. The road to finding this out will not be easy or short, and we will see an exacerbation of anticommunism long before we will see a new interest in Marx. But the workers' dialectical negation is absolutely necessary at this point; anticommunism East European-style is right now the only means available (other than the success of perestroika in the USSR) to fight Stalinism and hope for its defeat.

And only with the final defeat and burying of Stalinism can we finally come to grips with the problems of freedom and necessity in the transformation of society. In this way we can fully see our transformative aim as the realization of the kind of society envisioned by Marx and Engels in the *Communist Manifesto*: the one "in which the free development of each is the condition for the free development of all."

6

"The course and speed of events in Eastern Europe . . . call for an agonising reappraisal of widely held theories and deeply felt ideologies of socialism."

The Revolutions Force Socialists to Rethink Their Ideology

Andre Gunder Frank

Andre Gunder Frank is a professor of development studies and social sciences at the University of Amsterdam in The Netherlands. A well-known socialist theoretician, he also directs the University's Institute for Socio-Economic Studies of Developing Regions. He has written many books, including *The European Challenge, On Capitalist Underdevelopment, Reflections on the World Economic Crisis,* and *Capitalism and Underdevelopment in Latin America.* In the following viewpoint, Frank states that since thousands of Eastern Europeans suffered under and then rejected socialism, socialism's credibility is in question. He argues that socialists should respond to the revolutions in Eastern Europe by comprehensively reexamining their ideology.

As you read, consider the following questions:

1. Why does the author disagree with socialists who argue that Eastern Europe and the Soviet Union are not really socialist countries, thus socialism has not been defeated?
2. What specific issues and concerns must socialists rethink, according to the author?

Andre Gunder Frank, "Revolutions in Eastern Europe: Lessons for Democratic Social Movements (and Socialists?)," *Third World Quarterly*, vol. 12, no. 2, April 1990. Reprinted with permission.

The course and speed of events in Eastern Europe, which have surprised everyone (including their protagonists), call for an agonising reappraisal of widely held theories and deeply felt ideologies of socialism, of the nature of democracy and social democracy and of the role of social movements in both. Moreover, both the economic causes and consequences of these socio-political processes merit more attention than has been usual in the euphoric reception of the 1989 revolution. Their analysis offers at least a dozen important lessons, which are explored below. Hopefully, they can embolden us all to face, and act in, the future. . . .

An Important Transformation

Actually-existing socialism has undergone an important transformation because of these events and requires reconsideration. To account for these events and transformations, the prime determining factor has been the failure of actually-existing (non)socialism in Eastern Europe and the USSR to compete economically with the West. It is well known that the centrally planned economies achieved relative success through forced absolute growth. Heavy industry and, in some countries, large scale industrial agriculture boomed. Social services were provided and assured, but not individual services. It has become equally apparent that these inflexible economies were unable to promote intensive growth. It was precisely during the recent technological revolution, particularly computerisation in the West and in the East Asian NICs [newly industrializing countries] that the centralised economies of the USSR and Eastern Europe were unable to keep pace. On the contrary, they lost ground both absolutely and relatively. This was the most determinant starting point of the social movements and revolutions. As an economic failure, moreover, 'socialism' has proved to be no match for nationalism. First in Yugoslavia, Hungary and (above all) in Poland, then in the Baltics, Transcaucasus, Central Asia, the Ukraine, and elsewhere in Eastern Europe nationalism challenged the political economic order and demanded democratic self determination. With economic success neither these social and nationalist movements nor this (kind of) demand for democracy would have developed, much less this move to marketise the economies.

Such observations about Eastern Europe, however, require a brief, parenthetical, comparative glance at other parts of the world. It is noteworthy that economies throughout Africa, most of Latin America, and parts of Asia have recently suffered the same competitive failure, manifested in disastrously declining absolute living standards and relative marginalisation from the

99

world economy. Many of them have suffered even more than most economies in Eastern Europe. Perhaps Poland, Romania, Bolivia, Argentina (maybe Burma) and much of Africa top the sad list of greatest decline. Social movements have also developed in many of the other countries outside Eastern Europe, yet in none of them with similar results, or such far-reaching goals. . . .

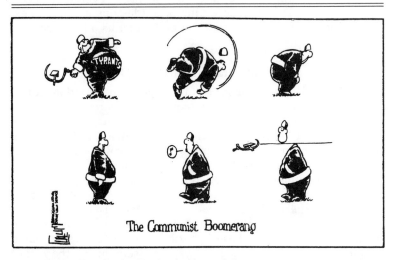

The Communist Boomerang

Cullum/Copley News Service. Reprinted with permission.

Of similar significance is the fact that in none of these other countries has there been a serious attempt to replace the obviously failing economic system by another, radically different one, let alone to replace the failure of capitalism by socialism. On the contrary, in terms of economic organisation there has been a move to the right, to marketisation (privatisation) everywhere. Moreover, the failure of 'socialism' in Eastern Europe can only accelerate marketisation elsewhere, no matter how socially costly run-away capitalism has already proved. None of the new democratic regimes in Latin America propose to reform, let alone to turn back, export-led growth (be it absolute growth as in Chile or absolute decline as in Argentina): the democratic opening is itself under threat from the repressive economic measures that democratic governments are obliged (not least by the intervention of the International Monetary Fund) to impose on their populations. . . .

Thus, the failure of socialist, but also of many capitalist and mixed, economies is marked above all by their inability to com-

100

pete adequately on the world market. Of course, this has always been the case; it is in the 'nature' of any competition that only few can win and many must lose. This process of selection operates largely irrespective of the capitalist or socialist 'system' that they use to compete, which is at best a contributory factor in the inevitable selection of winners and losers. Therefore, the economic failure and loss of 'socialism' *per se* is relative to both the success and also the failure of 'capitalism' to compete in the same ('capitalist') world market. The replacement of one 'system' by the other is no guarantee that any economy will then compete more successfully, most will continue to lose the race.

The move away from 'socialism', to the greater marketisation of East European economies and their further integration into world competition comes on the heels of recently increased and still-growing economic weakness. Therefore, they pose great economic and political dangers, not the least of further economic failure and of popular political disillusionment and backlash. . . .

The question arises of a possible, different socialism for the future. How and what would it come to be? An oft-posed issue, at least by some who consider themselves socialists, is whether the USSR and Eastern Europe (indeed any other place) has been socialist at all. Since their answer is a resounding 'no', they also argue that the long-standing failures and critiques of actually-existing socialism, which finally gave rise to the revolutions of 1989, were not really of socialism, but of Stalinism or some other aberration of, or imposter for, true socialism. The ideological implication of this argument is, of course, that these failures do not compromise the true socialist cause and do not oblige real socialists to undertake an agonising reappraisal. Real socialists, then, need only insist more than ever on their own critiques of actually-existing (non)socialism to differentiate 'us' (goodies) from 'them' (baddies). The 'practical' implication of this 'theory' is that, experience notwithstanding, true socialism is still around the corner—or at least down the road.

Preaching to the Converted

However, the real practicality and even theoretical coherence of this, perhaps well-meaning, argument clashes with all world social-political-economic reality. To begin with, if ever there was an argument that only preaches to the already (auto)converted, then this is it. It could not possibly convert those who have already experienced actually-existing socialism, even if it were really non-socialism: those amongst them who reject most of the previously-existing (non)socialism are likely to continue to reject any potential 'real' socialism. Indeed, many of them are likely to put their faith in the magic of the market and some, alas, in far-right politics. On the other hand, those who now lose the benefits of their previous experience will only yearn for the 'good old days' of order and stability and the (non)socialist *ancien régime*. Among these, those who had little and now lose even that will recall their modest benefits and ask for renewed order, if not of the old 'communist' variety, then perhaps of a new 'fascist' one. Only those who received much from the old party may now, under a new democratic socialist guise, try to hang on to as much of it as possible. The social democratic argument will also lack appeal for those elsewhere who never wanted themselves or any one else to experience 'socialism' or 'communism', of whatever kind. Therefore, it is wholly unrealistic to think that the damage of the whole experience to the idea of socialism, of democratic or whatever kind, can simply be wished away by latter-day professions of one's own purity against others' former sins.

No Viable Alternative

The fact is that today, no viable alternative to the dynamism of the world market has been developed. Given the collapse of communism, social democrats would now play a pre-eminent role if they could have demonstrated that there is an alternative. But, they haven't. . . .

It would be tragic for the Left to tarry long in its present wasteland of barren imagination. The Right, which always defends its own interests first, can allow itself the luxury of pragmatism and the short-term perspective. The Left, which struggles for the actualization of an idea about a more just society, is condemned to the long-term perspective.

Régis Debray, *New Perspectives Quarterly*, Spring 1990.

Second, however anti-Stalinist the subjective intent of this argument, its objective consequence is to stick to the guns of the Stalinist theory of socialism in one country (or even smaller community). Beyond disregarding the first problem and that of transition to this socialism in theory and praxis, this argument clashes with the same practical reality of having to compete in practice the whole world over. Yet the inability to do so was the fundamental failure and undoing of the Stalinist system, socialist or otherwise. Whatever the kind of socialism, capitalism, or mixed economy, Islamic political economy or other system that people may 'choose', they cannot escape world-wide competition; it is a fact of life. Cooperation as an 'alternative' is all very well, so long as it is more competitive.

Third, the (only?) alternative interpretation of 'real' socialism is 'world' socialism. Beyond its unreality for any foreseeable future, it is difficult to imagine what this might ever mean. What would distinguish this world socialism from world capitalism, so long as competition reigns as a fact of life in the future as it has for millennia in the past?

The Chances for Social Democracy

What of the chances for social democracy, if not democratic socialism? One time 'socialists' in the West and the East, including Mikhail Gorbachev himself, have found new appreciation for and interest in social democracy as the *desideratum*, which best combines both 'socialism' and 'democracy'. They, again including Gorbachev, look to Sweden, and sometimes to Austria, as the model for Eastern Europe and even for the USSR. In the architectural design for the new Common European Home, many socialists and social democrats would further provide for social democratic, if not democratic socialist, influences emanating from the East into the West. Thus, the whole of Europe would become another Sweden writ large. As Gandhi answered when he was asked what he thought of European civilisation, 'It would be a good idea.' Unfortunately, these good ideas take little account of some hard realities.

Thus, even disregarding the USSR, which is hardly realistic, the prospects for early Swedenisation in Eastern Europe are not very bright. On the contrary, it will take much effort by all, including Western Europe and even the USA and Japan, only to lay some—indeed, even to protect already existing—economic (social democratic) foundations for political social democracy in Eastern Europe. It is at best uncertain whether, and how much, a West German/European Marshall Plan would promote social democracy in Eastern Europe. Nor is it certain that such an enterprise would advance the progressive version of social democracy (with small or large 's' and 'd') and defeat conservative politics and parties in the West. Investment in good business (but not in unprofitable social investments) in the East could easily spell more polarisation in the West as well. Really 'new' social movements, East and West, could develop both to reflect and to propel such accelerated polarisation.

Dim Prospects

Thus, socialists are indeed obliged by the hard facts of life to rethink socialism, if they insist on sticking to their socialist ideology at all. We would not pretend to do this rethinking here and now, let alone do it alone. To be realistic, however, any such socialism would have not only to take account of competition, but to rewrite the rules of the (competitive) game under which it takes place. Gender, class, national, ethnic, religious, community, as well as economic, political, social, cultural, ideological and other interest groups and family or individual inter-relations would have to have new participatory social (movement) expressions and institutional protection of and guarantees for the mutual respect of their democratic expression and for the peaceful resolution of their conflicts of interest beyond anything hitherto known. Realistically, the prospects for any such 'democratic socialism, or otherwise, are still dim. Indeed, all the evidence is that things will, and will have to, get worse before they get better. However, things may get so much worse and so rapidly so that mankind may face a common economic-ecological and/or military-political and, therefore socio-cultural, crisis of such alarming proportions and absolute threat to physical survival, that we will finally be moved to get ourselves together.

Understanding Words in Context

Readers occasionally come across words which they do not recognize. And frequently, because they do not know a word or words, they will not fully understand the passage being read. Obviously, the reader can look up an unfamiliar word in a dictionary. However, by carefully examining the word in the context in which it is used, the word's meaning can often be determined. A careful reader may find clues to the meaning of the word in surrounding words, ideas, and attitudes.

Below are excerpts from the viewpoints in this chapter. In each excerpt, one or two words are printed in italics. Try to determine the meaning of each word by reading the excerpt. Under each excerpt you will find four definitions for the italicized word. Choose the one that is closest to your understanding of the word.

Finally, use a dictionary to see how well you have understood the words in context. It will be helpful to discuss with others the clues which helped you decide on each word's meaning.

1. A few *PERSPICACIOUS* Bolsheviks recognized that Soviet Communists like Stalin were setting up privileges for themselves.

   PERSPICACIOUS means:

   a) obnoxious   c) insightful
   b) ignorant   d) fussy

2. Astonishing, almost unbelievable events in 1989 rose to a *SURREAL* crescendo the last few months of the year.

   SURREAL means:

   a) foreign   c) intellectual and obscure
   b) big   d) fantastic and unreal

3. The magical *INCANTATIONS* of communist thinkers have proven to be nonsense.

   INCANTATIONS means:

   a) chants   c) prayers
   b) books   d) stern warnings

4. Socialist claims have been proven wrong when implemented in real life. Several cherished *SHIBBOLETHS* of Marxism were refuted by the events of 1989.

   SHIBBOLETH means:

   a) sword
   b) monument
   c) common idea
   d) unpopular belief

5. East European leaders might have been relatively *BENIGN* had they not been caught up in the brutal influence of Stalinism.

   BENIGN means:

   a) incompetent
   b) good-natured
   c) evil
   d) stupid

6. After suffering so long, Eastern Europe is now *RESURGENT.* The region is awakening to democracy and prosperity.

   RESURGENT means:

   a) stagnant
   b) regressing
   c) rising
   d) powerful

7. The gap between Solidarity's officials and common workers continues to widen; conflict between the *NOMENKLATURA* and *PROLETARIAT* is likely.

   NOMENKLATURA means:

   a) priests
   b) foreigners
   c) oppressed
   d) privileged class

   PROLETARIAT means:

   a) workers
   b) Poles
   c) business owners
   d) carpenters

8. Stalin allowed no one to disagree with him. His opposition to new information led to *OBSCURANTIST* claims in science, political thinking, and the arts.

   OBSCURANTIST means:

   a) profound
   b) mean
   c) outdated
   d) hidden

9. Communists are fooling the West and are now poised to take over the world, as predicted in George Orwell's *APOCALYPTIC* novel *1984.*

   APOCALYPTIC means:

   a) prophetic
   b) Biblical
   c) unusual
   d) hysterical

Periodical Bibliography

The following articles have been selected to supplement the diverse views presented in this chapter.

Timothy Garton Ash — "Eastern Europe," *New York Review of Books*, February 15, 1990.

George Bush — "People Are Demanding Freedom," *Vital Speeches of the Day*, December 15, 1989.

Jackson Diehl — "The Sparks That Set Off the Fires of Freedom," *The Washington Post National Weekly Edition*, January 22-28, 1990.

Milovan Djilas, interviewed by George Urban — "Milovan Djilas on Gorbachev's Future," *The New York Times*, December 3, 1988.

Mikhail Gorbachev — "Our Ideal Is a Humane, Democratic Socialism; Political Pluralism," *Vital Speeches of the Day*, March 15, 1990.

Meg Greenfield — "From Berlin to Budapest," *Newsweek*, February 5, 1990.

Gertrude Himmelfarb et al. — "Responses to Fukuyama," *The National Interest*, Summer 1989.

Christopher Hitchens — "How Neoconservatives Perish," *Harper's Magazine*, July 1990.

In These Times — "Remaking Eastern Europe," March 21-27, 1990.

Noel Malcolm — "The Song Remains the Same," *National Review*, March 5, 1990.

Arno J. Meyer — "Europe After the Great Thaw," *The Nation*, April 9, 1990.

Michael Novak — "The Revolution That Wasn't," *Christianity Today*, April 23, 1990.

Josef Škvorecký — "Czech-Out Time," *The New Republic*, December 25, 1989.

Socialist Review — "Reinventing Socialism," April/June 1990.

Paul M. Sweezy — "Revolution of '89: Is This Then the End of Socialism?" *The Nation*, February 26, 1990.

Caspar Weinberger — "A Noncommunist Eastern Europe Is Not Here Yet," *Forbes*, February 5, 1990.

World Marxist Review — "For Democratic and Humane Socialism," February 1990.

Z — "To the Stalin Mausoleum," *Daedalus*, Winter 1990.

What Economic Policies Should Eastern Europe Adopt?

EASTERN EUROPE

Chapter Preface

The term "market" often surfaces in discussions of economic reform in Eastern Europe. In this region, the market—the buying and selling of goods—has in the past been controlled by governments. Communist governments regulated what could be sold, how much of it, and at what price. Many people believe that excessive governmental interference harmed the economies of Eastern Europe.

The Austrian economist Ludwig von Mises predicted that centrally planned economies such as these would fail. He argued that these systems would be plagued by bad economic decisions because consumers' voices would not be heard. In an unregulated system, if consumers do not buy a product, the business stops producing it; if the product sells out quickly, more businesses rush in to start producing it. As von Mises's theory suggested, the lack of such a consumer-based mechanism in Eastern Europe led to extreme shortages of needed items and overstocks of useless or poor quality goods.

While many people agree that Eastern Europe's centrally planned economies did not work, few agree on how to reform them. Some experts advocate eliminating all restrictions on the market, while others argue that some regulations are necessary and beneficial. The following chapter examines the debate on this urgent topic facing the governments of Eastern Europe.

"The nations of Central Europe, far as they certainly have traveled, are still in need of painstaking education in the moral and legal foundations of capitalism."

Eastern Europe Should Adopt Capitalism

Juliana Geran Pilon

Romanian exile Juliana Geran Pilon is the executive director of the National Forum Foundation, an organization in Washington, D.C. that advocates a strong national defense. In the following viewpoint, she argues that Eastern Europeans should be encouraged to drop socialist ideas and adopt purely capitalist economic policies. Pilon contends that while the Eastern Europeans hate communism, they have not completely rejected socialist ideas.

As you read, consider the following questions:

1. What remnants of communist philosophy remain influential in Eastern Europe, in the author's view?
2. What evidence does the author find that suggests Poles have not fully embraced capitalism?
3. What characteristics do Central European intellectuals share, in Pilon's view?

The West has been watching, stunned, as a corroded Iron Curtain crumbles rapidly and irrevocably, the rust of its contradictory ideology finally giving in to the weight of time and irrelevance. Meanwhile the opposition in these countries is tasting power for the first time in nearly five decades and faces tough choices. It is now no longer enough merely to oppose Marxism. A positive plan must be forthcoming. And yet, while it is generally clear to the opposition that the free market is superior to a centrally planned economy, there is much talk about "the Swedish model," welfare rights, and, yes, equality. The nations of Central Europe, far as they certainly have traveled, are still in need of painstaking education in the moral and legal foundations of capitalism. Their encounter with democracy is, after all, not only geographically and historically distant but tarnished by decades of egalitarian indoctrination.

There is little doubt that Marxism-Leninism has long been discredited. The challenge before us is to rescue from under the rubble of its fatal misconceptions a philosophical base strong enough to see the long-mutilated nations of Central Europe emerge into Western civilization once again. For the logical leap from repudiating Marxism to defending capitalism is not apodictic. . . .

Progress in Rejecting Marxism

Some progress has occurred. The failure of Marxism has precipitated serious intellectual reexamination of first principles even among ordinary people with little or no philosophical training. As Josiah Lee Auspitz wrote in a June 1989 *Commentary* article, "Young Poles seem to understand that concepts like a legal person, freedom of contract, civic virtue, trust, separation of powers, and the rule of law must be reconstructed from the ground up, if prepared minds are to seize such opportunities as may present themselves."

The variety of philosophical schools that currently flourish in Poland is indeed testimony to the intellectual health of this nation newly emerged from communism. This is surely a momentous opportunity: There is a good chance that totalitarian ideology will be replaced by a healthy appreciation for pluralism, coupled with a rejection of simplistic scientism and ubiquitous, stultifying planning. For there is little doubt that communism, or socialism in its extreme form, has lost all credibility in the Soviet Bloc.

At the same time, the ideas of capitalism have made some inroads. British philosopher Roger Scruton explains in a journal article that what he calls "new right" philosophy (essentially, classical liberalism) has been infiltrating Central Europe for several decades now. Increasingly, he finds, this thought is influenced by "the phenomenology of socialist failure, the attempted return (perhaps in a state of unbelief) to Christian roots and to the 'symbolic order' which has grown from them, and the idea of the market as an expression of responsibility."

Steve Kelley/Copley News Service. Reprinted with permission.

Yet the capitalist credo is by no means dominant in Poland, members of the labor union Solidarity only recently having started to convert to nonsocialist ways of thinking, with still a long way to go. Neither has the Catholic Church traditionally been an enthusiastic supporter of capitalism. Miroslaw Dzielski, the late president of the Krakow Industrial Society, a free-market-oriented association, was initially shunned by the Catholic Church and later embraced only with reservations. Shortly before his untimely death in November 1989, Dzielski told me that the Poles are not yet ready to understand the significance of guaranteeing property rights. In an interview published by the Gdansk-based *Mloda Polska* journal on June 22, 1989, Dzielski said that "for the time being the left dominates the scene" in Poland, since "all [recent] democratic changes in Poland have been instigated by the left."

The problem, familiar to libertarians in the West, is that people see capitalism as an engine of material progress but not as a morally superior or politically attractive way of organizing human affairs. Dzielski told *Mloda Polska* that the 1980s have seen many changes in Poland; the concept of free enterprise has made great advances. The Krakow Industrial Society has gained respectability and influence, to the point that Dzielski could say that in fact "today there is no 'left' thinking in economy in Poland. In other words we seem to have succeeded." But, he admitted, "the left has a natural political and social support. This is the obstacle one finds hard to overcome."

Although the Krakow Industrial Society has been painstakingly educating Poles in the principles and mechanics of private initiative for nearly a decade, the road to privatization in Poland is still a thorny one. The society was legalized in 1988 and is gaining increasing official recognition, with three of its members in top government positions, including the minister of industry. Yet there is still far to go. Its proposal to create a credit bank to make small loans to entrepreneurs flounders for lack of a paltry $1.5 million in capital. Meanwhile, the Polish government asks Western governments for aid totaling billions of dollars—aid that, unlike the credit bank's loans, would likely not be repaid. Notes Polish free-market economist Rafal Krawczyk of the Catholic University of Lubin: "The Poles do not understand free enterprise. They apply it haphazardly and mix it with government controls."

Similarly, the statement of principles of the Hungarian Alliance of Free Democrats blends classical liberal ideals with welfare state rhetoric. So, for example, the Free Democrats declare, "we are heirs to European and Hungarian liberalism, which seeks to restrict the power of government over society, which desires an end to human defenselessness and which aims to realize the autonomy of the economic sphere." But they also say, "we are heirs to European and Hungarian social democracy, which was the first to discover efficacious means to protect working people against exploitation, making them conscious of their right to a decent living." The platform calls for "the right of individuals and collectives to have full jurisdiction over their property and . . . a free enterprise system." But it also speaks of "the right to minimum income" and "the right to prosperity."

Intellectuals' Distaste for Ideologies

Central European intellectuals, particularly in Hungary and Czechoslovakia, often not only have failed to fully understand free enterprise but have adopted a distrust of systems and ideologies in general. The Hungarian intellectual George Konrad, for example, writing in a "manifesto" entitled *Antipolitics,* opts for "a healthy pagan cynicism toward dedicated fanatics" of any stripe. Konrad favors a transcendent, transpolitical, or nonpolitical system of values—reflecting an abhorrence of all ideology.

Czechoslovakia's new president, playwright and former dissident Vaclav Havel, often couches his political writing in poetic language. In his 1984 essay, "Politics and Conscience," he decries Marxism as the most dangerous illusion of all, "a vision of a purely scientifically calculable and technologically achievable 'universal welfare.'" But his distrust of planning and science extends to a general suspicion of all ideologies, even, one might conclude, the nondirected system of capitalism.

Their Last Step

The nationalization of East European economies after the communist takeovers was a comparatively straightforward affair, but the restoration of capitalism is a much more complex and disruptive process. Structural reform will involve economic deterioration and social instability; the more far-reaching the reform, the more profound the dislocation. Western "carrots" should be geared toward lubricating the transition from socialist dictatorship to capitalist democracy. Talk of some "third way" is illusory and may simply preserve state control while manipulating capitalist elements to salvage their decrepit economies. . . .

The process of democratization and marketization must relegate the communist parties of the Soviet bloc to that infamous "dustbin of history" so often invoked by revolutionaries. The communists' "brave step forward" must indeed be their last.

Janusz Bugajski, *The World & I*, November 1989.

He resists ideological categories, deeming them out of date and too impersonal: "Or the question of socialism and capitalism! I admit that it gives me a sense of emerging from the depth of the last century. It seems to me that these thoroughly ideological and often semantically confused categories have long since been beside the point. The question is wholly other, deeper and equally relevant to all; whether we shall, by whatever means, succeed in reconstituting the natural world as the true terrain of politics, rehabilitating the personal experience of human beings as the initial measure of things, placing morality above politics and responsibility above our desires, in making human community meaningful, in returning content to human speaking, in reconstituting, as the focus of all social action, the autonomous, integral and dignified human I, responsible for ourself because we are bound to something higher, and capable of sacrificing something, in extreme cases even everything, of his banal, prosperous private life—that 'rule of everydayness' as Jan Patocka used to say—for the sake of that which gives life meaning. It really is not all that important whether, by accident of domicile, we confront a Western manager or an Eastern bureaucrat in this very modest and yet globally crucial struggle against the momentum of impersonal power."

On a less abstract level, the democratic revolution in Czechoslovakia seems to have been the work of young, largely apolitical students. Jailed with old-time dissidents in a crackdown last fall, the students learned the techniques of 1968 from their elders. But their anti-establishment fervor represented the rebellion of youth. Although they demanded elections and an end to the communist system, they offered no platform for what would come after. Alongside wall posters of Karl Marx, they hung pictures of Groucho Marx and John Lennon—neither exactly a symbol of a coherent philosophy.

Few Understand the Free Market

Opposition to authority clearly does not automatically translate into a libertarian philosophy. Karel Dyba, a senior researcher at the Academy of Sciences in Prague and former Communist Party member, observes that free enterprise has won the intellectual battle among many serious economists in Czechoslovakia. But, he adds, implementation of free markets will face many obstacles. Interest groups will undoubtedly be hurt as, for example, some prices increase. Already in Czechoslovakia, parliamentary deputies from mining regions have raised objections to free-market reforms that could put miners out of work.

But Dyba also notes that few people understand just what "the free market" entails. Deep-seated egalitarianism reinforced by decades of Marxist assumptions, may rouse people to oppose the privileges of the communist system. But it may also make them uncomfortable with the inequalities of capitalism—as Soviet citizens have begun to resent the prosperity earned by owners of private co-ops. . . .

An Experiment with Universal Relevance

The people of Central Europe have developed a deep love for their respective tortured nations, and a long, rich cultural heritage has fostered a sense of pride. Thus Havel, at least, does not beg for Western help, believing that the people of Czechoslovakia, in particular, must help themselves. Yet neither does he deny the universal relevance of what has happened there: for what is at stake is "the salvation of us all, of myself and my interlocutor equally. Is not the destruction of humans in Prague

115

a destruction of all humans?" What happened in Central Europe after the Second World War is the monstrosity of state control writ large. This experiment, therefore, has implications beyond Prague—or Budapest, or Warsaw.

It is not hard for me to imagine the state of mind of Central Europe. I recall that misty day in October, 28 years ago, sensing the despair I was leaving behind in my native Romania. In Romania, communism was born brain-dead, with little chance of ever gaining support. Yet as I left it, I had no appreciation whatever of capitalism. That knowledge would take years to gain, and longer yet to embrace.

"The social solidarity required . . . for modernizing the East European economies cannot be generated with an untrammeled 'pure' market economy."

Capitalism Will Hurt Eastern Europe

Bogdan Denitch

In the following viewpoint, Bogdan Denitch objects to the claims of American conservatives who insist Eastern Europe must become purely capitalist to succeed economically. Denitch argues that such a formula, in fact, would leave Eastern Europe with the same problems facing other capitalist nations: rich people becoming richer while poor people become poorer, rampant corruption, and social unrest caused by this unfair economic situation. Denitch is an author whose books include *The Socialist Debate*, *The End of the Cold War*, and *Limits of Change: The Crisis of Yugoslav Socialism and State Socialist Systems*.

As you read, consider the following questions:

1. What does the author mean when he states that Eastern European reforms may lead to "Mexicanization"?
2. What countries are most likely to succeed in their economic reform plans, in the author's opinion?
3. Why does Denitch believe that the ideas of such Western economists as Milton Friedman and Jeffrey Sachs threaten democracy?

Bogdan Denitch, "The Triumph of Capitalism?" reprinted with permission from the Spring 1990 issue of *Dissent*, a quarterly publication of the Foundation for the Study of Independent Social Ideas, Inc., 521 Fifth Avenue, New York, NY 10017.

The familiar debate about the prospects for capitalism and socialism has taken a sharp turn as a result of three new trends transforming the politics of the world. In brief, these are the collapse of the communist dictatorships in Eastern Europe, the end of the cold war, and the growing pace of European unification. Each by itself would represent a major development; the three together mark a profound historical change.

Changing Capitalism

One likely consequence will be a relative decline in the economic and military position of the United States, with a consequent loss of moral and political authority. This also means that the capitalism that will continue to dominate the world is likely to have new and peculiar characteristics, rather different from those propounded by Anglo-Saxon apologists. It will be a world capitalism without the familiar cold war; without the United States as dominant power; without a threat, real or supposed, of Soviet expansionism.

It will take some time for the magnitude of these changes to sink in. But, clearly, the capitalism likely to prevail in Europe will be different from the American and British models, perhaps in some instances sharply different. For capitalism is not an abstract entity, beyond the impact of time and historical change. Nor is it simply an economic system (whatever that might mean). It is a historically inflected and changing system, in which political, economic, and social arrangements interact.

Capitalism has its institutions and legal systems, its armed bodies of men, its dominant ideology, and certain kinds of political relations on a world scale. It is also a system in which the *political* rule of parties committed to its maintenance—as it exists in actuality, and not as a theoretical "model"—is necessary. This is true whether the dominant party is officially pro-capitalist or prolabor, conservative or social democratic. Seen from this perspective, capitalism is in considerable trouble in . . . Eastern Europe. . . .

Eastern Infatuation

Large sections of the East European intelligentsia, it is true, are now fascinated by the idea of "the market." That "market," however, has rather little to do with the market that functions in the real capitalist world. The talk about markets in former communist states often serves as a synonym or code word for seeing to it that the state and especially the party are deprived of control over the economy and society. In East European countries lacking a usable tradition of political democracy, the market that is now being introduced could well bring about

I SEE THAT FOLKS IN EASTERN EUROPE
WANT TO HAVE OUR WAY OF LIFE.
THEY CAN HAVE MINE ANYTIME.

Norman Goldberg/*People's Daily World*. Reprinted with permission.

what I'd call a process of "Mexicanization." Both Mexico and a
"Mexicanized" Eastern Europe have to cope with giant superpowers pressing down upon them; both are or will be mixed
economies with a powerful state sector, a corrupt yet vital private sector, an elite that includes technocrats, decent trade
unionists, corrupt trade unionists, as well as the rich and the
gangsters. We will have all of that in Eastern Europe, and whatever else, it will not be capitalism as described in textbooks or
the kinds of prose poems about the "free market" that have
been appearing in the American press. Rather, it will be a
highly politicized system, with political dominance manifesting
itself through the economy, although at least in part it will in-

clude a functioning market. But, *nota bene,* this market economy will be subject to considerable corruption as former bureaucrats of the nomenklatura join foreign investors in a scramble to grab the more lucrative chunks of the economy at knockdown prices. Happily, many of these people will lose their shirts—the fates are sometimes just.

Improving Welfare Systems

My prediction is that after the kissing stops, some very grim economic and social issues will come up. The prognosis for a decent democratic outcome is best for those countries with powerful, old-fashioned trade unions struggling to make sure that the burden of social transformation is not borne entirely by industrial workers and other employees. Whatever else, the upheavals in Eastern Europe did not take place in order to abolish the crude but almost universal welfare systems. To the contrary, *improvements* in services, health, education, and pensions, not to speak of living standards, are expected to result from toppling the party dictatorships—and sooner rather than later.

The idea of introducing the raw market of Thatcherite capitalism is therefore—short of authoritarian repression—politically unviable, even if it were morally and economically desirable. Since the communist parties are now disabled, an authoritarian repression could come only from the right, or from a curious union of communist technocrats and nationalist populists. In consequence, the optimistic prognosis for Eastern Europe would be for parliamentary democracies with strong unions, mixed economies, and a substantial socially owned or nationalized sector. In other words, a social-democratic type of neocorporatism, somewhat like the West European welfare states. The pessimistic prognosis is for a xenophobic nationalist-populist authoritarian neocorporatism with limited democracy. Neither represents quite the victory of capitalism now being celebrated in the Western press. And neither represents a victory of socialism. . . .

If, then, capitalism faces serious troubles, what has triumphed? What has triumphed is the notion that socialism is not something that can be wished into being overnight. What has triumphed is the notion that there may be an extremely long period of transition during which most countries will be a part of a single world market that is essentially capitalist. But what has not triumphed is the worldview of the Chicago school, Margaret Thatcher, Reaganauts, and the others; that peculiarly puritanical version of capitalism that is really a part of Anglo-Saxon exceptionalism.

In Eastern Europe the goal of democratic movements has to be the creation of a legal order where the judiciary system is independent of the state, a richly varied civil society autonomous from the state and the dominant political parties, genuine mass democratic trade unions, and a multiparty parliamentary democracy. These are necessary but not sufficient prerequisites for a genuine democracy, which should also move toward workers' control in the workplace, popular grass-roots participatory authority in the various institutions, and the abolition of gender oppression. Such democratic socialist goals are not to be counterposed to the institutionalization of a democratic polity. Fighting for these goals requires stable democratic institutions and development of a democratic political culture. A parliamentary democracy with powerful unions, parties, and social movements is the optimal terrain on which to work for democratic change. This requires tolerance, a virtue rare enough anywhere and positively priceless in Eastern Europe, where common sense argues against pushing political and national differences to the limit, at least until democratic institutions develop firmness and stability.

Begging the Question

To talk of Western market capitalism and the market economy begs these questions: which form of capitalism, which type of market economy?

Both Sweden and Argentina are capitalist states with free elections and market economies. So is the U.S. So is West Germany. So what? The differences between Swedish and Argentinian capitalism or between the welfare state and industrial democracy of West Germany and the squalid greed, poverty and illiteracy spawned by American-style market freedoms are immense....

Ninety-nine percent of the advice [Eastern Europeans] are getting encourages them to adopt a Latin American solution. Welfare subsidies should be cut, kindergartens and hospitals converted to private profit, wages driven down, a mentality of greed encouraged.

Denis MacShane, *In These Times*, March 21-27, 1990.

Tolerance of differences is essential in order to build stable democratic regimes. It is the precondition for a democratic civic culture. That means no vengeance, no matter how justified, against former communist hardliners, no attempts to illegalize communist parties, and above all no hunt for scapegoats in what will be grim times.

Eastern Europe is populated today with ghosts of chauvinist, populist, and right-wing corporatist parties. It is important to try to keep these ghosts quiet. Nationalism is the red meat of

121

the organic "genuine" Heideggerian national community, all too easy to mobilize against a mere "cool" legal and rational democratic universalism. It is therefore a continual threat to those who would build a multiparty democratic order. Nor does it help the prospects for democracy that many of the reformist intellectuals in Eastern Europe have fallen in love with the idea of the market. From love of that idea almost as much suffering may be visited on Eastern Europe as has been for the equally abstract idea of centralized planning. There seems to be no limit to how much suffering can be imposed on living bodies in the name of abstract ideas. That seems to be the original sin of intellectuals.

In Hungary national populists have already begun attacking "cosmopolitan," read Jewish, big-city liberals. Similar national populist attacks on economic reforms and pluralistic democracy, with or without anti-Semitic subtexts, can be expected in Poland, Romania, and Serbia. The road to democratization runs through perilous straits in Eastern Europe. That is why it is essential to help democratic institutions, trade unions, and civic groups with massive moral, political, and material support from the West.

Establishing Genuine Democracy

Genuine democracy requires at least minimal commitment to social justice. Effective political equality is not consistent with great differences in wealth. Wealth all too easily translates into political power. The social solidarity required to make the sacrifices necessary for modernizing the East European economies cannot be generated with an untrammeled "pure" market economy. There is no such thing as a "pure" economic policy that can be isolated from social and political consequences. Professors Milton Friedman and Jeffrey Sachs should be kept at a distance from policy making in Eastern Europe. Their policies are dangerous to democracy itself.

"A modern market system . . . doesn't necessarily mean capitalism."

Eastern Europe Should Adopt a Mix of Capitalism and Socialism

Valtr Komarek

Valtr Komarek is the deputy prime minister of Czechoslovakia. He was a key figure in the Czech government in 1968. That year the government, led by reformer Alexander Dubcek, attempted to assert some independence from Soviet control and to create a new, more humane socialism. In the following viewpoint, Komarek argues that communism's failure in the East Bloc shows that economies must use markets to encourage competition and efficiency. He maintains, however, that no market system is purely capitalist. Instead, the government adopts policies to redistribute income and provide all citizens with basic human needs like food, clothing, medical care, and shelter. He concludes that a combination of capitalism and socialism is the best system.

As you read, consider the following questions:

1. What is Komarek's assessment of the state of socialist ideology in Czechoslovakia?
2. Name three specific economic reforms the author advocates.
3. In the author's opinion, what is the significance of the Eastern European revolutions?

Valtr Komarek, "The Human Face of Socialism Returns," *New Perspectives Quarterly,* Winter 1990. Copyright © 1990, Los Angeles Times Syndicate. Reprinted with permission.

Everyone is surprised at how fast the regime collapsed in Czechoslovakia. Once the country stopped being just a garage for Soviet tanks, the regime's life depended on inertia alone. When the general population courageously stood up to the government after the brutality against pro-reform student demonstrators on November 17, 1989, the bravado of the Communist leaders melted away like a snowman in the rain.

Now that the people of Czechoslovakia have forced the Communist Party to give up its monopoly on power, what does the future hold?

The Communists Would Lose

If there were free elections today, the Communist Party would get perhaps 10 percent of the vote. Even great numbers of Party members wouldn't vote for the Party.

If the Party would abandon the Leninist principle of democratic centralism, which is incompatible with the democratic concept of citizenship, and if it united with groups on the socialist left, such as the Obroda Club comprised of former Communist Party members expelled from the Party after 1968, it might then, as part of a broad socialist coalition, gain a respectable share of power. But this is hard to forecast. Right now, as a consequence of its incapacity to react to events, the Communist Party is disintegrating as a political force with each passing moment. It is rapidly becoming a marginal party.

But what of socialism generally? As a theory or a model, socialism has collapsed completely. What people care about in this country is prosperity, democracy and clean air. They care about well-stocked markets and good theatres. In short, they are interested in mechanisms that can bring about these conditions, not grand models of society.

People are totally fed up with all the talk about socialism over the past decades; they feel antipathy toward it because they link it with repression. Socialism in Czechoslovakia can be discussed again in a more sensible way only if a new Social Democratic Party is formed along the lines of the Spanish or German Social Democrats; if the present Communist Party manages to transform itself into a modern party that tries to influence events exclusively by political means; and if a new all-European socialist left is formed that would give new meaning to this ideology. Only under such circumstances could socialists then compete persuasively with liberal and Catholic forces here in the same civil way they do elsewhere in Western Europe.

In making our transition from the past, we have the same aim as the other democratic movements that have coursed through

Eastern Europe: dismantling Stalinism in the political and economic system and returning to civilization. We all want a restoration of classical attributes, pluralist democracy and, above all, a modern market economy.

No Pure Capitalism

A modern market system, however, doesn't necessarily mean capitalism. Pure capitalism, after all, hasn't been around for a long while, even in the West. Rather, there are different mixes of the state and market.

The basic principles of a market economy are the same everywhere. At issue is the final social synthesis of pluralist democracy and the market economy. In a market economy, socialist ideals are expressed in the social, not economic, policies through redistribution of private profits for health care, child care, etc. We could conceivably end up with a "socialist synthesis" of the Swedish type, or a "liberal synthesis" of the West German type. Of course, what social system the new Czechoslovakia adopts will be determined by how well the political parties representing different programs fare in free elections.

Bruce Beattie/Copley News Service. Reprinted with permission.

In Czechoslovakia, we are particularly concerned to avoid the very serious problems of inflation and unemployment that have hit Poland, and, to a lesser degree, Hungary. The Czechs are used to full employment and social protection from the disruptions of a dynamic market, so we must avoid the situation we see elsewhere that leads to mass unemployment and too great a loss of social security. Our distinct advantage as a belated entrant into the reform era is that we can learn from the mistakes of others. While we obviously cannot reform without hardship, the experiences elsewhere in the East show that there must also be results very soon.

The brunt of hardship, I believe, should fall on the state enterprises that have been protected for so long: they must now face the economic pressure of competition. Surely, that will drive many of them into bankruptcy, no doubt causing unemployment for many thousands, but the consumer will benefit immediately from the broader selection of goods and the more flexible supply of the profitable firms that are able to respond to consumer needs and tastes. Pensioners and young families with children, on the other hand, should be most spared from the hardship of structural change, which is why we must avoid inflation. We must take a great deal of care that these most vulnerable groups are not asked to pay the bill for reform.

The New Reform Agenda

What Czechoslovakia needs is a program to de-bureaucratize the society, introduce market forces, stop the ecological destruction which has become very serious with pollution, and resume the effort to put a human face on Czech socialism.

On the economic front, we need to permit private ownership and private production, particularly in services—ranging from the telephone system to car repair—which are very underdeveloped. In the US, for example, some 70 percent of the work force, as compared to our 40 percent, is in services.

Private production would also introduce some variety and quality into our very gray array of textiles and foodstuffs. Our entire system of production has focused on mass production and average quality. The highest priority of the immediate future is to change this situation so that quality and variety in such goods as cars, textiles, electronics and other consumer goods become widely available.

We need to demonopolize and decentralize enterprises as well as introduce market competition. That means a proliferation of private, individual enterprises that operate by the rules of harsh competition. I envision thousands of small operations, some of which will succeed and others of which will go belly-up.

126

Such reform doesn't call for some monstrous plan. Economics is a matter of interests: it is a matter of people, ambition and a new social atmosphere that encourages individual initiative.

Redirect Investment

It is time to end the wasteful Stalinist attitude of production for production's sake. We should shift away from our foolish over-investment in mining, metallurgy and heavy chemicals to good quality, mid-range technologies such as advanced machine tools, which would fit the needs of Western markets.

Social Protections

It might surprise some Americans to learn that the collapse of communism has not turned East Europeans into partisans of American-style capitalism. As the specter of communism vanishes from Europe, it would be wrong to think that it means the end of the heritage of Marx. The demise of East Bloc communism and the convergence of Eastern and Western Europe will promote the victory of the other strain of socialism in a united, social democratic Europe. . . .

The people of Eastern Europe want political freedom, but they don't think that means giving up social protections such as free health care and free higher education or even government control of some institutions, particularly railroads, utilities and other vital monopolies.

Lucy Komisar, *Los Angeles Times*, January 2, 1990.

We also need to abandon autarky and liberalize foreign trade, opening up joint ventures with foreign companies. It is absurd that our goods—apart from Czech beer—don't even appear in Austria. Bratislava is a stone's throw away from Vienna, but you won't find Czech glass there. And our comparative advantage in tourism is tremendous. Instead of sinking scarce resources into hyperatrophied mining, the real goldmine is Prague itself, with its beautiful architecture, bridges and churches. It would cost us little to shift our resources in such a direction: the investment was already made in the 14th century by Emperor Charles IV! We would be able to compete very well with Vienna, which is such a short distance away and has such a lucrative tourist trade.

Naturally, greatly increased trade with the West requires a convertible currency, so we need to move quickly toward convertibility. The first step would be to join the International Monetary Fund and World Bank, either through an agreement with these institutions or perhaps through something like a new Marshall Plan. What we would be seeking initially is about $500 million worth of gold backing for the Czech crown in order to create a hard currency market. Once we have reached that first stage of convertibility, the basis for rapid trade expansion with the West will be in place.

A Real Europe

The Western European countries weren't ready for what has happened in Hungary, Poland, East Germany and Czechoslovakia. They imagined that Eastern Europe would stew in its own juices while they formed a common market. For them, "a common European house" was more an exalted figure of speech than something to be taken seriously.

All that has changed. Europe is suddenly emerging with a unified cultural tradition and political perspective. Adding 100 million new people to a nearly-integrated market of 350 million can make Europe a formidable competitor in the world economy to North America and the Pacific Basin. With East and West united again, the once unimaginable revival of European civilization will be at hand.

"The challenge to American business is to seize the historic opportunities . . . in the heart of Europe to demonstrate that free enterprise and freedom are but two sides of the same coin."

Eastern Europe Should Welcome Western Investment

Lawrence S. Eagleburger

Lawrence S. Eagleburger is the U.S. deputy secretary of state. In addition, President George Bush appointed Eagleburger to coordinate U.S. aid to Eastern Europe. The following viewpoint is taken from a speech he delivered to members of the American Chamber of Commerce. Eagleburger states that encouraging American businesses to invest in Eastern Europe is a key part of the Bush administration's plan to help these nations. According to Eagleburger, successful American businesses can demonstrate the benefits of the free market to Eastern Europeans.

As you read, consider the following questions:

1. What four objectives does the U.S. have for political and economic reform in Eastern Europe, according to Eagleburger?
2. In the author's view, what international agencies can help Eastern Europe? How?
3. What does Eagleburger believe should be the investment strategy of American businesses?

Lawrence S. Eagleburger, "America's Opportunities in Eastern Europe," speech delivered to the American Chamber of Commerce International Forum, Washington, D.C., February 16, 1990.

The year 1989 saw the most dramatic changes on the European Continent since the end of World War II. From the June elections in Poland, in which communist candidates were soundly defeated, to the fall of the Ceausescu dictatorship in late December, we have witnessed the steady march of democracy, freedom, and human rights across central and Eastern Europe.

However, the mind can only absorb so much change before numbness sets in and we begin to lose perspective. It is important, therefore, that we not lose sight of the fact that the democratic transformation of Eastern Europe represents the vindication not only of U.S. policy during the cold war but also of the commitment of American lives in two World Wars toward the making of a Europe which is prosperous, stable, and free. So our stake in the success of the East European revolutions is substantial. We are faced with the challenge and the opportunity to help assure the economic growth and stability which eluded the region in the wake of the First World War and to consolidate the freedom which was denied to Eastern Europe after World War II.

Careful Efforts

Make no mistake about it, this will be a tall order. But the United States cannot—and will not—shirk its duty. We are committing substantial resources to East European economic recovery, but we are doing so in a careful and calibrated manner. Our efforts should be focused on projects where we can make a difference, not dispersed over so many programs that none in the end will have a substantial impact. Our goal is to encourage reform and self-generating economic growth in the region and in a way which emphasizes close coordination with our allies to avoid duplication of efforts and to maximize our comparative advantages in the assistance field. Moreover, our blueprint for central and Eastern Europe accords perhaps the highest priority to the role that the American private sector will be called upon to play in the revolutionary transformation of these economies. . . .

A Framework for U.S. Assistance

The United States has been a leader among Western nations in providing assistance to Poland and Hungary. We must now expand our assistance efforts to the entire region of central and Eastern Europe, including Yugoslavia. We must develop a process and framework for managing the transformation of these countries from communist governments with centralized economies to pluralistic democracies with market-oriented economies.

The provision of U.S. assistance shall be based on the extent to which these countries are taking steps toward the achievement of four objectives that are very much in our mutual interests.

First, we want progress toward political pluralism, based on free and fair elections and an end to the monopoly of the Communist Party.

Second, we want progress toward economic reform, based on the emergence of a market-oriented economy with a substantial private sector.

Third, we want enhanced respect for internationally recognized human rights, including the right to emigrate and to speak and travel freely.

Fourth, we want a willingness on the part of each of these countries to build a friendly relationship with the United States. As President George Bush emphasized in his speech in Hamtramck [Michigan] in April 1989, hostile intelligence activities and technology theft are not friendly acts.

The Best Investment

I know that America has her own problems and difficulties, some of them very serious. We are not asking for charity. We are not expecting philanthropy. But we would like to see our country treated as a partner and a friend. We would like cooperation under decent and favorable conditions. We would like Americans to come to us with proposals of cooperation bringing benefits to both sides.

We believe that assistance extended to democracy and freedom in Poland and all of Eastern Europe is the best investment in the future and in peace, better than tanks, warships, and war planes, an investment leading to greater security. . . .

The decision by the Congress of the United States about granting economic aid to my country opens a new road. For this wonderful decision, I thank you warmly. I promise you that this aid will not be wasted, and will never be forgotten.

Lech Walesa, Speech before a Joint Session of Congress, November 15, 1989.

In deciding on the level and mix of assistance that we provide to each individual country, we shall be influenced by their movement toward these objectives.

I should add here that not all of our assistance will be conditional; some of it will be available to countries as they need it and are able to use it. In this category, I would place emergency and humanitarian aid, designed to relieve deprivation and give a new government some breathing room. The medical supplies we have provided to Romania and the food relief we have provided both to Poland and Romania are examples of this assistance. . . .

Beyond this first level of assistance, we are prepared to ease the barriers to trade and investment as the countries of Eastern Europe meet the requirements of U.S. laws. Bilateral trade and investment agreements, most-favored-nation (MFN) treatment, eligibility for export credit guarantees from our Export-Import Bank and Commodity Credit Corporation, authority for the U.S. Overseas Private Investment Corporation (OPIC) to operate in these countries—all these are tools which would benefit both the United States and the countries of Eastern Europe.

Finally, we are prepared to offer a third level of assistance to those countries which are committed to the difficult and painful task of institutionalizing political and economic reforms. We know that making the transition from a controlled, planned economy to a market-oriented economy is tough; in fact, it has never been done before. But we believe this is the only avenue to self-sustaining growth, and, therefore, we are prepared to extend transitional economic support to those countries which are willing to bite the bullet to help themselves.

Our approach includes bilateral measures such as money for stabilization funds designed to bring hyper-inflation under control and make possible a shift to convertibility of local currencies. It also includes the provision of capital to stimulate private sector development, whether on a bilateral basis through "enterprise funds" or through a willingness to consider participation in a new multilateral institution such as the proposed European Bank for Reconstruction and Development (EBRD).

Debt Relief

Debt relief can be an important tool as well; we are prepared to join our partners in the Paris group in providing such relief. Access to concessional trade programs, such as the generalized system of preferences (GSP), also fits into the category of transitional economic support. Finally, we believe international financial institutions, such as the International Monetary Fund (IMF) and World Bank, can provide important assistance in integrating Eastern Europe into the world economy. We will support the efforts of those countries committed to reform to join these institutions as they meet membership criteria.

Poland and Hungary have led the way on the path of reform and thus are beneficiaries of our new policy of differentiation. Czechoslovakia is clearly determined to move rapidly to institutionalize political and economic reforms, and Secretary of State James Baker announced a package of U.S. assistance measures in Prague which take account of this fact. The other countries of Eastern Europe—as well as Yugoslavia—are, to various degrees, preparing the ground for free elections and institutionalized political and economic reforms. We look forward to the time when they are clearly committed to representative democracy and a real transition to free markets. . . . We seek the flexibility to respond as these countries move into a new phase of political and economic developments. . . .

Direct Western Investment

The most important component of an economic agenda is direct Western investment. Joint ventures are one vehicle. Another is a mutual fund to invest in the shares of companies in those countries where this is possible. . . .

A second component of an economic agenda will be much stronger encouragement of Western companies' involvement in Eastern Europe. . . .

There are many concrete steps the West can take, and there is reason for hope. In Hungary, for example, from 1986 to 1988 the number of U.S. companies with offices in Budapest increased from seven to twenty, and the number of Western joint ventures in Hungary exceeded one hundred. The world fair, now planned to be held simultaneously in Vienna and Budapest in 1995, is an excellent example of the kind of bridging that is desirable and a U.S. company, Bechtel, has a contract to help set up the fair.

Mark Palmer, in *Central and Eastern Europe: The Opening Curtain?* 1989.

Building a sound infrastructure is a way of encouraging the flow of Western capital. In a time of budget constraints, we have deliberately sought to wield those instruments at our disposal—OPIC insurance and Export-Import Bank credits, above all—which will act as a catalyst for private sector investment. We are also working to reduce, and where possible eliminate, barriers to American business throughout the region.

Your expertise—as well as your financial resources—are vital to achieving our overall national objectives in Eastern Europe. Obviously there is much that we as a government can do, both in the area of resources and in terms of building democratic institutions. But Eastern Europe is never going to overcome its legacy of underdevelopment and instability unless East Europeans learn how to become self-reliant and self-sufficient economically. And this they must learn from you. It is you who can impart the genius of entrepreneurial success. Your trade, your know-how, and your investment can be the engine for economic growth and the political transformation of Eastern

Europe.

It is true that during the transitional phase ahead, foreign companies will face a difficult landscape. Laws and policies will be changing. New ideas will be clashing with old habits. Credit, banking, communications, and other facilities for doing business will be well below Western standards, at least in the beginning. The entrepreneurs you deal with are going to be inexperienced and often unrealistic in their expectations. And they will be constantly adjusting to change themselves.

An Unusual Opportunity

But with all that said, Eastern Europe presents an unusual opportunity. The needs are obvious, and the East Europeans are looking outward for investment and know-how. Our experience, our advice, and our capital are needed and welcome. Lech Walesa, in his visit to the United States, repeatedly stressed to U.S. businessmen the opportunities in Poland. A presidential mission to Poland, led by Secretary of Agriculture Clayton Yeutter, found numerous areas for Western investment, including agriculture, environmental technology, telecommunications, banking, housing, and energy.

The same needs exist throughout central and Eastern Europe. Privatization of state enterprises, badly needed infrastructure projects, the growth of private sectors, and the creation of capital markets all offer major openings for foreign firms.

The East Europeans, for their part, are moving quickly to open their economies to foreign investment. Poland has embarked on a major structural adjustment program approved by the IMF. Part of that effort includes a plan for making the zloty convertible and passing new laws on banking, foreign investment, and customs, all designed to work in the free-market system. East Germany has adopted legislation allowing joint ventures and in some cases majority foreign ownership of East German firms. Czechoslovakia is revamping its joint venture law to allow majority foreign ownership of companies. Hungary has created a stock market and is actively pursuing foreign investment; General Electric's deal with Tungsram is just one example of the opportunities in that country. Yugoslavia has made its currency convertible, created a stock market, and introduced a program of market-based economic reform.

I understand your responsibility to your companies and to your shareholders. Obviously, you have to be satisfied that the mix of risk and return on investment in Eastern Europe is competitive with other opportunities. And it may not be easy today to see when an investment in Poland or Hungary or Czechoslovakia will finally turn a profit.

What I would ask of you is to be both aggressive and patient at the same time. If you wait until Eastern Europe's markets fully stabilize before going in, you will probably find when you arrive that foreign competitors have beaten you to the punch. But by the same token, if you go into Eastern Europe expecting quick profits, you will probably be disappointed. Moreover, I can assure you that your West European competitors will decidedly not be aiming to make a quick buck. Thus, the most successful American firms will be those that move quickly to establish a long-term presence in Eastern Europe—a presence upon which our long-term national influence in the region will largely depend.

Remove the Barriers

To help supply capital and consumer goods for their economies, East European countries must open their systems to foreign investment and imports. Foreign investors not only must be allowed to bring their money into the country, they must be allowed to take out their profits and eventually their principal investment. This gives them greater assurance that their investments are safe against government abuse. This can be done by removing controls on the import and export of capital, removing tariffs and other protectionist measures, and providing legal guarantees against expropriation.

Edward L. Hudgins and Douglas Seay, The Heritage Foundation *Backgrounder*, March 13, 1990.

One of the first things Secretary Baker did at the State Department was to inform our diplomatic representatives overseas that improving American export performance is a top priority of this Administration. He told the chiefs of American overseas missions to be the principal commercial officer at their posts and to become personally involved in promoting U.S. exports and assisting U.S. business. He also instructed them to assure that each member of their mission is committed to promoting U.S. business interests. We are serious. We mean it. And we intend to succeed. . . .

Meeting the Challenge

The U.S. Government is meeting the challenge in Eastern Europe. We are supporting the establishment of democracy and free enterprise. The challenge to American business is to seize the historic opportunities which now exist in the heart of Europe to demonstrate that free enterprise and freedom are but two sides of the same coin.

"Those countries suffering the worst economic problems are . . . those most integrated with, and dependent on, western markets and western capital."

Eastern Europe Should Reject Western Investment

Paul Phillips

In the 1970s, many East Bloc countries borrowed large sums of money from Western banks. Unfortunately, the money did not generate economic growth in these countries and now many Eastern European governments cannot afford to pay back the huge debts. In the following viewpoint, Paul Phillips argues that advocating Western investment to alleviate the debt problem is the wrong strategy. Such investment would prevent Eastern Europeans from establishing independent, viable economies, he argues. Phillips teaches economics at the University of Manitoba in Winnipeg, Canada.

As you read, consider the following questions:

1. What are some of the reforms East Bloc economists are advocating? Why does Phillips believe the reforms will fail?
2. In the author's opinion, what are Hungary and Yugoslavia's options for dealing with their foreign debt problem?
3. Why does the author conclude that Eastern Europe may become a new Latin America? Why does he argue that this would be harmful?

Paul Phillips, "The Debt Crisis and Change in Eastern Europe," *Monthly Review*, February 1990. Copyright © 1990 by Monthly Review Inc. Reprinted by permission of Monthly Review Foundation.

The truly remarkable changes that have taken place in Poland and Hungary in 1989 have prompted many western observers to trumpet the return of capitalism to eastern Europe. Many on the left have watched these changes with comparable interest but with considerable concern that "the God had failed," that the socialist alternative to the inequality, injustice, and inhumanity of capitalism had proven unable to maintain itself in competition with capitalism. The declining standards of living and the shortages of food and consumer goods seemed to point to the failure of the communist countries to solve efficiently the basic economic questions of production and distribution. . . .

At a conference of Yugoslav managers in which I participated, the hottest debate was over the unique Yugoslav institution of social (collective) ownership and its relation to the country's current economic problems. One prominent economist maintained quite explicitly that all that was necessary to make enterprises efficient and profitable was to privatize them.

An Idealized View

Because of the isolation of eastern European economists from more critical western economic analysis, many of them tend to have the same idealized view of the capitalist market mechanism that informs neoclassical analysis and denies the reality of class, of political and economic power, and of all their related distributional problems. That isolation has led to a host of proposed or attempted economic reforms that promise to make current problems worse and more difficult to solve in the future, while destroying the egalitarian social and economic ideals of the original socialist vision.

This is not to deny that reforms of the Soviet-type central planning model are required. Central planning seems to be an inappropriate and inefficient institution for the provision and distribution of many, if not most, consumer goods and services. Large state enterprises have proven inflexible in responding to changing technology, consumer demand, and quality standards. Administered prices have failed to adjust to changes in the real costs of production, leading to irrational price structures. The profusion of transfers and subsidies and the virtual guarantees against unemployment and dismissal have provided such constraints on enterprises that there are few incentives to managerial efficiency and economizing on resources. Workers have little incentive to work hard or to produce quality goods. As a result countless enterprises are mired in losses, and by any rational accounting are bankrupt.

The policy response in many of the "reforming" socialist

economies has been to allow and encourage the emergence of a private sector, to promote foreign investment, and to foster the spread of unregulated markets. In Hungary, reforms include the legalization of private firms with up to 500 employees and the creation of a stock market. The reformers hope that markets will become more responsive to consumer demand and will exert constraints on state enterprises, and that the stock market will tap a pool of private savings to enhance economic growth.

"Help yourself!"

Lurie/Cartoonews International Inc. Reprinted with permission.

There are a number of reasons why these types of reform are almost certain to fail. Private markets in the Soviet Union have been reported to have elicited considerable negative response because of high prices and the emergence of pockets of wealth. Debate in the Soviet parliament has involved charges that the new co-operative (private) sector was "squeezing the workers dry" and was "widely despised for its high prices." Stock markets are ineffectual because there are few pools of private capital seeking investment opportunities. Of the less than 100 firms listed on the Hungarian stock exchange, almost all are state firms, although some are also joint private-state ventures. Eastern economists seem almost totally unaware of the dominant position of institutional investors in western capital markets. It is not surprising that the Hungarian stock market has had almost no effect in generating new capital and that trade on the exchange has been almost exclusively by state enterprises.

Potentially the most dangerous reform for future economic prospects is the encouragement of foreign direct investment because it threatens to worsen the debt problem and the reliance of the eastern European economies on western markets, a major cause of the existing crisis. Those countries suffering the worst economic problems are, for the most part, those most integrated with, and dependent on, western markets and western capital. In fact, I would argue that the most pressing cause of the current economic crisis in a number of the smaller eastern European countries is foreign (hard-currency) debt combined with peripheral absorption into the western economic system.

Different Systems, Similar Problems

The strongest evidence pointing to foreign debt as the critical element in the current economic problems of eastern (or central) Europe is a comparison of countries such as Hungary and Yugoslavia. While they have very different political-economic systems, both are undergoing severe economic crises, though the manifestations of these crises are somewhat different, reflecting their different institutions. . . .

Both countries have hard currency debts of approximately $20 billion, though Yugoslavia, with a population more than double that of Hungary, has less than half the per capita debt. In Hungary the debt was contracted during the 1970s to finance "goulash communism," the expansion of consumer goods production and increased trade with the West. Hungary developed a dependency on the West for goods, particularly for capital goods, yet saw its potential markets dry up in the 80s with recession and increasing protectionism.

In Yugoslavia, the great expansion in debt occurred in the last couple of years of the Tito era. With Tito obviously dying, there was considerable anxiety that the country would succumb to regional infighting based on very high regional income disparities. (The ratio of per capita income between developed Slovenia and underdeveloped Kosova is at least five to one.) To quell regional unrest, money was borrowed and spent, but with little lasting accumulation of productive capital. In short, the debt contracted was largely consumed. Yugoslavia was also hurt by western protectionism in the 80s. Both were victims of monetarism and the high interest rates that have prevailed during the 1980s.

The problem of foreign debt in these semi-developed industrial countries is, in my view, intractable. The interest alone on existing debt amounts to a minimum of 2 or 3 percent of the gross national product, or higher—perhaps 5 or 6 percent—if measured out of net social product. Moreover, this amount, in excess of $2 billion annually for each country, must be raised out of a trade surplus in goods and services with the West alone. And unless some principal is paid (or the debt somehow otherwise drawn down), this will be a drain in perpetuity. In the case of both countries, foreign trade is almost equally divided between the West and the Comecon countries, led by the Soviet Union. To further complicate matters, both countries run a trade surplus with the Soviet Union, paid in non-convertible credits, and a trade deficit with the West, thereby adding to their convertible currency debts. . . .

Cheap Labor

It's not surprising that for some of the dissidents the political freedoms they seek, the same ones existing in the West, are associated with the free-market economies of the Western nations. They believe the free market is the way out of their countries' economic regression, the way democracy will end their political repression.

But for many others, the appeal of free competition is muted by their correct awareness that Western-style capitalism means unemployment, harder work on the job and greater insecurity and stress in daily living. They are also wary of Western corporations moving in and taking over their national industries.

It is just this foreign investment that the Eastern-bloc bureaucrats are so hungry for as a quick fix for their ailing economies. Ironically, the major enticement these "socialists" have to offer the Western capitalists is cheap labor.

New Unionist, December 1989.

In short, Hungary and Yugoslavia share with a large number of other semi-industrialized, developing countries (including Argentina, Brazil, Mexico, Israel, and Poland) the burden of the international debt crisis. It is manifested in these countries in declining real incomes, hyperinflation (incipient or actual), real or suppressed unemployment, economic stagnation, and balance of payments problems. Both countries have resorted to conditional standby agreements with the International Monetary Fund (IMF) which involve more reliance on the market, but if anything this has made their problems worse. (It was the IMF requirement that Yugoslavia devalue and make its currency convertible that set off its hyperinflation, for example.)

These countries have limited options, and none of them is

satisfactory. The obvious option, further borrowing, is not at all attractive to the debtors themselves. Additional loans, even if they could be obtained, would quickly make the debt problem worse. At prevailing borrowing rates, it takes a trade surplus with western countries of at least 10 percent of the value of a loan just to pay the interest on it, and a much larger fraction if the loan is to be amortized. To create such a surplus, the authorities must suppress domestic consumption or slash public services. In countries where democratic forces can make political repression extremely problematic, this suppression of demand is not likely to be feasible. Even such oppressive regimes as South Korea and Chile are now finding it hard to repress their populations in the name of capital accumulation.

Promoting Foreign Investment

Economists in both Hungary and Yugoslavia have urged that their countries avoid the burden of higher interest and amortization payments by pursuing a second option, the promotion of direct foreign investment, including the sale of domestic enterprises to foreign investors and the establishment of joint ventures between foreign firms and state firms (in Hungary) or co-operatively-owned firms (in Yugoslavia). Success in attracting foreign investment has been very limited so far. This is probably fortunate, since this alternative only promises "long-term pain for short-term gain." Foreign firms invest in a host country for three main reasons: to take advantage of low-wage labor to produce labor-intensive manufactures for re-export, to get access to or control over raw material supplies, or to capture a share of the host-country market. But neither Hungary nor Yugoslavia has industrial regions with much unemployed labor, and neither is particularly well endowed with natural resources. And foreign investment to exploit domestic markets is perhaps the least attractive option. Such firms are likely to spend much of their initial investment on capital goods from the home country and to repatriate their substantial earnings and depreciation allowances. Many of their managers and technical personnel will come from the home country, so few good jobs are created. And judging from the Canadian experience, they will import an unusually large proportion of their material inputs. Thus the second option, to attract direct foreign investment, does little to alleviate the balance-of-payments problem that is at the root of the current crisis.

A third option was pursued in Romania: squeeze the living standards of the workers to the point where the import of consumption goods is drastically reduced, expropriate the domestic surplus and use it to pay off foreign debts. The human welfare cost, however, is enormous and would not be politically acceptable in the liberalized Hungary or Yugoslavia of today.

The ideal solution would be for the western industrial powers to cancel at least a considerable portion of the accumulated debts. Not surprisingly, their banks are reluctant to do this, though in fact they have done as much by unloading large amounts of it on a rapidly-depreciating secondary market. (Yugoslavia's debt in September 1989 was being sold for 55 cents on the dollar.)

An obvious solution, of course, would be to repudiate the debt, but this would conflict with the aim of both Hungary and Yugoslavia (and Poland, for that matter) to increase their economic integration with the West. As long as the Soviet economy wallows in the doldrums, these countries have few good alternatives to repudiation. . . .

Bad Trade

The real danger is that Yugoslavia, Hungary, and Poland will attribute their debt-induced problems to their political and economic institutions. If they do, and alter the latter without solving the former, they risk trading their relatively egalitarian societies and comprehensive welfare systems for the stagnation, inequality, and appalling poverty of so much of Latin America.

"The transformation of our economic system into a market economy . . . offers the greatest possibility for improving living conditions."

Poland Should Establish a Market Economy

Tadeusz Mazowiecki

Tadeusz Mazowiecki is a member of the Polish trade union Solidarity. He became Poland's prime minister in 1989 and advocated a controversial economic reform plan that is intended to quickly move Poland from a centrally planned economy to a market economy. The following viewpoint is excerpted from the first speech Prime Minister Mazowiecki gave before the Polish parliament, the Sejm. In it, he admits that reforming the economy will impose some short-term hardships, as food subsidies are cut and inefficient industries are eliminated. But these short-term hardships are essential, Mazowiecki argues, to provide food and jobs for all Poles.

As you read, consider the following questions:

1. What are the two main problems Poland faces, according to Mazowiecki?
2. What does Mazowiecki predict will be the consequences of policies intended to fight inflation?
3. For what reasons does the author feel confident that a market economy is ultimately the most successful system?

Tadeusz Mazowiecki, "Prime Minister Mazowiecki's Speech to Parliament," *Uncaptive Minds,* November/December 1989. Reprinted with permission of the Institute for Democracy in Eastern Europe.

I am convinced that the decisive majority of Poles understands as I do the goals toward which we should be moving, and that they carry in their hearts the same ideal of the nation as I. We wish to live in dignity in a sovereign and democratic state, subject to the rule of law, which everyone—regardless of ideological and political orientation—can regard as his own. We wish to live in a country with a healthy economy, where it is worthwhile to work and save, and where the satisfaction of basic material needs is neither arduous nor humiliating. We want a Poland that is open to Europe and to the world, a Poland without an inferiority complex, a Poland that contributes to the creation of material and cultural goods, a Poland whose citizens will feel they are welcome guests and not intruders when they travel to other countries of Europe and the world.

The Heritage of Solidarity

I come as a man of Solidarity, loyal to the heritage of August [1980, when Solidarity was born]. For me, this heritage represents a great call from all of society for sovereignty, the right to decide the nation's fate, and a readiness for united and decisive action in order to achieve these goals. But the heritage of August is also the ability to overcome disputes and divisions, to build partnership, to forsake revenge and the settling of accounts.

Much had to happen before I, a man of Solidarity, could stand before you today as prime minister. . . . This could not have come about without deep disturbances, which could have proven dangerous to the nation if the main political forces in our country had not shown imagination, good will, and a sense of responsibility. The Church also played a crucial role in this process.

Today, we confront two main problems: how to reconstruct the state and how to surmount the economic crisis. . . . I know how difficult it will be to reconcile the solutions to both of these problems and to implement them simultaneously. At any moment the construction of democracy in Poland, which has only just begun, could collapse if the economy breaks down.

We will enjoy our newly regained political freedoms for only a short time if we do not surmount the economic crisis. Society will judge democratic institutions useless if a clear change does not follow in everyday life.

We reject the political philosophy that assumes economic reforms can be introduced against society, over its head, in the absence of thoroughgoing democratic changes. Only a society of free citizens and a government that is granted trust by the clear majority of Poles can solve Poland's problems.

The transformation of society's attitude toward the state is of fundamental importance. . . . Recent history has led many Poles to believe that the state, as it has been shaped after the second world war, is an institution that does not serve the interests of the nation. The state sought to organize every aspect of social life; it sought to rule not just over the actions but over the minds of people. This philosophy still inheres in the structures and principles of many state institutions—and in our consciousness as well.

Now we are able to end the situation where the good of society is opposed to the interests of the state. Rebuilding society's trust in the state, however, is a task for the government. Our goal is to create a state which provides safe conditions for individual and social life, which only delineates [but does not otherwise impinge upon] the extent of individual and group rights . . . but which does not leave the weak without protection. . . .

We face the historic task of carrying out thoroughgoing changes in the economy that will keep pace with the political changes that are sweeping Poland. However, this task must be carried out in an extremely difficult economic situation. . . . We are threatened with massive inflation, which could lead to total economic chaos. We have decided to slow this process as much as possible. . . . Above all, we intend to reduce the budget deficit. Toward this end, it will be necessary to enforce tax collection. Many enterprises treat unpaid taxes as a form of cheap credit. This cannot continue. Credits are granted by the bank and not by the budget.

Reductions in state expenditures, however, will also be necessary. They will be accomplished by reducing subsidies, limiting centrally funded investments, partially transferring resources from the military to the civilian sector, and limiting the range of credit preferences. Limiting the growth of the money supply will be indispensable. The government will slow down the fall in the real value of savings. We will be forced to strictly enforce tax laws against enterprises that allow wages to rise faster than regulations permit. . . .

The Consequences of Fighting Inflation

It must however be stressed that there is no example in the history of the world where reducing such a high rate of inflation has been possible without serious social distress, the collapse of some enterprises, and unemployment. Unjustified subsidies to unprofitable economic enterprises will disappear as soon as unbacked money stops entering the economy. It is likely that this may cause a temporary fall in production and, in turn, a further decline in living standards.

The emergence or aggravation of certain social problems will place the trade union movement in a difficult position. We trust that the trade unions, aware of the country's difficult situation and the absence of simple solutions, will support the [proposed] reforms. . . . The government will do everything possible to alleviate the hardships resulting from the fight against inflation. We will concentrate on developing employment agencies and retraining centers to help workers develop new skills. We will also facilitate the creation of new jobs. Services, retailing, and small-scale manufacturing—all of which are poorly developed—should be able to create many new jobs.

We will introduce or strengthen other aspects of social welfare, including benefits for the unemployed. We must be aware, however, that such benefits are part of the budget, and their scope will be limited by the overall goal of reducing inflation. Aid will therefore be limited. We see a definite need to increase old age pensions and disability benefits, and to adjust other welfare payments for inflation, so as to prevent the further decline in living standards of the poorest social groups. . . .

Transforming the Economy

Together with adopting policies aimed at counteracting inflation, the government will take steps toward creating a modern market economy—the kind of economy that has been tried and tested by the developed countries. A government official will be appointed to oversee the transformation of property ownership. . . . The basic principle will be public and open sale, accessible to all citizens and institutions interested in efficient management. We are seeking ways to facilitate worker ownership of enterprises. There will also be a place for various other economically efficient forms of ownership.

A Great Chance

The implementation of our difficult economic programme is the primary issue. The programme is difficult but its implementation is a great chance for Poland. It is a great chance for working people. A chance to stop wasting work and boost the country economically. . . .

Now that we have halted inflation, our task is to proceed to economic transformations, first of all by means of privatizing and boosting our economy. And this can be only achieved by people who have faith in themselves.

Tadeusz Mazowiecki, Speech to the Second National Congress of Solidarity Delegates, April 19, 1990.

The principle of public and open sale will end the practice of the appropriation of state enterprises and property on the basis of informal ties and non-economic criteria. We must quickly set up a stock exchange, which is indispensable for transferring ownership. . . . Halting inflation and abolishing rationing, introducing market prices . . . and making all economic sectors equal before the law will improve the efficiency of state enterprises. . . .

Monopolies dominate our economy, and it is well known that monopolies and cartels render the market inefficient. That is why we will take decisive action to remove unnecessary and harmful economic structures—in particular in the food industry. . . .

Fundamental tax reform is a matter of great importance. It must include the introduction of a tax on personal incomes. This will not, however, conflict with the basic aim of mobilizing the tremendous but currently inert resources of human initiative and enterprise in our society.

We shall speed up the transformation of the banking system. . . . The current banking system must be raised to the level of those in economically developed countries. The obstacles to the formation of new commercial banks must be removed.

These steps will initiate the transformation of our economic system into a market economy, which might not be perfect but is recommended by experience. Such a system offers the greatest possibility for improving living conditions. It is a system that allows people to work at a less frenetic pace and at the same time more productively than has been the case up to now. . . .

A New Chapter for Poland

The Polish people must start a new chapter in their history. Hatred, a potentially destructive force, must be abandoned. As a nation we must overcome the feeling of hopelessness and take up the challenges facing us: surmounting the economic crisis and restructuring the state. The government the Sejm approves will take up this twofold task. We do not promise that it will be easy for everyone. As a nation, however, we cannot lose if we make an effort, have patience, and have the will to act. Let us have trust in the spiritual and material forces of the nation. I believe God will help us to take a giant step on the path that is opening before us.

7

"Poland needs . . . a strong social democratic party in order to defend the interests of the most endangered groups in society."

Poland Should Follow Socialist Principles

Jan Jozef Lipski

In the following viewpoint, Jan Jozef Lipski, a member of Poland's socialist party, argues that establishing a market economy does not guarantee Poland a bright future. In fact, Lipski believes the Polish economy will become more like the economies of Brazil and Malaysia than like U.S. and Western European economies. As Poland moves into a difficult period of economic reform, the nation needs a strong socialist commitment to providing all citizens with an adequate standard of living, Lipski contends.

As you read, consider the following questions:

1. Why does the author argue that it is unrealistic to demand that the Polish government not intervene in the economy?
2. Lipski writes that the state will guide Poland's economic reforms. What are his concerns about the process of making these reforms?
3. Why does Lipski believe that economic criteria alone are insufficient for making decisions on the reform process? Do you agree or disagree?

Jan Jozef Lipski, "In Defense of Socialism," *The Socialist*, March 1990. This article first appeared in the Fall/Winter 1989 issue of *Across Frontiers* and is reprinted with permission of *Across Frontiers*.

In our thinking about the economic changes underway in Poland, we seem overly impressed by the wealth of the U.S.A. and western Europe, where market forces rule (though not exclusively). We tend to forget that there are other countries in the world governed by the market, whose situation does not nearly approximate the U.S.A. or West Germany or France. Consider, for instance, Brazil and many countries of Southeast Asia.

Somehow, the dictatorship of the market (for this is what the extreme "laissez faire" position amounts to) functions one way in the highly developed countries of the Northern Hemisphere, another way among the poor of the Southern Hemisphere and in yet another in the countries of Southeast Asia. These latter are now making a great leap in development, producing goods competitive on world markets. This is made possible by the world's cheapest labor force, with its miserable standards of nutrition, clothing, and housing.

Everywhere social polarization grows wider. This, too, is a rule of the market.

A few years from now, will we be more similar to Brazil and Malaysia, or to West Germany? I believe the former is more realistic. And that ought to influence the direction of our economic proposals. They will, inevitably, take on either a Leftist or Rightist hue.

State Intervention Is Necessary

There are people in Poland who say we need an "anti-socialist" party. Whatever this party might look like, it would unquestionably push an extreme "laissez faire" program. This, as is well known, is the rallying cry of opposition to state intervention in the economy. Yet in virtually every corner of the earth the state intervenes in the economy: imposes taxes, collects custom duties, subsidizes certain sectors of production, e.g., agriculture, maintains price levels (such as the artificial reduction of farm production in the U.S.A.), sets monetary policy, undertakes welfare programs which entail economic consequences, etc. Our Polish laissez faire advocates, therefore, are simply demanding that we become the first country in the world to radically reject state intervention.

This constitutes a dangerous experiment, especially so for a country undergoing a protracted economic crisis in a context of deeper and deeper poverty.

Despite the laissez fairists, Poland needs to make decisions, arbitrary ones, that determine key features of the changing economic system. The state will make them—who else? Specifically, they will be the business of the executive bodies of government installed, as we all know, by a process that can be called neither free, universal, nor equal. The Polish "anti-socialists" have not thought much about this arbitrariness. This is not a situation that developed organically, in an evolution over decades or centuries! It is the displacement of one decision, imposed some 40 years ago, with another top-down dictum.

A Bad Choice

The choice among such fundamental decisions has to be based on more than economic criteria. If someone were to propose (without any assurance of long term benefit) to throw millions of people into a poverty and homelessness much worse than may be already the case, in order to create a glorious future—then that person should be told that that future ought to be slightly less glorious, or that it should be put off altogether, rather than to have it realized at the enormous price of today's suffering, hoping for distant future rewards. And let us not forget that such proposals are for the most part floated by people not themselves in danger of poverty, people who, on the contrary, often stand to make immediate profits.

Danziger for *The Christian Science Monitor* © 1990 TCSPS. Reprinted with permission.

Poland needs not only Solidarnosc but a strong social democratic party in order to defend the interests of the most endangered groups in society by the means available to a political party. The PPS (Polish Socialist Party) is unfortunately still too weak for the task. Until this changes, the PPS will have to limit itself to the role of a people's advocate.

Proposals to Privatize Industry

Let's now turn to the proposals for the re-privatization of Polish industry. Some have objected that this will amount to doling out gifts rather than being a business proposition (there have already been instances of "enfranchisement of the nomenklatura" [party bureaucrats]). But there is more at stake.

Every worker, indeed, every Pole, has a right to say that in large part this will not be a "re-privatization," but a privatization of that which, for better or worse (the latter, as a rule), had been built through the effort and sacrifice of working people. It is their property that will be sold off, because it is entirely the product of their labor. Where did the FSO [large automobile plant in Warsaw] come from? It was not appropriated from anyone, and in a real sense we built it together, paying for it through a lowered standard of living for all. Sold it will be, or leased (to whom?) for our own good, conveniently overlooking that what is being sold factually and morally belongs to someone. If the economic reform is not accompanied by the enfranchisement of working people, they will have little reason to give it their support.

The Well-Off and the Destitute

But above all, we must concentrate our efforts on halting the rapidly widening polarization which is dividing our society into the well-off and the destitute. This is a minimalized "egalitarian" program. Such decisions ought to be based not only on purely economic criteria, but on moral ones as well. Clearly, neither economy nor politics should be confused with morality, but they should not be held completely separate either. Both politics and the economic system can have criminal effects—in which case they ought to be challenged and changed.

I am afraid that this will not be easy. After years of politics insulated from moral criticism, what might lay ahead is an analogous situation in which economic practices are exempt from moral criteria.

Socialists can never accept such a condition, and in this I believe they will win strong social support.

8

VIEWPOINT

"Yugoslavia's troubles offer a foretaste of the difficulties that could await its neighbors as they attempt to restructure their economies while hanging onto . . . socialism."

Yugoslavia's Economy Proves Socialism's Failings

Craig Forman

After breaking from the Soviet Union in the 1950s, Yugoslavia began integrating the capitalist idea of market competition into its predominantly socialist system. Yugoslavia's experiment is important and controversial. Experts disagree on what happened in Yugoslavia and what lessons Yugoslavia offers for other East Bloc reformers. Craig Forman, a reporter for *The Wall Street Journal*, argues in the following viewpoint that Yugoslavia's experience shows the drawbacks of trying to hold on to socialism. He contends that Eastern Europeans must decentralize their economies completely and allow the market to rule if they are to avoid repeating Yugoslavia's mistakes.

As you read, consider the following questions:

1. What point does Forman make by beginning the viewpoint with a discussion of the Feni ore smelter?
2. Why does the author believe it would have been better to attach conditions to the aid Western countries gave Yugoslavia?
3. Why does Forman contend that it will be difficult to eliminate state interference in East Bloc economies?

Silhouetted in winter sunlight, the nickel smelter's hulking buildings tower hundreds of feet, their canted roofs forming a jagged industrial skyline. Two smokestacks soar even higher. A conveyor belt as wide as a roadway stretches away from the plant, for 24 miles over mountainous terrain, to the Feni mine.

One of the most spectacular engineering feats in the Balkans, the Feni smelter swallowed $300 million in Western capital during construction. Its giant conveyor belt carried, along with ore, the dreams of impoverished residents for more jobs and a better life. But in 1985, having never broken even in its brief 26 months of operation, it came to a halt, with the government still owing $200 million on the project. Many wonder if the smokestacks will ever smoke again.

The Feni smelter, a technical marvel but a commercial flop, starkly illustrates the flaws in Yugoslavia's approach to economic modernization. Those flaws aren't of concern just in Belgrade. As change sweeps Eastern Europe, Yugoslavia's troubles offer a foretaste of the difficulties that could await its neighbors as they attempt to restructure their economies while hanging onto at least a piece of socialism.

Yugoslavia was a pioneer of economic reform among communist lands. Decades ago it asked the kind of questions being confronted now by the likes of Poland, Czechoslovakia, Romania—even the Soviet Union. After breaking early with Stalinism, the non-aligned Yugoslavia under Tito fashioned a more market-oriented economy. It got rid of central planning. It welcomed foreign investors. It opened its borders to the free movement of labor.

However, Yugoslavia also spent freely on ill-advised projects, without fully subjecting them to the rigors of the marketplace. It never tackled the systematic problem of allowing bureaucrats with little understanding of free enterprise to make big decisions about allocating resources.

Today, after having outrun other countries in its region by most economic yardsticks a decade ago, Yugoslavia is a winded laggard. Its output has fallen a total of roughly 6% over eight consecutive years, economists say. Its labor productivity is down 20% and real personal income off 25%. Inflation has surged to 1,500%.

So now, as the rest of Eastern Europe strives to modernize, economists are looking to Yugoslavia for lessons.

Halfway Measures

"The lesson of Yugoslavia is that there is no compromise between a market economy and a centrally planned economy," says Ivan Ribnikar, an economist at Yugoslavia's University of

Ljubljana. "One must have a true market economy. It can be harder, like America, or softer, like Sweden or Austria. But it surely shouldn't be like Yugoslavia."

"Yugoslavia is the sad story of 40 years of missed opportunities," adds Prof. Ljubo Sirc, the Yugoslav-born director of London's Center for Research into Communist Economies. Nations that follow in its footsteps, he warns, "risk repeating the same nonsensical development."

In January 1990, the government enacted a tough austerity plan to halt the economic decline and cool inflation. It is freezing wages and many prices. It has made its currency, the dinar, convertible into dollars and West German marks, a first for Eastern Europe.

© Thompson/Rothco. Reprinted with permission.

Already, the people are howling. Croatian and Serbian workers have staged wildcat strikes for higher wages. Though the government says Yugoslavs are hoarding dinars, depositors in a Belgrade branch of Investbanka on a recent morning seemed to be selling as many dinars as they were buying. "I think prices will still go up," said Marja Paulovic, who was buying marks. The mood could worsen if the government is forced to devalue the currency, a move that could shake confidence in the austerity plan.

The fate of the plan will determine whether Premier Ante Markovic's government survives or falls, many think. The government seems to think so, too. "There is no alternative" to the economic program, says Zivko Pregl, the vice president of the federal government and a Slovene economist. "By the end of the 1970s, Yugoslavia was pushed into a situation where it had to earn its own living, and our system showed itself to be inefficient. It took all the 1980s to realize we were in a crisis. Now, we have no choice."

Although the plan is welcomed by Western experts, the odds against success are high. The continuing economic chaos is aggravating Yugoslavia's deep-rooted regional and ethnic tensions, which in turn are exacerbating the economic chaos. Few nations are more divided than Yugoslavia, whose 23 million people are partitioned by two alphabets, three religions, four languages and five nationalities into six republics and two autonomous regions.

In northern Slovenia, which is closer to Munich than Belgrade in ways beyond mere geography, well-dressed businessmen drive German cars on superhighways to Alpine chalets. In the poorer south, peasant farmers drive horses and wagons on dirt roads. Northerners burn cordwood to be trendy. Southerners burn scrap wood to be warm.

Simmering feuds are escalating. Serbia and Slovenia are boycotting each other economically. You can't buy a Slovene refrigerator in Belgrade or a Serbian table in Ljubljana. Ethnic violence is on the rise. Tone Valas, the director of a consumer-products company called Emona, says his firm finds it easier to expand in New York and Munich than elsewhere in Yugoslavia. "You invest where there is a positive business environment," he says. "We don't have enough courage to expand around Yugoslavia."

Lesson Number One

Yugoslavia's most obvious lesson for its East European neighbors is that decades of throwing money at problems doesn't solve them. More than half of its $20 billion foreign debt went to subsidize consumption or was wasted on projects providing no real return, Prof. Ribnikar says. Yet many people, in both the East and the West, are asking Western governments, banks and companies to open the credit tap again.

Already, industrialized nations have pledged more than $5 billion in loans and aid to the East Bloc, and new loans are announced almost weekly. The Japanese have promised an aid package totaling $1 billion for Poland and Hungary. West Germany has offered $3.5 billion to East Germany. European Community Commission President Jacques Delors says six East Bloc countries could require as much as $17 billion in Western aid annually for a decade.

Meantime, General Motors wants to build cars in Hungary. So does Suzuki. Ford, Volkswagen and Renault are thought to be not far behind in their East Bloc planning. General Electric's brighter idea is to make light bulbs.

In an elegant office in Ljubljana, Joze Kunic, a Yugoslav development banker, is skeptical. "A lot of people are willing to lend money," says Mr. Kunic, a former executive vice president of Yugoslavia's Bank for International Economic Cooperation. But after 40 years under communism, he adds, Poles, Czechs, Hungarians and Romanians "don't know what is profit, what is a market. They don't know what it is to compete. Will they be able to pay the loans back? I doubt it."

Danica Purg, the director of a Yugoslav business school, notes one of her country's mistakes: "When others were closing steel plants, we built them." She adds: "You must develop areas in which you can be a world leader. None of the East Bloc countries realize this."

Free Elections and a Free Market

Most people believe that the complex problem has an easy answer: free elections and a free market economy. This is the road being taken by Slovenia, and to a lesser extent by Croatia. Proper representation would allay the fears of the non-Slavic people, especially the large ethnic groups of Albanians and Hungarians. If they had the right to freely present their views, these groups would be able to join the process of democratization, thus reducing tensions.

Sami Repishti, *The Christian Science Monitor*, November 20, 1989.

Such observers warn that capital will be put to productive use only if tough strings are attached—by investors or lenders who set specific goals and ride shotgun to see that they are met. Without such discipline, new funds could subsidize economic half steps unlikely to produce long-term improvement. Economists unimpressed by talk about a new Marshall Plan for Eastern Europe warn that in these countries, which lack a modern free-market tradition, change may take decades.

Lesson Number Two

And that suggests the second lesson of Yugoslavia: Easy money is spent too easily. At the Feni smelting plant, one enters the offices via a beautiful pink-marble stairway, and the halls and many offices have marble floors, too. The production equipment is the best that America had to offer—induction motors from Westinghouse, an IBM 4341-series mainframe, a cooling system from Marley Cooling Tower Co. of Mission, Kan. But in the huge equipment shed, two giant tractors for moving the ferronickel ore sit idle, each with only 20,000 miles on its gauge.

"In the West, you invest the minimum amount of money for the maximum return. At Feni, it is just the opposite," says Ljubo Milevski, a retired professor of metallurgy at the nearby University of Skopje. "Politicians wanted to leave monuments. We have to pay for such megalomaniacal investment."

He blames Feni's failure mainly on the low nickel content of its ore, which is only a third that of mines elsewhere. In addition, he says, the project demanded too much costly electricity, relied on an expensive new technique and could have been designed more cheaply. "Production is justified only if you receive more in the marketplace than it costs you to produce," he notes. But Feni had to show only that nickel could be produced, not produced at profit. . . .

At that time, the experts—including economists and bankers from 35 Western institutions, such as the U.S. Export-Import Bank, Bankers Trust and Manufacturers Hanover—seemed more concerned with recycling petrodollars than laboring over harsh commercial projections, Feni people say.

Lesson Number Three

Yugoslavia's third major lesson is that all the administrative and legal reforms in the world don't necessarily amount to the free-market deregulation that economists and bankers say is vital if the East Bloc is to restructure successfully.

Nearly every East Bloc country is introducing new laws to encourage foreign investment. But it may take decades to reduce the bureaucratic interference. Meanwhile, disputes will still be resolved by judges who owe their positions to the previously dominant Communist Party elite.

When Yugoslavia ended government ownership of enterprises in the mid-1970s, it didn't establish legal protections for private ownership. Instead, it introduced more worker self-management and collective ownership; in effect, the state continued to control the means of production. And at plants such as Feni, production costs soared as politicians ordered that hundreds of extra workers be put on the 1,800-person payroll.

Now, the smelter seems deserted. Weeds sprout beside the road that once was the bustling main artery along which the giant tractors hauled ore. A skeleton crew spot-checks the equipment once a month.

"This was something great to work for. It was very busy. The salary was good," says Branko Jovanovski, a 53 year-old watchman who left his mountain village and started working at Feni more than a decade ago. "Now, it's bad. I make one-third of what I did. And it's seven years until I retire."

*"A genuinely communist vanguard [must]
. . . . reforge the fraternal links among the
Yugoslav working people so badly eroded by
decades of 'market socialism.'"*

Yugoslavia's Economy Proves Capitalism's Failings

Workers Vanguard

Workers Vanguard is a biweekly newspaper published by the Spartacist League, an American Communist group. In the following viewpoint, the staff at *Workers Vanguard* write that when Yugoslavia's experiment with market socialism failed, Yugoslav leaders turned to Western capitalists for more money. These capitalists demanded that Yugoslavia adopt harsh economic reforms which ultimately hurt Yugoslav workers. The authors conclude that the failure of these reforms and of market socialism proves that true communism, established by a revolutionary working class, is the only feasible economic system.

As you read, consider the following questions:

1. What similarities do the authors see between the Soviet Union and Yugoslavia?
2. How have economic problems aggravated Yugoslavia's nationalist conflicts, according to *Workers Vanguard?*
3. What do the authors mean when they advocate proletarian internationalism?

Excerpted, with permission, from "Workers' Protests Spread, Nationalist Agitation Deepens: Yugoslavia Inflamed," *Workers Vanguard*, October 21, 1989.

Invoking the catchword *perestroika*, Mikhail Gorbachev proposes "market socialism" as the nostrum to cure the ills brought about by over six decades of Stalinist usurpation and misrule in the USSR. But Gorbachev's panacea has already had a trial run—in Yugoslavia. After decades of "market socialism," Yugoslavia is bankrupt. The multinational workers state was forged through great sacrifice by the Yugoslav workers and peasants in securing the victory of Tito's Communist partisans over the Nazi occupation during World War II. Today it is a powder keg threatening to explode sooner rather than later. While workers strike over starvation wages ordered by Belgrade on behalf of the imperialist banks, bureaucratic manipulation could spark bloody, internecine national conflict opening the road to possible capitalist counterrevolution. . . .

Today the country is saddled with a foreign debt of over $21 billion owed to the imperialist loan sharks; inflation is raging at over 200 percent annually; and unemployment approaches 20 percent of the workforce. Fixed investment and industrial production have spiraled down, and the workers have seen their standard of living drop by more than 40 percent since 1980. The liberal-Stalinist policies of Tito and his heirs have brought the Yugoslav deformed workers state to economic ruin and provoked the dangerous rise in national antagonisms. Together these disastrous developments pose pointblank the urgent and desperate necessity for proletarian political revolution.

Capitalist Bankers Take Over the Economy

In 1987 Yugoslavia literally ran out of money. The Yugoslav bureaucracy, hat in hand, went begging to the imperialist bank cartel, the International Monetary Fund (IMF). In exchange for a financial quick fix the Yugoslav government imposed a savage austerity program on the workers, freezing and cutting wages while raising prices 25 to 60 percent. In response 150,000 workers in over 1,000 enterprises walked off the job. By year's end over 1,500 strikes had taken place, including one by Croatian coal miners that lasted for two months, the longest strike in the country's postwar history. And the strike wave has not abated. In 1988 strikes erupted in all areas of the country.

A big impetus to the latest round of strikes was another set of IMF-dictated austerity measures imposed in spring 1988. The intent is to dismantle the system of "workers self-management." Subsidies to money-losing enterprises would be cut off. Personal capital investment in the economy through bonds, shares and stocks would be permitted, while restrictions on foreign investments are loosened. This raises directly and inevitably the rapid spawning of a layer of petty entrepreneurs linked to the imperialist financial centers and ultimately bent on capitalist counterrevolution.

Already Yugoslavia has been racked by corruption scandals . . . linked with foreign trade. Now a millionaire businessman has been awarded the "Order of Labor," an honor "customarily reserved for shock workers of Communism" (*The New York Times*, 29 September 1988). Most ominously, "bankrupt" state enterprises are now to be sold off. Yet from the standpoint of the world market almost all Yugoslav firms are "bankrupt." To whom do Slobodan Milosevic and the Croatian and Slovenian party leaderships intend to sell these assets?

Strikers Protest Government Policies

As inflation soared at an annual rate of 859 percent in June 1988, wages remained frozen or were cut by up to 30 percent. Taking their cue from a late May march on the federal parliament by 400 striking Bosnian coal miners, in June and July tens

RUSSIA UNDER KHRUSHCHEV: AN ANTHOLOGY FROM *PROBLEMS OF COMMUNISM*, Abraham Brumberg, ed. (Praeger Publishers, New York, 1962.) Reprinted with permission.

of thousands of strikers marched on Belgrade and demonstrated outside parliament in bitter protests against the government's IMF starvation policies. . . .

Resurgence of Serbian Nationalism

Along with the massive working-class unrest there has been a dramatic escalation of nationalist agitation.

The bureaucrats and intellectuals of Slovenia—the most developed region bordering Austria—have long complained about subsidizing the poorer regions to their south. Increasingly, Slovenian nationalists want to link their future to a German-dominated Central Europe. In fact, all things German (including the language) have become very fashionable in Slovenia. At the opposite end of the national spectrum are the Albanians of Kosovo, who resent being the poor stepchildren of the Yugoslav federation and bridle at Serbian overlordship of their "autonomous province." And now we are seeing the spectacular eruption of Serbian nationalism, that is, the nationalism of the dominant people. This is partly economic resentment at pouring money wastefully into the impoverished regions of Kosovo and Macedonia and partly is a backlash against the vocal pro-Western nationalism of the Slovenes.

The wave of Serbian chauvinist demonstrations, ostensibly in defense of the Serbian minority living in Kosovo, are far from spontaneous, but rather have been whipped up by Milosevic. Milosevic, a former director of the Belgrade Bank, purged the Serbian party of his anti-nationalist opponents in 1987, and is now intent on buttressing his power by overturning the 1974 constitutional provisions that removed the autonomous provinces of Kosovo and Vojvodina from the direct administrative control of the Serbian republic.

Six years before his death in 1980 Tito, in an effort to curb the growing national antagonisms fostered by his regime's economic policies, imposed on both the Yugoslav state and the League of Yugoslav Communists (LCY) a completely federated structure. Thus, for example, the Yugoslav presidency is a collective presidium shared among the six republics and two autonomous provinces. Chairmanship of the presidency rotates annually. Likewise any one of the eight constituent republics can veto any measure before parliament. What made the whole unwieldy structure work while Tito was alive was that he, elected president for life, served as the arbiter. With his death the whole system has spiraled into autarky and paralysis worthy of the Hapsburg Empire in its final years.

Former bank director Milosevic is perhaps one of the LCY's strongest advocates of what the IMF calls the "structural reform" of the Yugoslav economy. Thus Milosevic is encouraging the nationalist demonstrations to put himself in the role of arbiter, "first among equals" of that utterly corrupt wing of the Yugoslav bureaucracy intent on bailing out their regime by selling the country to the imperialist bankers at bargain-basement prices. The nationalist outbursts also deflect attention from the economic misery that he and his cothinkers have been and are planning to inflict on the Yugoslav working class, not least the powerful and militant Serbian proletariat.

The Market Failed

The reforms introduced a limited market economy which created a grave unemployment problem. To solve joblessness, borders were opened and people encouraged to leave their homeland, sometimes their families, and seek jobs in western Europe. (There are still approximately one million Yugoslavs working in the West, many of whom are seeking political asylum rather than return to the regimen of life in Yugoslavia with its uncertain future.) And Yugoslavia fell further into debt to western banks. Thus, the experiment with "a little bit of the market" and even less democracy only aggravated economic ills and heightened political repression.

Sonja Licht, *New Politics,* Summer 1989.

Milosevic and his cohorts in the Communist League of Serbia have seized upon the Kosovo question precisely to whip up the most extreme Serbian chauvinism. For diehard Serbian nationalists Kosovo *is* the Serbian question. Cradle of the medieval Serbian kingdom and site of the definitive albeit glorious defeat of the Serbs (along with their Albanian allies) by the Turks in 1389, it is woven into the national literature and messianic national myth of the Christian Serbs defeated yet steadfastly resisting the Turkish infidels for 500 years. . . .

Since the late '60s national tensions in Kosovo have escalated dangerously. In 1981 the region was hit with a wave of angry Albanian protests. Many were bloodily suppressed and some 3,500 Albanian nationalists imprisoned. Today Kosovo is populated by 200,000 Serbs and 1,800,000 Albanians. It is the poorest, least developed area in Yugoslavia, with an unemployment rate of over 35 percent. The billions of dinars in "development funds" which have been poured into Kosovo have mainly been squandered on palatial government buildings. Since 1981 some 34,000 Serbs and Montenegrins have left the area, many claiming they were driven out by Albanian terror tactics. Certainly there have been incidents as the Albanian nationalists work on reversing the terms of oppression. Charges of arson, rape, robbery and murder abound, and are vastly exaggerated in the superheated atmosphere of national animosity. . . .

So far Milosevic has been able to ride the wave of Serbian chauvinism he has unleashed in his intra-bureaucratic struggle for power. He has managed with impunity to openly defy an LCY party presidium directive against nationalist rallies. He forced the resignation of the Vojvodina party leaders who tried to oppose his Great Serbian chauvinist policies, while mass pro-Milosevic rallies demanded the resignation of the Montenegrin party leadership as well.

Milosevic has provoked a strong backlash from among other elements of the Yugoslav bureaucracy. Now, as verbal battles escalate in the Politburo, this crisis is coming to a head. . . .

Bureaucratic Corruption

Big sections of the liberal-Stalinist Yugoslav bureaucracy are worried about Milosevic's "extraparliamentary" mobilizations. They have been the occasion for giant outpourings of proletarian outrage over the bureaucracy's corruption and mismanagement of the economy. A September 22, 1988 demonstration at the Serbian industrial town of Kraljevo, for example, was as much a protest over economic conditions as a nationalist rally. Speaking at the meeting, the local union chief at the railway car factory, the town's main industry, said:

> We don't want imposing villas, planes, yachts and private beaches. You are not our comrades because you do not line up at dawn to buy 'people's bread.' You don't share our destiny on the first, second or third shift. You don't go down in the mine shafts; you don't climb high to build bridges. You are not our comrades.

> —*The New York Times*,
> 23 September 1988

According to the *Times* report the crowd responded enthusiastically, shouting "Thieves!" "Down with those who sit in armchairs!" and "The people should judge them!"

It's clear that Milosevic's Kosovo demonstrations are heavily fueled by plebeian outrage. Such mobilizations may blow up in this miserable demagogue's face when the masses discover that their fool's gold of Serbian nationalism purchases them an IMF shock treatment—administered by a former bank executive in a pin-striped suit sitting in his own armchair in Belgrade and himself not lacking in access to Mercedes, villas or yachts. . . .

The fundamental inability of any Stalinist bureaucracy to resolve the national question is strikingly demonstrated by the eruption of nationalism and national conflict in the Soviet Union, fueled by Gorbachev's *perestroika*. Yugoslavia *prefigures* what could happen in Russia. The most aggressive nationalist movements are in the richest, most advanced regions—Estonia and Latvia—analogous to Slovenia in Yugoslavia. The Baltic nationalists want to get even richer (at the expense of other Soviet peoples). At the same time, there is certainly a potential for resentment among the poorer, more culturally backward Turkic-speaking peoples of soviet Central Asia, analogous to the Albanians of Kosovo.

But the greatest danger lies in resurgent nationalism among the *dominant* people—the Russians, like the Serbs in Yugoslavia. The nucleus of such a nationalist movement already exists in the nativist Russian fascist organization Pamyat, which is protected by sections of the bureaucracy. As we wrote on 23 September 1988, "The Pamyat Nazis must be crushed before this festering sore becomes a gangrenous cancer threatening the Soviet state and its multinational people."

The danger of the Soviet Union ripping apart through national conflict still lies in the future. In Yugoslavia that danger exists right now! It is the absence of a revolutionary leadership in Yugoslavia today that permits the inept, increasingly corrupt and nationally fractured Yugoslav Stalinist bureaucracy to divert the natural unity of the Yugoslav workers in struggle into the dead end of bloody national conflict. And it will take a revolutionary internationalist leadership to repudiate the country's foreign debt to the imperialist bankers.

A Socialist Federation of the Balkans

Clearly the massive nationwide strike movement presents a crucial opportunity for a genuinely communist vanguard to reforge the fraternal links among the Yugoslav working people so badly eroded by decades of "market socialism." As Trotskyists we stand for equality among peoples on the basis of increased material well-being. This can only be achieved through a proletarian political revolution to establish workers democracy, soviet power, central planning and a rational allocation of investment resources. Above all this requires a definitive break from the Stalinist dogma of "socialism in one country," and its replacement with the program of proletarian internationalism. As Trotsky stated in a discussion with his Greek supporters in the early 1930s: "A revolutionary perspective is impossible without a federation of the Balkan states, which obviously will not stop here, but rather will extend into a federation of the United Soviet States of Europe."

Recognizing Statements That Are Provable

From various sources of information we are constantly confronted with statements and generalizations about social and moral problems. In order to think clearly about these problems, it is useful if one can make a basic distinction between statements for which evidence can be found and other statements which cannot be verified or proved because evidence is not available, or the issue is so controversial that it cannot be definitely proved.

Readers should be aware that magazines, newspapers, and other sources often contain statements of a controversial nature. The following activity is designed to allow experimentation with statements that are provable and those that are not.

The following statements are taken from the viewpoints in this chapter. Consider each statement carefully. *Mark P for any statement you believe is provable. Mark U for any statement you feel is unprovable because of the lack of evidence. Mark C for any statement you think is too controversial to be proved to everyone's satisfaction.*

If you are doing this activity as a member of a class or group, compare your answers with those of other class or group members. Be able to defend your answers. You may discover that others will come to different conclusions than you. Listening to the reasons others present for their answers may give you valuable insights in recognizing statements that are provable.

P = provable
U = unprovable
C = too controversial

166

1. The Krakow Industrial Society has been educating Poles about private enterprise since the late 1970s.

2. Central European intellectuals distrust systems and ideologies in general.

3. The Poles do not understand free enterprise and apply it haphazardly and mix it with government controls.

4. If there were free elections in Czechoslovakia today, the Communist Party would get perhaps 10 percent of the vote.

5. If the Communist Party united with other groups on the socialist left, it might regain a respectable share of the power.

6. Adding 100 million new people from Eastern Europe to a nearly integrated market of 350 million in Western Europe can make Europe a major competitor in the world economy.

7. Eastern Europe will end up with an economy more like that of Latin America than like that of the United States or Western Europe if it wholeheartedly embraces a free market system.

8. The year 1989 saw the most dramatic changes on the European Continent since the end of World War Two.

9. The fall of communism in Eastern Europe means that the policies of the U.S. in the Cold War were right.

10. Poland has embarked on a major program to restructure its economy and this program has been approved by the International Monetary Fund.

11. Workers in the communist system have little incentive to work hard or to produce quality goods, thus many enterprises are bankrupt.

12. Of the less than one hundred firms listed on the Hungarian stock exchange, almost all are state owned.

13. The Polish Church played a crucial role in the revolution against the ruling Communist Party in Poland.

14. A market economy offers the greatest possibility for improving the living conditions of the Polish people.

15. A great gap between rich and poor is a consequence of a market economy.

16. Ethnic violence in Yugoslavia has hurt the country's efforts to encourage foreign investment.

17. Eastern European countries will not be able to pay back their debts to Western countries.

Periodical Bibliography

The following articles have been selected to supplement the diverse views presented in this chapter.

Piotr Brozyna and Mark Lilla — "Dismantling Socialism in One Country (II)," *The American Spectator,* April 1990.

Mitchell Cohen — "Creating a New-Old Europe," *Dissent,* Spring 1990.

Christopher Farrell and Gail Schares — "Blueprints for a Free Market in Eastern Europe," *Business Week,* February 5, 1990.

Otto Karl Finsterwalder — "From Marxism to Market," *Vital Speeches of the Day,* May 15, 1990.

Milton Friedman — "Four Steps to Freedom," *National Review,* May 14, 1990.

John Kenneth Galbraith — "Which Capitalism for Eastern Europe?" *Harper's Magazine,* April 1990.

John Greenwald — "New Kids on the Bloc," *Time,* July 2, 1990.

John B. Judis — "Market Socialism: The Makings for Practical Politics—Particularly in U.S.," *In These Times,* May 9-15, 1990.

Wallace Katz — "The Flawed Triumph of Social Democracy," *Commonweal,* February 9, 1990.

John Kifner — "Poland's Changes to a Free Market Show Early Gains," *The New York Times,* March 3, 1990.

Vaclav Klaus, interviewed by John Fund — "No Third Way Out," *Reason,* June 1990.

Robert Kuttner — "A Little Pragmatism in Eastern Europe," *The Washington Post National Weekly Edition,* January 8-14, 1990.

Joanne Landy — "Revolution and Us," *Tikkun,* March/April 1990.

Frederick Painton — "Where the Sky Stays Dark," *Time,* May 28, 1990.

Philip Revzin — "Ventures in Hungary Test Theory That West Can Uplift East Bloc," *The Wall Street Journal,* April 5, 1990.

Jeffrey Sachs — "Lack of Solidarity," *The New Republic,* August 7-14, 1990.

Michael Scammell — "Yugoslavia: The Awakening," *New York Review of Books,* June 28, 1990.

How Will a United Germany Affect Europe?

EASTERN EUROPE

Chapter Preface

A throng of East Germans [was] dashing across the no man's land. The first to reach the wall was a young man in a brown jacket. He seemed to land on top of it in a single bound. The crowd parted and cheered as he raised his arms in triumph and danced along the concrete slab that hours before had imprisoned him.

This account, by NBC television anchorman Tom Brokaw, captures the drama and joy felt in Germany and worldwide on November 9, 1989, the night the Berlin Wall fell. Brokaw wrote that the young East German "transformed the wall from a sinister symbol of oppression to a platform for celebration and liberation." The dismantling of the Wall signified the beginning of the end of forty-five years of a divided Germany. While many people rejoice at the dismantling of the Wall, its implication—a newly united Germany—also raises fears about Europe's future.

Fears of a united Germany are rooted in the past. During the seventy-four years Germany was one nation (1871-1945), it was a leading antagonist in two world wars. During World War II Germany was ruled by Adolf Hitler, a dictator who ordered the killing of over six million Jews and other "undesirables." Hitler threatened to turn the rest of Europe into a miserable gulag. During his rule, German forces took over or invaded fifteen other European countries. The atrocities committed by Hitler's Germany have not been forgotten by other Europeans.

These old fears have now resurfaced. Uniting East and West Germany creates a population of 78 million—one of the largest in Europe. The combined East and West German military numbers 1.8 million regular and reserve troops—also one of Europe's largest. Third, now that the East and West German economies have been combined, they account for almost one-third of the gross domestic product of the European Economic Community. The strength of the West German economy has already given the nation a more influential voice at international economic conferences. With this much size and power, clearly Germany will play an enormous role in Europe's future.

The fall of the Berlin Wall in November 1989 raised a host of questions about the future of Germany. The authors of the following viewpoints debate whether the fear of a united and strong Germany is justified. They also analyze the effect this powerful nation will have on the rest of Europe.

"The Federal Republic of Germany is a trustworthy partner in the task of building a peaceful order in Europe."

German Unification Will Promote Stability in Europe

Helmut Kohl

Helmut Kohl has been the chancellor of West Germany since 1982. In the fall of 1989, as hundreds of East Germans fled their country, Kohl responded by advocating the unification of West and East Germany into one united nation. The following viewpoint is taken from a speech he gave at a meeting of the World Economic Forum. In it, he maintains that West Germany's postwar record proves a united Germany would be a responsible country. Kohl states that Germans have established a strong democracy, been reliable allies, advocated peace, and participated in and respected international agreements.

As you read, consider the following questions:

1. What connection does Kohl draw between the French Revolution and the changes in Eastern Europe?
2. According to Kohl, what role should the U.S. play in Europe?
3. Why does the author believe requiring Germany to be a neutral country would be wrong?

Helmut Kohl, "Europe—Every German's Future," speech delivered at the World Economic Forum, Davos, Switzerland, February 3, 1990.

Our old continent Europe is back again—with fresh energy and a new self-confidence. First we have disproved the gloomy forecast of the 70s and early 80s about "Eurosclerosis." Today the world focuses on Europe. It is once more the subject and no longer merely the object of world politics. The process of European Community integration continues. Media headlines are about radical political, economic and social reforms in central, Eastern and South-Eastern Europe.

In the center of Europe, in Germany, we are witnessing the first peaceful revolution in our history. The question of German unity is unmistakably on the agenda.

Masters of Their Own Fate

Indeed, 200 years after the French Revolution a historic change is taking place in Europe. The peoples of this continent are again becoming masters of their own fate.

As in 1789, in the Declaration of the Rights of Man and the Citizen, attention centers on the demands for respect for human rights and human dignity, for freedom and free self-determination. And in admirable contrast to 1789 this is taking place in the form of powerful but peaceful civil rights movements and demonstrations. . . .

In short, the post-war system which Stalin forced upon the nations of Europe is disintegrating. Something new is emerging. We Europeans have a historical responsibility to guide these developments along the right path.

Those who, at this truly historic turning point, mourn after the status quo, or indeed equate it with stability, misread the events of 1989. Nothing is more destabilizing than denial of reform! In the Europe of today stability can only be achieved by means of consistent, forward-looking reforms.

A Pan-European Significance

I speak deliberately of stability in Europe, not just in a particular country, because the reforms that have been set in motion have a pan-European significance. Every successful reform in one country is a step towards greater stability in the whole of Europe. In our own interest, therefore, we are banking on the success of these reforms. . . .

The developments taking place in central, Eastern and South-Eastern Europe are conducive to the goals and values of free democracies: human rights and human dignity. Free self-determination. A democratic system. Private initiative. And market economy. These goals are components of a future peaceful order spanning the whole of Europe, designed to overcome the division of Europe and hence of Germany as well. We

172

are therefore well advised to stay on course. We must calmly stick to our well-tried political principles and at the same time look to the future.

Support for NATO

First, the Federal Republic of Germany unswervingly supports NATO [North Atlantic Treaty Organization], the community of free democracies whose values we share and which guarantees our security. Our alliance set its goal as long ago as 1967 in the Harmel Report: a lasting and equitable peaceful order in Europe. The cornerstone of this alliance is and will remain our friendship with the United States. We accept President George Bush's invitation to play a leading role in partnership with the United States and view this as a serious obligation. We seek the closest possible coordination between the United States and the European Community. Today we face challenges similar to those at the time of the Harmel Report. Then the aim was to overcome the Cold War. The task now is to design the architecture of Europe's future security as a key element of a peaceful order.

Closer Integration

The necessity for the German people to be united is now being fuelled by sentiments that can no longer be bridled. It has become the only possible way to prevent a drift in the centre of Europe that might be even more destabilizing than the situation that presently exists. The countries of the European Community have expressed the hope in Strasbourg that this may come about in the framework of closer Community integration and a strengthening of the principles of the Helsinki Final Act. Integration, with all the difficult compromises and negotiations that this entails, will necessarily take longer than the phenomena that are now conspiring to forge the unity of a people divided by a long distant war, but the parallel between German unity and the unity of Western Europe still holds good. The CSCE, moreover, is the only context that can offer the political framework for German unity and the certainty that it can be achieved against the background of maximum international stability.

Gianni De Michelis, Address to the "Open Skies" Conference, February 12, 1990.

This future security architecture must make allowance for the legitimate security interests of every country, irrespective of its size and geography, and of all Europeans. It must manifest the conviction that no country can build up its own security at the expense of someone else's but that all must together guarantee their security. The disarmament process must be accelerated.

Not least, wise policies must at long last remove the causes of tension, diminish mistrust, and lay a new, solid foundation of mutual confidence. . . .

Bringing about the "unity and freedom of Germany" on the basis of free self-determination is our objective, as proclaimed in our Basic Law adopted in 1949. Even then, over 40 years ago, the path to German unity was linked to our commitment to European unification and world peace. That aim has not changed one iota. It is in keeping with the wishes and hopes of the overwhelming majority of Germans.

The dynamic developments in the GDR [German Democratic Republic] since the autumn of 1989 now offer us Germans the prospect of attaining this objective. With my ten-point program for German unity I have outlined a natural development in which the future architecture of Germany will form part of the future architecture of Europe. . . .

The Germans do not want to go their own, nationalistic way. That is why I am also strictly against the idea of German neutrality. Such a proposal is contrary to the logic of the process of pan-European unification. A united Germany in the heart of Europe should not have any special status which would isolate it.

A solution can only be achieved within the framework of the CSCE [Conference on Security and Cooperation in Europe] process and by the continuation of disarmament and arms control negotiations. The aim, as I have proposed, must be security structures in Europe spanning both alliances.

This is also the best way to cater for the legitimate security interests of all concerned in East and West, not least the Soviet Union.

In return we expect them to respect the right of the German people to free self-determination and to facilitate the process of unification.

I therefore warmly welcome Mr. Mikhail Gorbachev's commitment to a responsible settlement of the German question.

Moving Toward Unification

The road to German unity is not a mechanical process which can be arranged with the help of a timetable and stop watch. Least of all can the rate of progress be accelerated. An attempt to do this would be totally unhistorical and irresponsible. However, we can all visualize the demonstrations involving many tens, indeed hundreds, of thousands of our fellow countrymen in the GDR. Their chants of "We are the people!" and "We are one people!" are their program. They are defending it with growing impatience. Thus it would be just as unhistorical and irresponsible to try and oppose their interests and wishes.

What is needed is a continuous dialogue with the people, with the opposition groups, and with the new parties, as well as sensible proposals for reform, in which free, equal and secret elections will play a key role. And not least the people need to see tangible economic and social improvements. My government is willing to provide help on a new scale.

United Germany, United Europe

In the course of 40 years a free democracy has matured in the Federal Republic of Germany. In the GDR, the people had to obtain democracy by a peaceful revolution for freedom. A united Germany will be a free democracy based on the rule of law. The position that we seek for a united Germany is defined in our constitution, the Basic Law. Its preamble expresses the desire of the German people to serve the peace of the world as an equal partner in a united Europe. The door has been opened to German unity. Difficult problems still lie ahead. To solve them, we need clear-cut goals, imagination, a sense of responsibility and circumspection. But we can be quite certain now that we shall achieve German unity.

Hans-Dietrich Genscher, Policy Statement to the Bundestag, May 1990.

The alternatives to a course of reason, dialogue and tangible change are obvious:
• the possibility of crisis, which could overshadow the first peaceful revolution on German soil, and
• a continuation of the mass exodus which, the longer it lasts, the worse will be the opportunities for economic recovery. This in particular makes it abundantly clear that the only guarantee of stability lies in an energetic, forward-looking reform policy.

In this connection I also sincerely request our Western partners to help us in this stabilization process. . . .

We Germans realize that even within the framework of an integrating Europe the prospect of a Germany growing together again arouses misgivings, even fears, in some people in the East and West. Burdens endured in the past intermingle with fear for one's own future position. All responsible German politicians are well advised to take these arguments very seriously and do their best to dispel them.

Let us stick to the facts:
• In over 40 years the Federal Republic of Germany has proved itself to be a stable, free and democratic state based on the rule of law and social justice.
• It has proved itself a predictable and reliable friend and ally.
• It has from the very beginning placed its national objec-

tive—the freedom and unity of all Germans—into the larger European framework.

• It has shown itself to be a resolute champion of European union and of the CSCE process.

• And it has always been and will remain an advocate of disarmament and arms control. In my very first policy statement as head of government in 1982 I called for a world with fewer weapons. In 1990 we will come much closer to that goal.

A Trustworthy Partner

The Federal Republic of Germany is a trustworthy partner in the task of building a peaceful order in Europe. That peaceful order must manifest for all Europeans—including all Germans—the great vision expressed in the American Declaration of Independence over 200 years ago: "life, liberty and the pursuit of happiness."

That Europe is every German's future!

"A united Germany is so powerful an idea that it threatens the balance of power in Europe merely by existing."

German Unification Will Promote Instability in Europe

Walter Russell Mead

Walter Russell Mead argues in the following viewpoint that the very idea of a united Germany is destabilizing. Uniting East and West Germany creates a geographically large and economically dominant superpower in the heart of Europe, Mead points out. Whether a future united Germany is aggressive or peaceful, he maintains that its size and economic might will make the rest of Europe uneasy. Mead is a senior fellow of the World Policy Institute, an organization that promotes the study of foreign policy issues. His book is *Mortal Splendor: The American Empire in Transition.*

As you read, consider the following questions:

1. What historical incidents does Mead believe support his contention that a united Germany will destabilize Europe?
2. Why does Mead contend that the 1990s will be the German decade?
3. How will the United States be affected by a united Germany, in the author's view?

Walter Russel Mead, "Germany: In Unity, a Past Threat," *Los Angeles Times,* January 21, 1990. Reprinted with permission.

The exorcists have finally removed the specter that Karl Marx said would haunt the chancelleries of Europe: Communism no longer keeps statesmen tossing in their beds late at night. But they still aren't sleeping soundly—a new set of spirits rattles chains in the basement. Night after night the ghosts stalk through Europe bringing nightmarish visions of Germany past, Germany present and Germany to come.

A Powerful Idea

It isn't all Germany's fault that reunification gives its neighbors insomnia. A united Germany is so powerful an idea that it threatens the balance of power in Europe merely by existing. A prosperous Germany—as in the years 1871 to 1914—threatens the economic and political interests of its neighbors by economic dynamism and growth; an impoverished Germany, as in the Weimar Republic years between world wars, keeps Europe in turmoil.

Everyone understands that the long-term solution to the "German question" involves integration of a united Germany into a united and prosperous European—ultimately global—economy. Unfortunately, this is something world statesmen have never managed to achieve. The Soviet Union—and the United States—fudged the issue after 1945, making reunion impossible on terms the Germans were prepared to accept. Now the world must try once again for the right answer to the German question and, as German politicians and all parties have made clear, this time Germany's wishes will be impossible to ignore.

Fooling Ourselves

The West thought peace was made with Germany in the 1960s, but it was fooling itself. We made peace with rump steak, not the real thing. The Germany we have known since the war has not been itself; it was not only small, it was humble.

We have had half a century of German silence. A silence built on policy, because Germany feared to antagonize the victors; a silence of preoccupation, because Germans were too busy rebuilding the ruins of their nation to interest themselves in foreign affairs; last and most profound, a silence made of shame. Total defeat was bad enough, but for the nation to have surrendered itself so abjectly to Adolf Hitler was humiliating beyond words.

It has been 50 years since Hitler started his war, 45 years since he shot himself under the ruins of Berlin. German teenagers called up for service in the last days of the Reich are now in their 60s; surviving war criminals and Nazi officials are in their 80s and 90s, tottering toward the grave—and to whatever tribunal lies beyond it. There, we may hope, they will meet the justice so many evaded on earth.

© Wicks/Rothco. Reprinted with permission.

But for the generation of Germans who came of age since the war, another prospect is opening. The 1990s will be their decade: probably the years in which Germany reunifies, certainly the years of reborn German pride. We are entering the *Ich* Decade, the German counterpart of the Me Decade, to be marked by the end of the German silence and the beginning of German self-assertion. Free from all personal responsibility for the crimes of the Nazis, sustained by the economic miracle of Germany's recovery, made confident by the establishment of the strongest German democracy since the days of the Teutons, the Germans are back. And ready to lead.

The world will change in the German decade ahead of us. The German language will become, once again, important in business and scholarship. German leaders, intellectuals, economists and historians will again raise their voices. Berlin will be a great world city again, the metropolis where East and West meet, a center of all that is new and disturbing in the arts.

But other features of this new world will be more unsettling for other countries. Germany will voice doubts about the leadership of others with increasing frequency, asserting its own international interests with less hesitation as the decade goes on.

A Blow to U.S. Pride

The French seem to spend the most time worrying about the *Ich* Decade, but the United States is also likely to have trouble with the new Germany. The recovery of Japan has been a severe blow to U.S. pride; as Germany moves to take its natural place in the world, we're going to feel even more miffed. At the extreme, Germany could push the United States out of Europe, into inglorious isolation in the Western Hemisphere. But even short of that, the new Germany will be less willing to follow a U.S. lead. . . .

To hear Germans tell it, George Bush is a cipher, Ronald Reagan was a clown, Jimmy Carter a disaster and Gerald R. Ford a ghastly accident. During the years that the U.S. political system produced one leader after another whom Germans held in contempt, our economy lost supremacy and we became the world's largest debtor. This is not a record the Germans see much need to respect and they are going to be speaking their minds more often and more clearly. We will often not like what they say, but we owe them so much money and depend so much on the German Central Bank that we shall have to listen attentively.

Whether Germany will conduct itself deftly enough, and others summon the necessary magnanimity to welcome Germany back to its rightful place among the leading nations, will be the next great questions. For countries like France and Poland, a unified Germany—even a nice one—is a bad dream come true. Americans, flushed with triumph in the Cold War, will have to acknowledge new limits on their global role. For people everywhere, still numbed by Hitler's barbarism—and by the corollary horror that Nazi thugs were supported by most Germans of that generation—the prospect of a louder German voice remains, at best, a little terrifying.

The world made peace with a divided and defeated Germany in the 1950s and '60s. In the 1990s we contemplate the more exacting task of making peace with a united and increasingly self-confident Germany: richer, stronger, more advanced than ever—and still at the center of Europe.

"The United States needs to fight the known enemy of Soviet expansionism and Marxist communism, not the chimera of an aggressive reunified Germany."

German Unification Will Reduce Soviet Influence in Europe

Patrick Buchanan and Marx Lewis

In Part I of the following viewpoint, syndicated columnist Patrick Buchanan contends that supporting German unification is in America's best interests. He argues that if the U.S. supports German unification, the Germans will unite with the West against the Soviet Union. However, if the U.S. tries to delay the unification process, Buchanan warns, the Germans may ally with the Soviets. In Part II, Marx Lewis states that a united Germany allied with the West will prevent the Soviet Union and communism from becoming more influential in Europe. Lewis was a writer and the chairman of the Council for the Defense of Freedom, a Washington, D.C. organization that opposes communism.

As you read, consider the following questions:

1. What lesson does Buchanan draw from examining the 1922 Rapallo Treaty?
2. According to Lewis, what has been the traditional goal of Soviet policy toward Germany?

Patrick Buchanan, "United States Runs Risk of Losing Germany," *Conservative Chronicle*, January 3, 1990. Reprinted by permission: Tribune Media Services. Marx Lewis, "German Reunification Needs Quick Resolution," *Washington Inquirer*, October 27, 1989. Reprinted with permission of the *Washington Inquirer*, 1275 K St. NW, Washington, DC 20005.

I

Before the end of 1921 nationalists had new cause for wrath when the League of Nations announced that Poland was to receive that part of Upper Silesia where four-fifths of the mines and heavy industries were located. Winter and the steady deflation of the mark with its attendant hardships aggravated German discontent. On Easter Sunday, 1922, the atmosphere of violence was heightened by Foreign Minister Walther Rathenau's startling turn to the East; he signed a treaty with the Soviet Union at Rapallo. . . .

Rapallo! Inevitable consequence of Germanophobia. With it, Weimar gave up on the West: "Germany and Russia agreed to resume diplomatic relations, to renounce all claims for reparations on each other, and to resume trade. Neither was to enter into an economic agreement affecting the other without prior consultation. Russia was in need of modern technology.

What recalls these passages, from John Toland's biography of Hitler, is [the] inexplicable about-face by the United States.

Before Malta, America was the enthusiast of anti-Communist revolution, Mr. George Bush the Western champion of German reunification.

Suddenly, panicked at the speed of events, the U.S. joined the reactionaries of Europe, Marxist and Socialist, desperate to slow the revolution. Suddenly, our hope is for "stability," latest code word for keeping the Germans down.

Inviting a Second Rapallo

Before you may be one nation again, the President and Mr. James Baker now tell the Germans, you must meet conditions: You must remain inside NATO [North Atlantic Treaty Organization]; you must give up your claims to lost territory in the East; you must prove yourselves good Europeans by subordinating German sovereignty to the Socialist superstate, Economic Community '92 rising in Brussels. By putting America's loyal ally of 40 years on moral probation, Messrs. Baker and Bush are inviting a second Rapallo.

What will we do, if, having advanced Moscow's agenda to keep Germany divided, Moscow double-crosses us, sends a secret envoy to Bonn, and offers German unity, in exchange for Bonn's withdrawal from NATO, neutrality, and expulsion of the United States?

Moscow demanded and got a Four-Power Conference in Berlin. Purpose: Send the German people the message that their country's destiny is for British, French, Americans and Russians to decide. We lined up with our enemies, against our allies.

"Now, we know who our friends are," one German muttered.

Ironically, Mr. Baker is not only risking a double cross by Moscow, he is dealing cards to the German Right, which, now that Chancellor Helmut Kohl is being forced to back off his 10-point plan, will emerge as the new champion of rapid German reunification.

Why are we doing this? Why, on the way to Cold War victory and crushing defeat for communism, has America suddenly become the leading force for "stability" in the world?

President Bush put us behind Mikhail Gorbachev at Malta; Messrs. Brent Scowcroft and Thomas Eagleburger rushed to Beijing to do their kowtow to Deng Xiaoping, Mr. Baker goes to East Berlin to embrace Hans Modrow.

Seeking Their Destiny in the East

Forty-four years after Hitler's suicide, West Germany is a new nation. Prosperous and free, West Germans are fed up having their noses rubbed in the half-century-old horrors of a dead dictator, by allies who never rub Russian noses in the atrocities of J.V. Stalin. . . .

America has nothing to fear from a United Germany. But if we secretly seek permanent American presence in a divided Germany, that will become clear; and we may expect, soon, from our German allies a long goodbye, as they seek their new destiny in the East.

Patrick Buchanan, *Conservative Chronicle*, May 17, 1989.

Weeks ago, we wanted communism swept into the dustbin of history, and Germany reunited. Now, undebated, we have a new foreign policy: Prop up the "reform" Communists of Central Europe, the Soviet Union and China; and, keep Germany divided. Paris, London, Moscow and Beijing are cheering, but where is the correlation between this new policy and U.S. national interest?

Britain and France want reunification put off indefinitely, because they, too, fear a powerful, prosperous, united Germany; but why are we carrying the hod for them? Tying the mighty West Germany economy to EC '92 is what every European Socialist dreams of: but, why is America advancing an EC '92 designed to challenge our own economic primacy? Keeping U.S. troops forever on German soil is what Europe wants (i.e. automatic U.S. involvement in any future European war); but, why is that in America's interest?

NATO was created to shelter West Europe from the Red Army

until the shattered continent could undertake its own defense. That purpose is achieved, and, if the Cold War is over, the United States should turn NATO over to the Europeans, bring our troops home, and disengage from the coming ethnic and border conflicts of Europe in which not a single national interest of our country is engaged.

The U.S. Is Being Used

Let it be stated bluntly. The United States is being used, used for narrow national purposes by allies and enemies alike; we are being conscripted on behalf of causes that do not remotely square with our vital interests, or best traditions.

Mr. Baker's "new architecture"—keeping U.S. troops in Europe for decades, turning NATO into a political alliance, signing onto the Socialist superstate, EC '92—adds up to a permanent diminution of sovereignty, a permanent loss of American freedom of action, and endless U.S. entanglement in quarrels that are none of our business.

Have we forgotten the dream at the outset of this Cold War?

Was it not of a free, united Germany restored to the West, of a Central Europe empty of Russian troops, of Baltic Republics restored to the family of nations, of a Russia and Ukraine free of the demonic grip of Lenin's party—so we could go home.

What first tied the German people to the United States was the great Berlin airlift. America risked war with Stalin to save German lives and defend German freedom. Maintain that spirit, and we will keep that friendship. Abandon that spirit for the vindictive spirit of Versailles, and like the victors of Versailles, we will lose Germany.

II

Ever since the Soviets divided Germany, as they divided other countries they could not subjugate, it was thought that the German problem could be solved by reunification of the two parts. The East German leaders and the Soviets would have none of it, unless they could have control of the both parts. They continued to believe that by imposing restrictions on the Western powers with whom they shared the government following WW II, they could drive the U.S. out of Germany, and eventually, out of Europe.

Stalin tried it as soon as the war was over. In violation of the agreements reached prior to the end of the war, he tried to drive us out of West Berlin. He imposed the blockade which President Truman defeated by the Berlin airlift.

Since then, the Soviets have continued to try to achieve the neutralization of West Germany. This neutralization would create an imbalance that could threaten the peace in Europe, instead of promoting the stability that is needed there. Fears that a reunited Germany will recreate an aggressive military which will again provoke a European war are now being voiced by critics of reunification. . . . But this ignores many hard facts of history and the behavior of the Germans who have immigrated to this country. Certainly there is no reason to believe that the German character by itself is a threat to European stability and peace.

Nothing to Fear

A unified, democratic Germany is no threat to the United States or to democracy in Europe. The Soviet Union has a powerful vested interest in preserving East Germany. The United States does not. The Bush Administration has already tilted too far in support of Gorbachev's position and away from that of West German Chancellor Helmut Kohl. . . .

Americans should not fear a reunified Germany, a shrunken Soviet Union or a united Europe without a need for NATO. These have long been the goals of U.S. foreign policy. Now, on the eve of their fulfillment, it is time to welcome change even when it rouses old fears and stirs new anxieties.

Jeane Kirkpatrick, *Los Angeles Times*, January 29, 1990.

A partitioned Germany, however, has proved to be a danger to the stability of Europe, for it was partly to seek its pre-WW I boundaries and readjust what it thought to be the unfair settlement established at Versailles, that Hitler was able to unite his country for the prosecution of the Second World War. A continued artificial division is as likely to cause problems as a perceived notion of German aggressive tendencies. The German people have over the past 40 years proven that they are capable of democratic self-government.

For five decades the United States has stood for the right of self-determination and for the abolition of totalitarian brutality in Europe. . . . If we fail now to support German unification and the end to Soviet hegemony in the area, we run the risk of alienating both the East and West Germans.

If, on the other hand, we continue our stand against totalitarianism, we may well witness the end of the Soviet Empire, and we may see the reconstruction of a strong bulwark of democratic capitalism that will help keep all Europe in that path.

The United States needs to fight the known enemy of Soviet expansionism and Marxist communism, not the chimera of an aggressive reunified Germany.

"[The Soviet Union] has an inalienable right to expect . . . efforts to ensure that our country should not sustain either moral or political or economic damage from German unification."

German Unification Will Not Reduce Soviet Influence in Europe

Mikhail Gorbachev, interviewed by *Pravda*

Mikhail Gorbachev became the Premier of the Soviet Union and the Soviet Communist Party's leader in 1985. He soon proposed wide-ranging reforms in the Soviet economy, political system, and in Soviet foreign policy. One of the most startling changes in Soviet policy, however, was when Gorbachev did not intervene in Eastern Europe to prop up the faltering regimes of other communist leaders. The following viewpoint is excerpted from an interview he gave to *Pravda*, long an official newspaper of the Soviet government. Gorbachev states that while the Soviet Union supports uniting East and West Germany, the legitimate interests of the Soviet people must be respected. He points out that the Soviets lost many people in World War II at the hands of German soldiers, and contends that the Germans should affirm that they will never again threaten their neighbors.

As you read, consider the following questions:

1. Why does the author argue that the Soviet Union has never denied the Germans' right to unity?
2. What circumstances in Europe must German unification consider, in the author's view?

Reprinted from a February 21, 1990 *Pravda* interview of Mikhail Gorbachev, published by the Soviet Embassy Information Department's *News and Views from the Soviet Union,* February 22, 1990.

Question: *Pravda* is continuing to receive letters from readers asking for explanations on the German unification issue. Diverse opinions have also been expressed in the West on this issue, as well as on the results of your meeting with Chancellor Helmut Kohl. What could you say on this score?

Answer: The issue is very important indeed, being among the overriding ones in modern international politics. I would single out two of its aspects.

The first is the Germans' right to unity. We have never denied them this right. And I would like to recall that even right after the war, which brought our people both the legitimate pride of victory and immeasurable grief, along with a natural hatred of those who had caused it, the Soviet Union was opposed to the partitioning of Germany. The idea was not ours and we are not responsible for the path events took later, during the cold war.

The USSR's Traditional Support for German Unity

Let me add to this that even after two German states appeared, the Soviet Government, jointly with the German Democratic Republic, continued to uphold the principle of German unity. In 1950 the USSR supported the GDR's proposal for restoring common German statehood.

On March 10, 1952, the Soviet Government put forward a plan for the unification of Germany into a single democratic and neutral state. The West rejected that proposal as well. At a Foreign Ministers' Conference in Berlin in 1954 we suggested again the creation of a united demilitarized Germany. And once again, we were given the cold shoulder.

A year later, on January 15, 1955, the Soviet Government proposed the creation of a united Germany with a freely elected government, with which a peace treaty would be signed. That proposal was left unanswered as well.

In 1957-1958 the West would not even consider a proposal for a German confederation, which was put forward by the German Democratic Republic and actively backed by us. Another Soviet proposal followed at the four powers' foreign ministers conference in 1959. It was for a peace treaty with a single united Germany that would not be part of any military-political group, but have a certain military potential. The result was the same as before.

Even when concluding the Moscow treaty, the USSR did not rule out overcoming Germany's split sometime in the future. One illustration is the adoption by our government of a "letter on German unity," which was used by Willy Brandt and Walter Scheel to accompany their signing of the treaty.

These are the facts as they stand.

As you can see, the issue is nothing new to us. We proceed from the premise—and I have had many an occasion to say this both in public and in contacts with German politicians—that history has decided that there be two German states and that it will also decide which form of statehood will finally be adopted for the German nation.

Weighty Interests and Rights

The problem of German unity has a bearing not only on Germans. It must be decided in the context of the existing European and world realities, taking into consideration the interests of other countries and, certainly, the lessons of tragic history.

It goes without saying that in this case the Soviet Union has very weighty lawful interests and rights. The Soviet Union lost 26 million people. Tens of thousands of Soviet cities and villages were destroyed. Hardly any family in the Soviet Union was spared by war. No one can disapprove of us for the fact that we treasure the memory of our dead. . . .

All peoples, particularly the people of the Soviet Union, should have a right to the guarantee that the threat of war will never come from German soil. I believe they will accept and support German unity only if they are certain of this.

Eduard Shevardnadze, *News and Views from the USSR*, February 5, 1990.

History has suddenly been accelerated. In these conditions we affirmed once again that the Germans should themselves decide on the ways, forms and time-frame of their unification. This was discussed also in meetings with Hans Modrow and shortly afterwards with Kohl. But this is just one side of the matter and the meetings covered more than that.

Question: What do you mean?

Answer: First of all, the fact that the unification of Germany concerns not only the Germans. With all respect for their national rights, the situation makes it impossible to imagine that the Germans will come to terms among themselves and then let the others merely endorse decisions already made.

There are some fundamental matters which the international community is entitled to know about and which must leave no room for ambiguity.

It should likewise be made clear right from the start that neither the process of rapprochement between the Federal Republic of Germany and the German Democratic Republic nor a united Germany should spell a threat or harm to the national interests of neighbors or anybody else for that matter.

And, of course, any encroachment upon the borders of other states must be ruled out.

In addition to the inviolability of the postwar borders, which is most important, it also had other consequences. Nobody took away the responsibility of the four powers. And only they themselves can decline it. There is still no peace agreement with Germany. It is this agreement that can finally determine Germany's status in the European structure in terms of international law.

Security, however it can be, has been maintained for a long time by the existence of two military-political alliances—the Warsaw Treaty and NATO [North Atlantic Treaty Organization]. Prerequisites for forming a fundamentally new system of security in Europe are only emerging now. Therefore these alliances retain their role although it is radically modified as the armed confrontation decreases, the military component of security diminishes and political aspects of its activity increase.

Consequently, the reunification of Germany should take account of these circumstances, namely the inadmissibility of disrupting the military-strategic balance of these two international organizations. There should be complete clarity on this.

And the last thing. It follows from what has been said that the process of German unification is organically linked and must be synchronized with the general European process, with its core—the formation of a fundamentally new structure of European security which will replace the one based on blocs.

The Two-Plus-Four Talks

Question: It is known that foreign ministers agreed in Ottawa on the mechanism of discussing the German issue with the participation of the Soviet Union, United States, Britain, France, West Germany and East Germany. Could you say how the role of this mechanism was conceived?

Answer: Indeed, the point at issue is a certain form of discussing the German issue by the six mentioned states. Incidentally, the idea of such a procedure was born in Moscow and Western capitals simultaneously and independently of each other. We spoke about it with Hans Modrow and then with Helmut Kohl. Any references to "priorities" seem hardly appropriate.

Its legal basis is linked with the results of the war, with the four powers' responsibility for Germany's future role in the world. At the same time it takes account of the great changes that have taken place since then in Europe and the world, and in the two German states themselves, and therefore includes them in the formula of this mechanism, conventionally called "two plus four."

189

The task is to discuss in a comprehensive and stage-by-stage way all the external aspects of German reunification, to prepare the issue for inclusion into the general European process and for considering the fundamentals of the future peace agreement with Germany.

Moreover, the effectiveness of such consultations and their prestige depend on the degree of trust and openness between all parties involved. Naturally sovereign states can exercise any contacts, including on the German issue, on a bilateral and any other basis. But we rule out an approach whereby three or four parties will initially arrange things and then tell the other participants the already agreed-upon position. This is unacceptable.

The Danger of a Return to the Past

The public in both Germanies should understand that the two states and especially a united German state will be accepted favourably in Europe only if they do not become "troublemakers."

It is our duty to say this openly, and not only because the Soviet Union is one of the victor powers. People cannot be ordered to become democrats. Germans themselves should realize the danger of a return to the past.

Lev Bezymensky, *New Times*, no. 4, January 23, 1990.

Question: Isn't there an element of discrimination against other countries that also took part in the war?

Answer: The question is quite legitimate. It is exactly for this reason that, without belittling the historical right of the four powers, we link the "two plus four" mechanism with the general European process and at the same time understand the special interest of other countries left out of this formula, and, consequently, their legitimate right to protect their national interests. I refer primarily to Poland; the inviolability of its postwar borders, like the borders of other states, must be guaranteed. Only an international legal act can provide such a guarantee.

Understandable Anxiety

Question: What do you think of the certain anxiety among Soviet people and also other European peoples about the prospect of the emergence of a united German state in the heartland of Europe?

Answer: This concern is understandable both historically and psychologically, although there is no denying that the German people learned lessons from Hitler's rule and the

190

Second World War. New generations matured in both German states. Their view of Germany's role in the world is different from the one that existed over the past one hundred odd years, particularly in the period of nazism.

It is certainly important that the whole world was told more than once not only by the public of West Germany and the German Democratic Republic, but also by officials of the two countries that war should never emanate from German soil again. Helmut Kohl has an even more binding interpretation of this formula: Only peace should come from German soil. He said so when we had a conversation.

This is so. However, no one has a right to ignore the negative potential formed in Germany's past, especially as it is impossible to fail to consider people's memory of war, of its horrors and losses. Therefore it is very important that Germans, deciding the question of unification, should be aware of their responsibility and of the fact that not only the interests but also the feelings of other peoples should be respected.

This applies particularly to our country, to the Soviet people. It has an inalienable right to expect and the possibility to exert efforts to ensure that our country should not sustain either moral or political or economic damage from German unification and that the longstanding design of history would in the long run be realized.

The Need for Soviet-German Cooperation

History determined that we should be neighbors, linked our peoples by ties and profound mutual interests, made our destinies cross, sometimes in tragic circumstances. In conditions of the new epoch, history has given us the opportunity to trust each other and cooperate fruitfully.

*"It is hard to imagine that a united
Germany, . . . possessing one of the world's most
productive economies, would be content to
remain a passive neutral in . . . Europe."*

German Unification Will Ruin the Peace Established by Superpower Alliances

A. James Gregor

Although few regard the Cold War as a good era, some commentators have pointed out that during this period no major fighting broke out in Europe. The author of the following viewpoint, A. James Gregor, contends that Europe was relatively peaceful during the Cold War because the alliance established between the U.S. and Western Europe prevented Soviet expansionism. But now that East and West Germany are being united, the viability of the Western alliance is threatened, he believes, thus also threatening peace. Gregor teaches political science at the University of California at Berkeley and is a researcher at the University's Institute of International Studies.

As you read, consider the following questions:

1. How does the author use historical incidents to support his argument that international organizations are less effective in deterring war than the balance of power system?
2. What are the elements of Mikhail Gorbachev's new thinking in foreign policy, according to Gregor?

A. James Gregor, "The Balance of Power Conflicts of Eurasia," *Global Affairs*, Spring 1990. Reprinted with permission.

From the earliest times, and characteristically during the past two centuries, the major nations of the world have attempted to maintain international peace by deterring violence with the threat of countervailing force. A balance of power was consciously sought that was calculated to deter conflict by making fighting a war more costly than anything that might be achieved by winning it. Deterrence through a balance of power is predicated on the conviction that no state will embark on armed conflict if it is likely that the costs of pursuing a military resolution to international disagreement would be greater than any costs involved in negotiation, compromise, and tolerance.

Treaties, pacts, and arms control agreements seem to supplement, but not substitute for, a balance of deterrent power. That balance is sensitive to rapid change; for once lost, it is hard to restore. In the recent past, "new thinking" has frequently attended major changes in policy on the part of one or another principal in a power balance. What such changes imply seems reasonably clear. The history of modern Europe is suggestive of what is involved.

Bismarck's Adept Use of the Balance of Power

Prince Otto von Bismarck was one of Europe's most adept practitioners of the art of balancing power in order to maintain peace or reduce conflict to the lowest possible level of complexity and lethality. For decades, Bismarck maintained a series of alliances in Europe that balanced power and interests sufficiently to reduce the possibilities of an outbreak of international carnage on a grand scale. Between 1871 and 1890, when he was dismissed by the new Kaiser, Bismarck was the architect of a policy that served to guarantee the peace of Europe.

Only with his dismissal did Germany embark on a "new policy"—a foreign policy enterprise that undid the prevailing balance. Almost immediately following Bismarck's disappearance, the Russo-German neutrality pact, the Reinsurance Treaty, lapsed—setting in motion the forces that were to destabilize Europe and the world for the next quarter-century—until the outbreak of World War I. At their last meeting, Bismarck told the Kaiser that "the crash will come twenty years after my departure if things go on like this"—a prophecy fulfilled almost to the day.

The German leadership that succeeded Bismarck was responsible for the "new thinking" that unsettled the balance of power that had afforded Europe a long interval of peace. The consequence of Germany's new policy was a progressive collapse of international security. As instability increased, there were efforts at international arbitration to defuse critical tensions (Algeciras, Agadir, Bosnia), attempts to effect arms reductions (negotiations to secure a reduction of the German naval construction program), the crafting of new treaties and informal agreements, in the forlorn effort to restore the lost military balance. Germany's post-Bismarckian new "world policy" had thoroughly destabilized what had been an effective balance of power. The mobilizations that took place in the final days before the outbreak of World War I were the last failed efforts to reestablish the deterrent balance.[According to G.M. Gathorne-Hardy,] "The final stage before the First World War was not the application, in any real sense, of the principle of the balance of power, but a frantic and hopeless attempt . . . to redress the balance for which no sufficiently powerful counterpoise was then available." World War I was the result of the inability of the nations of Europe to restore the balance that had become undone after Bismarck's departure.

"Pardon me, I'm looking for the entrance."

© Simpson/Rothco. Reprinted with permission.

The war ended with the disintegration of three of the great empires that had sought to preserve the peace of Europe after the Napoleonic wars. Austria-Hungary dissolved into its components, while czarist Russia collapsed as a consequence of defeat and revolution. In Eastern Europe, where there had been seven nations before World War I, the arrangements that followed the war produced fourteen—each driven by its own "sacred national egoism."

Germany was defeated, disarmed, stripped of generous portions of its national territory, divested of its meager overseas holdings, and humiliated by the requirement that it assume all responsibility for the onset of the most devastating war in history. Czarist Russia, transformed into the Soviet Union, committed itself to the revolutionary destruction of the prevailing world system.

The Failure of the League of Nations

All of this was to be held together in peace and security by the good intentions and the putative "common interests of mankind" embodied in the Covenant that accompanied the founding of the League of Nations. Collective violence was to be rendered impossible and stability assured by the collective declaratory commitments of the members of the League.

Almost immediately, it became evident that the security promised by the Covenant was illusory. There was little hope of producing a credible general system of security; attention was once again directed to the necessity of regional arrangements and their associated balance of power.

The victorious allies sought to stabilize the security environment with the Locarno accords. The boundaries of Belgium and France were to be guaranteed by treaty; and France, Poland, and Czechoslovakia entered into a pact of mutual assistance in the event of German aggression. Behind the accords was the reality of compulsory German disarmament.

The Soviet–German Alliance

The renegade Soviet Union sought common cause with the defeated Germans in the Rapallo arrangements of May 1922. While Lenin advocated peace and universal harmony on one hand, he connived with wounded nationalism and destabilizing revolutionary organizations on the other.

The Soviet-German treaty of Rapallo provided Moscow with the opportunity of exploiting what it understood to be a promising conflict within the "capitalist camp." It also allowed the Germans to begin the reconstruction of the shattered *Wehrmacht*. The Soviet strategy was to take "advantage of the conflict and antagonisms among the imperialists and to slowly accumulate strength,"[Theodore von Laue has written].

Meanwhile, fewer and fewer of the major powers seemed to have confidence in the abilities of the League of Nations to maintain international peace and security. Nevertheless, the industrial democracies (with the exclusion of the United States, which had opted not to become involved) continued to pay lip service to the international organization. Moscow persisted in its declaratory policy of advocating general disarmament, an improved League of Nations, and a more equitable international distribution of natural resources. . . .

The Western powers continued to tout the League of Nations as the guarantor of peace, but for their own security they depended on treaty arrangements and a preponderance of military capabilities. Those arrangements and that preponderance were designed to contain any threat from a resurgent Germany and/or a revolutionary Soviet Union. The Locarno agreements, the network of security ties with the lesser nations of Eastern Europe, and the attempts at the Four Power Pact were all intended to maintain a balance of political and military power that would deter misadventure.

The U.S. Must Act

Unless George Bush stops mealy-mouthing meaningless phrases of congratulation, Europe is in for a serious period of instability. The American president must act—and act fast—to assure that the process of East Europe's liberation and Germany's potential reunification doesn't upset the continental balance of power. . . .

A unified Germany, . . . with its size and strength, would pose a threat to its neighbors in both the East and West. Germany started two world wars this century. As much as the Germans now may protest that they have been transformed into peaceniks, they should not be put into a position where their power can be misused.

William Echikson, *The Christian Science Monitor*, November 16, 1989.

None of these accommodations and arrangements persisted into the 1930s. Even before the advent of Adolf Hitler, Germany had scrapped its reparations obligations, and in December 1932 Germany's right to equality in arms capabilities was recognized. With Hitler's accession to power, a new constellation of German foreign policy objectives destabilized Europe's security environment. "Collective security" immediately recommended itself, but mutual suspicions, diplomatic bungling, and discrete national interests all conspired to make the search for such security extremely difficult. . . .

In 1931 and 1932, in the pursuit of security in the face of a potential German threat, the Soviet Union embarked on a series of treaties with France, Poland, Estonia, Finland, and Latvia in which Moscow was prepared to provide active assistance to the victim of aggression in an effort to contain the anticipated German threat. It required a threat from Germany to alter the overt thrust of Soviet foreign policy. The Soviet Union no longer identified its interests exclusively with the revisionists; it now became an ally of "capitalist" France and one of the most eloquent advocates of the pacific principles of the League of Nations. At the same time, the Comintern continued its revolutionary interventions, and Soviet leadership remained ambivalent. The Rapallo arrangement and the German-Soviet pact of neutrality and friendship of 1926 remained in force; they were prolonged in 1931, to be ratified in May 1933 after Hitler had become chancellor. In the rapidly changing environment, the Soviet Union was not certain what would best assure its security. Joseph Stalin continued to suspect that the French and the British had acquiesced in the revival of German militarism because they intended to turn Germany against the Soviet Union.

By March 1939, Stalin was convinced that the Western industrial democracies were grooming Hitler's Germany for an attack on the Soviet Union. He insisted that the policies of the West were designed not for "collective defense" but to "embroil" Germany "in a war with the Soviet Union; to allow all the belligerents to sink deeply into the mire of war, to encourage them surreptitiously in this; to allow them to weaken and exhaust one another, and then, when they have become weak enough, to appear on the scene . . . to dictate conditions to the enfeebled belligerents." Because the Soviets continued to conceive "capitalism" their principal enemy, Stalin's policies remained confused and confusing.

Stalin Allies with Hitler

In the fall of 1939, all this came together in Stalin's fateful "new thinking"—calculated to frustrate the international "capitalist plot" against the Soviet Union. On August 23, 1939, the Soviet Union entered into a non-aggression treaty with National Socialist Germany, in effect providing Hitler with the assurance of security on the eastern front. The fragile balance of power had been irreversibly subverted. World War II became an inevitability.

By the time Poland had been dismembered, the Soviet Union and Hitler's Germany supplemented their non-aggression pact with a treaty of friendship whose purpose was "to reestablish peace and order" in Poland. Stalin went on to affirm, in a joint closing declaration, that the Soviet-German arrangements would bring international peace unless the Western industrial democracies insisted on a continuation of an unnecessary war. Stalin informed the world that the "new thinking" that had allied him to Hitler would assure peace. What his policy *had* done was to destroy the last semblance of a sustainable balance of power—and there was no escaping global conflict.

The end of World War II found the major powers confused about future relations among the victors. Many of the U.S. leaders at that time were "universalists" opposed to the conception of organizing international relations around any notion of a "balance of power." Cordell Hull, Sumner Welles, Adolf Berle, Averell Harriman, and Charles Bohlen all deplored any process that would make postwar international relations between the Soviet Union and the West a prisoner to those same tactics that in the past had proved unreliable in fostering and sustaining peace.

Nonetheless, by the end of the 1940s and the beginning of the 1950s, the security policies of the United States reflected the convictions of Dean Acheson, George Kennan, Robert Oppenheimer, and Paul Nitze. Central to those convictions was a notion that conflict between the Western powers and their former ally could be averted only if the Western powers maintained a retaliatory capacity sufficient to impose such costs on the leaders in the Kremlin so as to nullify any disposition to employ Soviet military power as an instrument of foreign policy. . . .

A Dangerous German–Russian Alliance

America's vital interest is to see a stable, peaceful Europe, not an unstable German–Russian dominated one. That means striking a deal with Gorbachev . . . to keep newly–freed Germany from reuniting too quickly.

William Echikson, *The Christian Science Monitor*, November 16, 1989.

In the West, the war-devastated industrial democracies of Europe entered into the military alliance of the North Atlantic Treaty Organization (NATO). The balance of power in Europe rested on the credibility of the military might of NATO forces and the evidence of determination to use that might in response to aggression. The United States and its allies followed the prudent rule in statecraft that inclines nations and associations of nations to a balance of power. The United States and its allies could find security only if the Soviet Union lacked the military means to embark upon coercive initiatives—or if the prospective costs that would attend any such enterprise could be kept at what Moscow could only perceive to be prohibitive levels.

For almost four decades, the peace of Europe was maintained by the deterrent balance of military power deployed along the border that, with absolute clarity, separated Warsaw Pact forces from those of the industrial democracies. Where the major powers had not drawn a clear line of demarcation, and where the balance was uncertain, the United States and its allies found themselves drawn into military conflict.

When the United States appeared uncertain as to the boundaries of its interests, the Soviet Union and its allies undertook initiatives. The conflict on the Korean Peninsula was largely the consequence of the United States' unwillingness to commit itself to the defense of South Korea. . . .

Gorbachev and Stability in Europe

Almost from the moment he secured authority in the Soviet Union, Mikhail Gorbachev advocated "new thinking" in Soviet foreign relations. At the Twenty-seventh Party Congress and in an article in *Pravda* in 1987, Gorbachev proposed a "comprehensive system of international security" predicated on an expanded role for the United Nations; advocated strict observance of the U.N. Charter; and proposed the creation of an international agency that would monitor, supervise, and mediate international disputes. It would verify compliance with international arms agreements through on-site inspections. . . .

Corollary to that is Gorbachev's proposal that the Soviet Union undertake to "strengthen" the "peace potential which unites the countries of socialism, the international working-class and communist movement, scores of newly-free independent states and broad anti-war democratic movements." That is coupled with an explicit appeal to the Federal Republic of Germany to separate itself from the "aggressive military bloc" that threatens world peace. Gorbachev insists that "the Soviet Union attaches much importance to its relations with the Federal Republic of Germany." As a consequence, the Soviet Union appealed to West German economic interests with the promise of lucrative bilateral agreements. The West Germans' response was positive. Franz-Josef Strauss, the late leader of the Christian Social Union, announced that "we have nothing to fear from the Soviet Union. The postwar period is over. A new era has started." In February 1988, Lothar Spaeth, deputy chairman of Chancellor Helmut Kohl's Christian Democratic Party, informed Gorbachev that West Germany was prepared to embark on closer economic relations with the Soviet Union. West Germany has, in fact, become Moscow's major supplier of untied loans, has developed into one of Moscow's major trading partners, and is the source of a great deal of its imported advanced technology.

West German Assertiveness

Gorbachev has supported growing West German assertiveness with the suggestion that the nations of Europe "speak more definitely and confidently on [their] own behalf." There is, in fact, growing confidence on the part of West German spokesmen. They have begun to question whether German interests continue to fully coincide with those of the "Anglo-Saxons"—the British and Americans. . . .

Reason to Be Concerned

More than that, as Gorbachev's new thinking stampedes change in Eastern Europe, the issue of German reunification, long suppressed, has resurfaced. Henry Kissinger announced that such reunification "in some form has become inevitable." . . .

The implications of such a development are transparent. All the neighbors of a reunited Germany would have reason to be concerned. It is hard to imagine that a united Germany, with a population of more than 80 million and possessing one of the world's most productive economies, would be content to remain a passive neutral in a Europe destabilized by Gorbachev's new thinking.

Whatever the case, without Germany's presence, NATO could not be sustained long. At the same time, given the changes sweeping Eastern Europe, the integrity of the Warsaw Pact appears to be in equal jeopardy. The disintegration of the two alliances would reinvoke all the ethnic, territorial, resource, and marketing problems that undermined the peace of Europe between the two world wars. That would reintroduce a full measure of instability portentous in its magnitude. The more "successful" Gorbachev's new international policies prove to be, the more emphatic the threat of instability.

Whatever else it was, the Brezhnev Doctrine—of limited sovereignty for socialist states within the international socialist community—controlled the expressions of nationalism and inter-ethnic strife that had destabilized Eastern Europe for the past two centuries. NATO controlled German rearmament and produced the protracted stability that provided the foundation for the German "economic miracle." What the world is now facing is the end of the postwar European system and the balance of power it represented. What will take its place remains uncertain. What appears probable is that whatever does take its place will carry vast instability and tension in its train.

"The explosive birth of a new and huge Germany in the center of the continent immediately undercuts the entire movement toward European confederation."

German Unification Will Ruin the Chance for European Unity

Charles Krauthammer

Charles Krauthammer is a contributing editor to *The New Republic*, a well-known columnist, and the author of several books. In the following viewpoint, he argues that German unification disrupts the progress Europeans were making toward uniting all of Europe into a cooperative community of nations. Now instead of a united and stable Europe, Krauthammer predicts that the Europeans will argue among themselves and create temporary, destabilizing alliances in an effort to keep Germany from becoming too powerful.

As you read, consider the following questions:

1. Why does the author disagree with the idea that the Germans have an aggressive national character?
2. What does the author mean when he states that German unification signals the end of the decline of sovereignty?
3. What does Krauthammer mean when he refers to balance of power politics? What evidence does he see that this type of diplomacy is being resurrected?

Charles Krauthammer, "The German Revival," *The New Republic*, March 26, 1990.
Reprinted by permission of THE NEW REPUBLIC, © 1990, The New Republic, Inc.

The great intervening parties of modern history, although by no means the only ones, have been the great powers, and a great power is, among other things, a power that cannot be intervened against. . . .

—Hedley Bull

Overnight and once again Germany has become a great power. Not for long will it continue to be intervened against. All that is left to negotiate is the mode of liquidating the Big Four's half-century intervention in Germany. Beyond those negotiations lies the other half of the great power equation: In what ways and to what extent will Germany once again become an intervening power?

Pervasive Anxiety

German intervention, or, shall we say, German external intentions, are the major item on the European agenda. Because these intentions are as yet indeterminate, the fear of Germany, once the great subtext of European politics, is now the text. German reunification changes all geopolitical calculations. It colors plans for the single European market of 1992. It infuses dead organisms, like the Warsaw Pact, with new life. (The Solidarity prime minister of Poland asked Soviet troops to stay in his country until the "German problem" is solved.) Most chillingly, it evokes old memories. Who would have thought that we would live to see, again, a headline reading: "Polish Official Vows to Defend [German] Border" (*The New York Times,* February 21, 1990)?

Anxiety about Germany is so pervasive and seems so self-explanatory that it often escapes analysis. What exactly is the nature of the German danger? The answer presents itself in three distinct parts: military, economic, and political. The first two have been widely advertised and widely exaggerated. The third, the subtle effect German reunification will have in the realm of geopolitical ideas and institutions, is apt to prove the most serious.

Military Concerns

At the most concrete level, the fear of Germany has to do with borders. Much territory was stripped from Germany to punish it for starting World War II, and to diminish it as a hedge against World War III. With a reunified Germany dominating the continent, with Russia and America having gone home, who will stop Germany when it invokes a statute of limitations on World War II and demands restoration to its former, pre-Hitler self? . . .

Europeans, with memories of the Wehrmacht crisscrossing

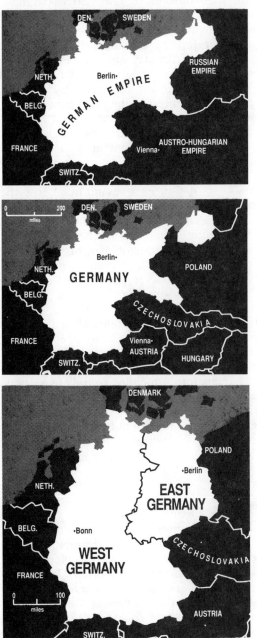

After the Franco-Prussian War in 1871, Bismarck molded German areas outside Austria into an empire under Prussian domination. The territory of present-day Poland had been split earlier between the Russian, Austro-Hungarian, and Prussian empires.

After World War I, Germany became a republic. Under the punitive Treaty of Versailles, the country lost roughly 10% of its population and territory, including the industrial Saar Basin in the west and the eastern Polish Corridor.

After World War II, Germany was split into four zones overseen by the Allies. In 1949 the Federal Republic (West) and the Democratic Republic (East) were created. Berlin, though deep inside East Germany, retained a major Western presence.

the continent, fear for their borders. If that fear is paranoia, then we must count Lech Walesa, Mikhail Gorbachev, most people in between, and much of Western Europe, too, as paranoid. Political philosopher Johnny Carson put it best. "The Berlin Wall is down," he noted the day after the event. "That means that all Germans are now free to go wherever they want in Europe. Hey, wasn't that the problem back in 1939?". . .

Germany will no doubt be required as the price for reunification to pledge adherence in perpetuity to its current borders. Yet no one can be absolutely sure that Germany ten or twenty years from now will not dismiss this agreement as the relic of a weakness long passed, as it did the Versailles agreements in the 1930s.

At the root of this fear of German revanchism lies the German national character, or more precisely, the belief in a German national character. The fear is that left to themselves Germans will revert to Teutonic barbarism, that German romanticism—the peculiarly fevered romanticism of the worker bee—will again seek fateful expression in politics and history. Beside this fear, forty years of democracy, forty years of peaceful accommodation to neighbors—in short, forty years of history—count for little.

One cannot definitively disprove this fear. How does one prove the negative proposition that Germans do not suffer from some peculiar character defect that inclines them toward expansion and aggression? One can only say that invoking national character as an explanatory principle or predictive device should always be cause for skepticism. The psychological interpretation of nations is even more unreliable than the psychological interpretation of individuals, itself a notoriously unreliable enterprise. By this reckoning, how do we account for the fact that the French disposition toward romantic expansionism, which took them all the way to Moscow in 1812, was abruptly banished in 1815?

The Triumph of History

We account for it as the triumph of history over "character." As Daniel Pipes says, there is no cure for total ambition quite like total defeat. Before there was a German problem, there was the French problem. Waterloo was its solution. Who worries about French national character now? There is no certainty, of course, that the German problem was solved in 1945 as surely as the French problem was solved in 1815. But the last forty years of German history cannot be so easily dismissed. (And security guarantees, such as a continued American presence on the continent, should provide sufficient reassurance until the new Germany has the time to demonstrate that it is indeed heir to the Federal Republic and not to more archaic German forms.)

The more realistic fear of the new Germany is economic and, as a result, cultural. As Rita Klimová, the Czech ambassador to the United States, said, "The German-speaking world"—by which she meant the two Germanys and Austria—"will now achieve what the Hapsburgs, Bismarck, and Hitler failed to achieve: the Germanization of Central Europe." She added, "Through peaceful and laudable means, of course. And by the logic of commerce rather than conquest." Her point was clear. The dynamism of German commerce is already being felt in the weak economies of Eastern Europe. Czech schools, she explained, had just abolished Russian as the second language. The only question now was whether the new second language would be English or German. She urged the United States to send English teachers.

A Dominant Power

The problem is that a united Germany, or even a confederated Germany, would be the hegemonic power in an independent Europe. Consider the evidence. The West Germans have built from rubble the most powerful economy in all Europe. Yet an even greater feat may have been performed by the East Germans. They have created a relatively productive economy under the impossible, absurd conditions of Marxist economics. Put these two together and you have what all of Europe understands will be its dominant power.

This does not, of course, mean German armies retracing the path of the Wehrmacht. But it does mean Germany coming to dominate the political economy of the Continent. Would such a Germany continue to, in effect, sustain and subsidize much of the European Community? Would it accept in perpetuity its shrunken postwar borders? Would it continue to abjure nuclear weapons?

Charles Krauthammer, *Time*, September 25, 1989.

Eastern Europe fears outright domination by the German dynamo. Western Europe—Britain and France in particular—fear eclipse. This will be an economy of 80 million people producing fully forty percent of the European Community's gross domestic product. As the economic powerhouse of the continent, it will dictate policy to its neighbors even more powerfully than it does today.

One can understand the origin of these fears without granting them undue respect. The fear of being outcompeted by a peaceful commercial republic operating on fairly equal terms is a fear of which a nation ought not be proud. It characterizes, for example, the rather hysterical and occasionally racist American hostility toward Japan. German economic domination of the continent may be an injury to the pride of the British and the French. And the spread of German automobile manuals may be unwelcome to Czechs and Poles. But neither development constitutes a menace to anyone's standard of living (in market systems, prosperity is not a zero-sum game), or a threat to anyone's national existence, or an argument against German reunification.

Political Concerns

What then is the real problem with German reunification? It will reverse one of the most salutary European developments of the last fifty years: the decline of sovereignty. German reunification will constitute the most dramatic rebirth of sovereignty in the postwar era. In this era, Europe has enjoyed a historically unprecedented period of peace largely because the sovereignty of its warring nations was suppressed, brutally in the East and benignly in the West, by the advent of two great empires. Whatever else it did, the cold war division of Europe into a pax Sovietica and pax Americana did have the virtue of suppressing internecine European conflict.

But the imperial suppression of sovereignty must be temporary. Empire is not forever. Hence the post-cold war question: How to remove the artificial suppression of sovereignty by the superpowers, without then risking the national explosions that follow almost universally—in our time, in Asia and Africa—whenever the imperial power withdraws? Western Europe thought it had found the answer. Over the last forty years it has gradually built up transnational institutions, most notably the European Community. The great project accelerating toward completion was the formation of the single European market by 1992 that would transform the economies of the Twelve into an economic unit almost as free of legal barriers as that of the United States. Ireland and Greece would trade as freely as Maine and Texas.

Giving Up Political Autonomy

But the importance of Europe '92 is not just economic. It involves one of history's greatest peacetime transfers of sovereignty. By giving up enormous economic, social, and regulatory power to a central European authority, the countries of Western Europe are consciously giving up much of their political autonomy. That is precisely why Margaret Thatcher so resists the process. She knows that EC monetary union, for example, may soon lead to a common currency, which will lead further to a common economic policy, which will lead inexorably toward political confederation. Talk of a United States of Europe is premature. But it is not farfetched. That is the trajectory that Western Europe is following.

Or was until November 9, 1989, the day the Berlin Wall fell. Europe '92 was to substitute the diminished sovereignty imposed by European integration for the diminished sovereignty once imposed by American domination. It was to be a transition from imperially- to self-imposed community. The great hope was that an integrated Europe would begin to acquire some of the internal stability of a federal country such as the United States. By diminishing the sovereignty of each country and centralizing more and more authority in "Europe," the national rivalries that led to centuries of European wars would become obsolete. It would be as if Texas went to war with Maine.

Returning to the 19th Century

As we welcome the rebirth of a diverse Europe, let us not forget that this rebirth brings with it the pangs of our old nationalisms. In short, the 19th century awaits us at the dawning of the 21st.

Régis Debray, *New Perspectives Quarterly*, Winter 1990.

German reunification challenges the idea and derails the process. West Germany, pledged to diminish its sovereignty by joining this single European market, is about to swallow the East, an incorporation that will augment its population, territory, economy, military strength, political centrality, and diplomatic clout. It is about to become the new giant on the continent. Leave aside potential territorial claims against its neighbors. Leave aside the possibility of Germany acquiring nuclear weapons. The simple fact of the explosive birth of a new and huge Germany in the center of the continent immediately undercuts the entire movement toward European confederation.

A German Confederation

Such a Germany is its own confederation. Absent any malice, ill will, or "romanticism" on the part of its leadership, it will necessarily begin to act in accord with its new power—independently and with the kind of assertiveness and regard for distant interests that characterizes the other great powers, notably the United States and the Soviet Union.

The real danger posed by a reunified Germany is not that a new Bismarck or Hitler will arise. It is that the birth of a new giant in the middle of the continent will arrest Europe's great confederational project and produce in its place, as *The Economist* put it, a "revised version of a previously destructive balance-of-power system," a recapitulation of the kind of international system of the late nineteenth and early twentieth centuries that ended in catastrophe.

We can see the new balance-of-power system taking shape already. The shape is disturbingly familiar. The Western European powers are maneuvering to reestablish pre-war links with the ex-Soviet colonies of Eastern Europe, not just in pursuit of economic opportunity, but quite consciously to prevent Germany from dominating the region. . . .

As the Europeans begin to maneuver to find partners to balance and contain Germany, each country is forced into a kind of reactive nationalism. Margaret Thatcher "is practicing a very narrow brand of nineteenth-century nationalism," complained a West German diplomat to *The Washington Post*. "The danger is that when one country does this, others may be forced to follow." She might reply, We didn't start this. But no matter. Wherever one chooses to place the blame, the result is the same: the movement toward integration, federalization, and dilution of sovereignty is halted. Europe invented the idea of sovereignty, suffered its consequences, and was about to demonstrate how to transcend it. Now Europe is heading back the other way. For a continent consisting of twenty-nine sovereignties speaking forty-five languages, that way is not just an anachronism, it is a prescription for instability.

The Revival of Sovereignty in Eastern Europe

To be sure, this revival of sovereignty had already begun elsewhere. In Eastern Europe the erosion of Soviet power is already giving rise to reassertions of contentious and conflicting nationalisms. The withdrawing Communists leave behind a myriad of territorial and other grievances and no structure to moderate these conflicts. Not surprisingly, the most advanced case of malignant nationalism can be seen in the place from which Soviet influence was first expelled. Yugoslavia, Eastern Europe's oldest Moscow–free zone, is home to ethnic strife of truly heroic depth and irrationality.

Everyone is aware of the dangers of these revived Eastern and Central European nationalisms. But there was a hope: that a powerfully united Western Europe would draw the Eastern countries into its orbit and that, as they attached themselves individually to this new stable center, their intramural conflicts would be tempered. The key to a pax Europa was to be a deeply integrated European Community: a core confederated Western Europe attracting and taming the newly freed sovereignties of the East.

That was the vision of the new Europe. In fact, it became the very definition of the word. When Vaclav Havel says that he wants Czechoslovakia to "rejoin Europe," he means not just a reunion with Western culture and political tradition, but something very concrete as well. He means joining the enterprise launched by the European Twelve and institutionalized in the framework of the European Community. He means the Council of Ministers in Brussels, the Parliament in Strasbourg, the Court of Justice in Luxembourg. . . .

In October 1989, when writing about a post-cold war world, I ventured that among the great powers of the new multipolar order would be "Europe." It was possible then to imagine a confederated Europe emerging from the structure of the EC. It is harder to imagine that now. Not because Germany is by policy its enemy, but because the rebirth of a great German nation within Europe is provoking a rebirth of national self-assertion throughout Europe. In this climate, it is impossible to think of a "Europe" emerging. As we head toward multipolarity, the pole that was to be "Europe" will instead be greater Germany. It is possible that Germany might still choose to subsume itself in Europe, but in the first flush of post-(cold)-war independence, that is hardly likely.

The Wall Fell Too Soon

The Berlin Wall came down too soon. Had East Germany been the last Soviet province to fall, as we thought the Kremlin would insist, it might have been but a small piece digestible by a new and stable Europe. Having come so quickly, German unification threatens to disrupt the whole by creating in the heart of Europe a greater Germany that Europe cannot contain.

The danger is not that greater Germany will march across Europe but that its birth turns the twilight of sovereignty into a new dawn. It derails a process by which Europe was hoping to make itself safe from itself. We return instead to the old Europe, balance of power Europe, the Europe that produces more history than it can consume.

"The Jew in me is troubled, even worried. Whenever Germany was too powerful, it fell prey to perilous temptations of ultranationalism. "

German Unification Threatens the Jewish People

Elie Wiesel and Arye Carmon

Part I of the following viewpoint is by Elie Wiesel, a survivor of the Nazi concentration camps, Auschwitz and Buchenwald. The novelist wrote about his experiences in the camps in the memoirs, *Night.* He won the Nobel Peace Prize in 1986 for his commitment to human dignity and freedom. The second part of the viewpoint is by Arye Carmon, the president of the Israel-Diaspora Institute at Tel Aviv University. He is also the publisher of *Israeli Democracy*, a magazine supplement to *The Jerusalem Post International Edition.* Wiesel and Carmon argue that Jews have good reason to fear a united Germany. They worry that Germans have forgotten the Holocaust and may be susceptible to the racism and nationalism that fifty years ago resulted in the deaths of six million Jews.

As you read, consider the following questions:

1. Why does Wiesel believe Germans do not remember the past as well as they should?
2. Why does Carmon contend that even though West Germany is now a democracy, Jews still have reason to fear German unification?

Elie Wiesel, "I Fear What Lies Beyond the Wall," *The New York Times,* November 17, 1989. Copyright © 1989 by The New York Times Company. Reprinted by permission. Arye Carmon, "Beware of Euphoria," *Israeli Democracy,* Winter 1990. Reprinted with permission.

I

Like most people who abhor imposed separation and oppression, I am happy for the citizens of East Berlin. And for those of West Berlin. Watching on television the tens of thousands of young Germans celebrate freedom was a moving and rewarding experience. Whenever and wherever liberty is victorious, people everywhere ought to rejoice. The Berlin wall was a disgrace. An abomination. Its murderous shadow, a nightmare.

Most of the faces we saw on the TV screen were young. One couldn't help but share their joy and excitement. Their parents and grandparents had placed unbearable burdens and dark complexes on their shoulders. It was not easy for them to grow up wondering: "What did my father do during the war?" They deserve the chance to begin again, I thought. No one ought to begrudge their exuberance. They are entitled to their day in the sun. No one ought to spoil it.

A Symbol of Hope

The fact that it happened in Berlin lent, in a way, the remarkable event a special meaning. What was, 50 years ago, history's capital of absolute evil has so suddenly become a symbol of hope. If this is possible, I thought, why despair of seeing a similar occurrence in other areas of the world—the Middle East, for example?

Then, as always, emotions gave way to political considerations. Commentators and analysts began asking obvious questions: What next? Will this unexpected turn of events lead to a reunification of Germany? If so, when? What will its impact be on the international scene? Will a united, powerful, new Germany break away from the conquest-thirsty demons that dominated the old Germany?

I cannot hide the fact that the Jew in me is troubled, even worried. Whenever Germany was too powerful, it fell prey to perilous temptations of ultranationalism.

Nazis Still Exist

Does my worry mean that I do not trust Germany's youth? I do. I hope they will have learned the lessons of World War II and will be shielded by that memory. But as long as the old generation is still around, one must be vigilant, on the alert. Remember: Reactionary, anti-Semitic journals are still being published in Germany; former Nazis still have their own associations, one of their leaders has been elected to high office in Berlin.

The general trend points toward "normalization" in political awareness and history as well. Should this trend go unchecked, will it lead to the "normal" impulse of turning the page? If so, is the pace of events too fast? Does the acceleration of history suggest danger?

In other words, what is happening in Berlin troubles me because of its possible effect not only on the future, but also on the past. In fact, the past has already been affected. "Nov. 9 will enter history," declared the Mayor of West Berlin. Others echoed his statement in every media around the globe. They forgot that Nov. 9 has already entered history—51 years earlier it marked the Kristallnacht.

The intense joy of the present has overshadowed the past. No one in Berlin, or in our own country for that matter, made the connection. That is why I am worried. I wonder: What else will be forgotten?

Is my fear unfounded? Is it due to my background as a Jew who has been traumatized by what, once upon a time, rulers in

Berlin had willed and ordered against my people?

What should one feel when hearing old-new Germany's anthem — "Deutschland, Deutschland Uber Alles"?

II

The question of the reunification of Germany must be addressed by the Jewish community, and as soon as possible. Events of 1989—in what was Yalta, Central Europe—will certainly be described in text-books of the future as a major watershed of modern civilization. The 1990s have suddenly become not just a chronological turning point, but a fundamental historical milestone. All this has caused both bewilderment and euphoria. We, however, cannot afford to be euphoric.

I am a Jerusalemite, who grew up in a divided city, and a student of Nazi history, who has spent considerable time in divided Berlin. The dismantling of walls has affected my own biography, as it has so many others': We have learned that man cannot erect barriers between different viewpoints, cultures, or even human desires. The disappearance of this barrier is a triumph of freedom, one which comes at the end of a long, turbulent century. But we should not be misled.

No one knows if the disappearance of the Berlin wall is indeed a joint celebration of liberty by the two German states. It could, by the same token, provoke a repetition of German aggression. The current revolution in Berlin marks the failure of one system, but it does not prophesy an alternative. Twentieth century German history provides no guarantee that reunification will be accompanied by notions of liberty and tolerance and their accepted codes of behavior. Twice in this century a united Germany was responsible for outbreaks of the most devastating violence. The civilized world was startled by the rabid growth of racism under Weimar. This was the consequence of Germany's first experience in democracy.

Today's Germany

Today, as the other Germany stands on the precipice of freedom, the continued suppression of these instincts is the central issue. While liberal democracy has met most of the challenges it confronted during this century, it failed to solve the problem of extreme nationalism and its perversions.

We can hardly predict what political forms will evolve from the nations of the collapsing Eastern Bloc. We can only be sure of our knowledge that it is the cultural and moral values of a given national heritage that will dictate collective behavior. Past expressions of collective behavior in a unified Germany are only too well known. Whether or not they will resurface is a question that should be left untested.

The 1990s are to be the prologue to a new century. It will most likely be a decade of interregnum for Germany, a period to be closely watched—particularly by the Jews. Only 45 years ago, half way through the 20th century, Jewish sovereignty was established in Israel. Since then, the Jewish state has fostered democracy and a modern western Jewish identity. At the same time, the same western world that witnessed the Holocaust has granted an unprecedented degree of freedom to the Jews, as it has restrained its own anti-Semitic traditions. Yet, the major feature of the Jewish ethos remains "survival," both in Israel and the Diaspora. For this reason Jews must be wary of the current euphoria and conscious of the perils of naivete. Freedom for the German nation should not be permitted to become a renewed German nationalism. Germany should not be reunited!

"The Jewish people cannot forget the suffering inflicted upon them. . . . We Germans, too, remember, conscious that we cannot master our future by forgetting the past."

German Unification Does Not Threaten the Jewish People

Hans–Dietrich Genscher

The following viewpoint is an excerpt from a speech West German Foreign Minister Hans–Dietrich Genscher delivered to a conference of American newspaper editors. Genscher argues that the German people have been peaceful and responsible world citizens since 1945, the year the allies invaded and toppled the government of Nazi dictator Adolf Hitler. Genscher contends that the Germans remember the Jew's suffering during World War II. Consequently, he believes that a united Germany will not endanger Jewish people.

As you read, consider the following questions:

1. How does the author support his argument that the Germans have made responsible use of the freedom they regained in May 1945?
2. What points does Genscher make by discussing his birthplace?
3. Why do the two German nations want to be united, according to Genscher?

Hans-Dietrich Genscher, "The Future of a European Germany," speech delivered to the American Society of Newspaper Editors, Washington, D.C., April 6, 1990.

I address you as Foreign Minister of the Federal Republic of Germany and as a member of a nation which was divided for decades but has now embarked on the path of unification and wants to complete its unification in freedom, democracy and human dignity.

It is not only their common history, their common culture and their common responsibility for all that has happened in the past that makes the Germans one nation; it is their unshakable commitment to the values of a free society, and it is their responsibility for Europe's future.

The German Constitution

Since May 8, 1945, the Germans in the Federal Republic have made responsible use of the freedom they regained. They gave themselves the most liberal constitution in our history, which requires the people to achieve German unity, to seek the unification of Europe, and to serve the cause of world peace.

It is a constitution which uniquely directs the political establishment of our country to pursue a policy of responsibility and denounces the pursuit of power.

But that constitution is not yet valid for all Germans. Seventeen million Germans living against their, and our, will in a different state, the GDR [German Democratic Republic], had to wait a long time for freedom and democracy.

In 1989 they achieved that freedom by peaceful means, like the people in the other Central and East European countries.

Moving Experiences

Two hundred years after the French Revolution the people have brought about the great peaceful revolution for freedom in Europe. In those months during the second half of 1989 I had some of the deepest impressions and most moving experiences of my life.

I am the Foreign Minister of the Federal Republic of Germany, but I was born in a town which still belongs to the GDR, Halle on the river Saale. There I lived until I was 25, that is, until 1952, when I had to leave the GDR.

You can imagine what it meant to me when, on September 30, 1989 I was able to tell 5,000 Germans from the balcony of our Embassy in Prague that the way to freedom was open.

At that moment the whole world realized that seventeen million people could not be locked up forever behind a wall and barbed wire.

On February 16 of 1990, in the historic market square of my home town Halle, with its monument to Georg Friedrich Händel and the five towers which Lionel Feininger's painting had made known throughout the world, I spoke to nearly 100,000 people about freedom, democracy and the market economy.

The Link Between Germans and Americans

I thanked all those who had stood by us Germans in good and in difficult times, first and foremost the United States of America.

The people in Halle's market square felt just as the telephone operator in my ministry felt when, during the evening of the day the Berlin Wall was opened, I telephoned James Baker to thank America on behalf of the Germans. Before connecting me, she said to the Secretary of State of the United States: "Thank you, Mr. Secretary. God bless America." With those words she expressed the sentiments of millions of Germans.

An Important Lesson

It must never be forgotten that under the national socialist tyranny it was from Berlin that the genocide perpetrated against the European Jews was prepared and directed.

During the last few decades, however, Berlin has also come to symbolize the fact that the desire for freedom, human rights and self-determination cannot be suppressed in the long term. We recall with gratitude the efforts of the Americans, the French and the British to safeguard the freedom and viability of West Berlin. . . .

Only those who are prepared to face the whole truth, however painful, will acquire a true understanding of the value and dignity of freedom stemming from a sense of responsibility. This is one of the most important lessons we in Germany have learned since 1945.

Helmut Kohl, Speech at a joint meeting of the World Jewish Congress, European Jewish Congress, and the Central Council of Jews in Germany, May 6, 1990.

Thus the link between the Germans and the Americans has become closer and, in the positive sense of the word, more emotional than many people thought possible at the end of the terrible World War II.

No one in Germany has forgotten that on September 6, 1946, in that momentous speech in Stuttgart, American Secretary of State James F. Byrnes extended a helping hand to the former enemy.

The essence of our relationship is that to us Germans in the Federal Republic of Germany, our new beginning and our link with the United States are two sides of the same coin, that is to say, our irrevocable commitment to freedom and human dignity and hence to democracy and to the community of democracies.

We Germans are aware that there is concern among our neighbors in Europe, and in the United States too in connection with German unification, and that questions are being asked. Questions like: What do the Germans want? What are the implications for Europe and the world if nearly 80 million Germans live together again in one state?

Considering all that has been done in the name of Germany, I can understand these questions. And I can understand them especially when they are asked by Jewish people, for November 9, 1989 is not only the day when the Wall disintegrated, or the day in 1918 when the Weimar Republic was founded. November 9 also marks the pogrom night of 1938, which is often innocuously described as the "Night of the Broken Glass" but was in fact an evil omen of the holocaust.

In his famous speech marking the 40th anniversary of the end of the war, Federal President Richard von Weizsäcker spoke of the importance of remembrance in the Jewish faith.

The Suffering of the Jews

We Germans appreciate that the Jewish people cannot forget the suffering inflicted upon them, that they continue to remember. We Germans, too, remember, conscious that we cannot master our future by forgetting the past.

We can assure everyone that the joy we felt at the ending of a decades-long separation will neither extinguish nor conceal our memory of the suffering brought upon especially the Jewish people by Hitler in the name of Germany.

We Germans desire no more than to live in freedom and democracy and at peace with all our neighbors.

On behalf of Germany's European neighbors, Czechoslovak President Vaclav Havel said: "The time has come to join hands in friendship so that we will no longer have to fear one another."

Through unification the Germans will achieve even greater harmony among themselves and with their neighbors. The awareness of our European identity will grow even stronger. In this sense the unification of Germany does not create but rather solves a problem which affected the whole of Europe.

To be frank, the word "pride" has often been abused in the history of my people, but I admit to being proud of the fact that the people in my native region, in the place where I grew up, have step-by-step won their freedom, their democracy, their human rights, peacefully and without hatred.

Evaluating Sources of Information

When historians study and interpret past events, they use two kinds of sources: primary and secondary. Primary sources are eyewitness accounts. For example, the diary of a survivor of Auschwitz describing her experiences in the concentration camp would be a primary source. A book about Auschwitz by an author who used the survivor's diary would be a secondary source. Primary and secondary sources may be decades or even hundreds of years old, and often historians find that the sources offer conflicting and contradictory information. To fully evaluate documents and assess their accuracy, historians analyze the credibility of the documents' authors and, in the case of secondary sources, analyze the credibility of the information the authors used.

Historians are not the only people who encounter conflicting information, however. Anyone who reads a daily newspaper, watches television, or just talks to different people will encounter many different views. Writers and speakers use sources of information to support their own statements. Thus, critical thinkers, just like historians, must question the writer's or speaker's sources of information as well as the writer or speaker.

While there are many criteria that can be applied to assess the accuracy of a primary or secondary source, for this activity you will be asked to apply three. For each source listed on the following page, ask yourself the following questions: First, did the person actually see or participate in the event he or she is reporting? This will help you determine the credibility of the information—an eyewitness to an event is an extremely valuable source. Second, does the person have a vested interest in the report? Assessing the person's social status, professional affiliations, nationality, and religious or political beliefs will be helpful in considering this question. By evaluating this you will be able to determine how objective the person's report may be. Third, how qualified is the author to be making the statements he or she is making? Consider what the person's profession is and how he or she might know about the event. Someone who has spent years being involved with or studying the issue may be able to offer more information than someone who simply is offering an uneducated opinion; for example, a politician or layperson.

Keeping the above criteria in mind, imagine you are writing a paper on how a united Germany affects the rest of Europe. You decide to cite an equal number of primary and secondary sources. Listed below are several sources which may be useful for your research. *Place a P next to those descriptions you believe are primary sources. Place an S next to those descriptions you believe are secondary sources.* Next, based on the above criteria, *rank the primary sources assigning the number (1) to what appears to be the most valuable, (2) to the source likely to be the second-most valuable, and so on, until all the primary sources are ranked. Then rank the secondary sources, again using the above criteria.*

P or S		*Rank in Importance*
_____	1. A speech by a former French president who argues that German history shows the dangers of allowing Germany to be united.	_____
_____	2. The book *An Analysis of Post-War East Germany* written by a Soviet historian.	_____
_____	3. An editorial by an American military officer stationed in West Germany.	_____
_____	4. Viewpoint three in this chapter.	_____
_____	5. Transcripts of a meeting between Helmut Kohl and Mikhail Gorbachev concerning German and Soviet differences on foreign policy.	
_____	6. A pamphlet published by a neo-Nazi group advocating that united Germany reinstate the policies of Adolf Hitler.	_____
_____	7. The diary of an East Berliner who witnessed both the erection and dismantling of the Berlin Wall.	_____
_____	8. An article in a weekly magazine interpreting the effects German unity will have on European culture.	_____
_____	9. Viewpoint one in this chapter.	_____
_____	10. A German college student's research paper titled, "How Germany Overcame the Nazi Legacy."	_____
_____	11. A documentary series on public television covering German history from 1870 to 1990.	_____
_____	12. A reporter's account of meetings between German and Polish officials regarding the borders of the two nations.	_____

Periodical Bibliography

The following articles have been selected to supplement the diverse views presented in this chapter.

Christoph Bertram "The German Question," *Foreign Affairs,* Spring 1990.

Julian Bullard "Surviving the New Germany," *The Spectator,* April 28, 1990.

James Chace "Answering the German Question," *The New Republic,* December 11, 1989.

Ian Davidson "The Search for a New Order in Europe," *International Affairs,* April 1990.

Joachim Fest "The Silence of the Clerks," *National Review,* April 16, 1990.

Marc Fisher "In a New Era, a Continuing Need to Confront a Dark Past," *The Washington Post National Weekly Edition,* April 9-15, 1990.

Julio Godoy "Nowhere at Home," *Mother Jones,* February/March 1990.

Steven Greenhouse "German Unity Revives Vision of a Great Continent Reborn," *The New York Times,* April 3, 1990.

Richard Helms "What's the Big Deal?" *The Washington Post National Weekly Edition,* March 5-11, 1990.

Josef Joffe "One-and-a-Half Cheers for German Unification," *Commentary,* June 1990.

Robert D. Kaplan "The Lost Sheep," *The Atlantic Monthly,* March 1990.

Henry A. Kissinger "Living with the Inevitable," *Newsweek,* December 4, 1989.

Tom Mathews et al. "The Long Shadow," *Newsweek,* May 7, 1990.

New Perspectives Quarterly "The Next World Order," Spring 1990.

Daniil Proektor "A Reunited Germany—A Threat to Europe?" *New Times,* March 6-12, 1990.

Henry Ashby Turner "Baseless Fears of a United Germany," *The New York Times,* February 11, 1990.

James M. Wall "In Germany, the Debate About Values Isn't Over," *The Christian Century,* February 28, 1990.

The Wall Street Journal "Two Germanies United Would Pose Challenge to Other Economies," November 13, 1989.

Is European Unification
Possible?

EASTERN
EUROPE

Chapter Preface

Internationalism is the belief that humans can transcend their allegiances to individual nations and work together to create a peaceful world order. The philosopher Immanuel Kant expressed the hopes of many people when he wrote in 1795, "Since reason condemns war and makes peace an absolute duty, and since peace cannot be effected or guaranteed without a compact among nations, they must form an alliance." This alliance among nations "may be called a pacific alliance," Kant wrote, that would "forever terminate all wars." Kant is one of many people who have believed that if nations can unite, conflict may be avoided.

Obviously, establishing this alliance has never been an easy task. Humans have more often gone to war than established lasting alliances to guarantee peace. But the close of the twentieth century has brought hope that at least one region that has experienced warfare and division—Europe—may be able to unite into a pacific alliance. Three events have led to this hope. First, the nations of Western Europe are already moving toward uniting their economies. Europe 1992 refers to a plan to establish one market among twelve Western European nations. The plan's advocates maintain that this economic collaboration will encourage other forms of cooperation. Second, the fall of Communist governments in Eastern Europe ends the political division of Europe. No longer do Western and Eastern European nations have fundamentally different and opposing political systems. Third, the unification of Germany may also spur cooperation. Many European leaders, including French president François Mitterand and Italian foreign minister Gianni De Michelis, argue that Europe must unite and include Germany in that unity, so that the powerful nation of Germany remains committed to peace in Europe.

World trends are not easy to discern or predict. Controversy surrounds the move toward European unity. Is a united Europe truly possible? More fundamentally, can nations and peoples transcend their narrow interests and establish an alliance for peace? These are some of the questions debated in the following chapter.

"Our nations are looking for a way to democracy and independence."

Establishing Democracy in Eastern Europe Will Unite Europe

Vaclav Havel

For years playwright Vaclav Havel has been one of Czechoslovakia's most famous dissidents. During Communist rule in Czechoslovakia, Havel's plays were censored and he was arrested and jailed many times. He is a founder of the human rights movement Charter 77. *Letters to Olga* is a collection of notes Havel wrote to his wife while in jail. One month after a peaceful revolution toppled the nation's Communist government, Havel became Czechoslovakia's president. The following viewpoint is excerpted from a speech he gave before the U.S. Congress shortly after assuming office. In it, he states that Eastern Europeans are working to establish democratic governments that respect human rights.

As you read, consider the following questions:

1. What are the implications of the revolutions in Eastern Europe, according to the author?
2. What experiences have given Czechs and Slovaks insights on democracy that most Americans do not have, according to Havel?
3. What does Havel mean when he argues that salvation lies within the human heart?

Vaclav Havel, speech delivered to a joint session of the U.S. Congress, February 21, 1990.

224

The last time they arrested me, on October 27, 1989, I didn't know whether it was for two days or two years. Exactly one month later, when the rock musician Michael Kocab told me that I would probably be proposed as a presidential candidate, I thought it was one of his usual jokes.

On the 10th of December 1989, when my actor friend Jiri Bartoska, in the name of the Civic Forum, nominated me as a candidate for the office of President of the Republic, I thought it was out of the question that the parliament we had inherited from the previous regime would elect me.

Twelve days later, when I was unanimously elected President of my country, I had no idea that in two months I would be speaking in front of this famous and powerful assembly, and that what I say would be heard by millions of people who have never heard of me and that hundreds of politicians and political scientists would study every word I say.

When they arrested me on October 27, I was living in a country ruled by the most conservative Communist government in Europe, and our society slumbered beneath the pall of a totalitarian system. Today, less than four months later, I am speaking to you as the representative of a country that has set out on the road to democracy, a country where there is complete freedom of speech, which is getting ready for free elections, and which wants to create a prosperous market economy and its own foreign policy.

It is all very strange indeed. . . .

Rapid Changes

We are living in very odd times. The human face of the world is changing so rapidly that none of the familiar political speedometers are adequate.

We playwrights, who have to cram a whole human life or an entire historical era into a two-hour play, can scarcely understand this rapidity ourselves. And if it gives us trouble, think of the trouble it must give to political scientists, who spend their whole lives studying the realm of the probable.

Let me try to explain why I think the velocity of the changes in my country, in Central and Eastern Europe, and of course in the Soviet Union itself, has made such a significant impression on the face of the world today, and why it concerns the fate of us all, including you Americans. I would like to look at this, first from the political point of view, and then from a point of view that we might call philosophical.

Twice in this century, the world has been threatened by a catastrophe; twice this catastrophe was born in Europe, and twice you Americans, along with others, were called upon to save Europe, the whole world and yourselves. The first rescue mission — among other things — provided significant help to us Czechs and Slovaks.

Thanks to the great support of your President Wilson, our first president, Tomas Garrigue Masaryk, could found our modern independent state. He founded it on the same principles on which the United States of America had been founded, as Masaryk's manuscripts held by the Library of Congress testify.

UnRaveling

At the same time, the United States was making enormous strides. It became the most powerful nation on earth, and it understood the responsibility that flowed from this. Proof of this are the hundreds of thousands of your young citizens who gave their lives for the liberation of Europe, and the graves of

American airmen and soldiers on Czechoslovak soil.

But something else was happening as well: the Soviet Union appeared, grew, and transformed the enormous sacrifices of its people suffering under totalitarian rule, into a strength that, after World War Two, made it the second most powerful nation in the world. It was a country that rightly gave people nightmares, because no one knew what would occur to its rulers next and what country they would decide to conquer and drag into their sphere of influence, as it is called in political language.

All of this taught us to see the world in bi-polar terms, as two enormous forces, one a defender of freedom, the other a source of nightmares. Europe became the point of friction between these two powers and thus it turned into a single enormous arsenal divided into two parts. In this process, one half of the arsenal became part of that nightmarish power, while the other—the free part—bordering on the ocean and having no wish to be driven into it, was compelled, together with you, to build a complicated security system, to which we probably owe the fact that we still exist.

So you may have contributed to the salvation of us Europeans, of the world and thus of yourselves for a third time: you have helped us to survive until today—without a hot war this time—but merely a cold one.

And now what is happening is happening: the totalitarian system in the Soviet Union and in most of its satellites is breaking down and our nations are looking for a way to democracy and independence. The first act in this remarkable drama began when Mr. Mikhail Gorbachev and those around him, faced with the sad reality of their country, initiated their policy of "perestroika." Obviously they had no idea either what they were setting in motion or how rapidly events would unfold. We knew a lot about the enormous number of growing problems that slumbered beneath the honeyed, unchanging mask of socialism. But I don't think any of us knew how little it would take for these problems to manifest themselves in all their enormity, and for the longings of these nations to emerge in all their strength. The mask fell away so rapidly that, in the flood of work, we have literally no time even to be astonished.

An Irreversible Process

What does all this mean for the world in the long run? Obviously a number of things. This is, I am firmly convinced, an historically irreversible process, and as a result Europe will begin again to seek its own identity without being compelled to be a divided armory any longer. Perhaps this will create the hope that sooner or later your boys will no longer have to stand on guard for freedom in Europe, or come to our rescue, because Europe will at last be able to stand guard over itself. But that is still not the most important thing: the main thing is, it seems to me, that these revolutionary changes will enable us to escape from the rather antiquated straitjacket of this bi-polar view of the world, and to enter at last into an era of multipolarity. That is, into an era in which all of us — large and small — former slaves and former masters — will be able to create what your great President Lincoln called "the family of man." Can you imagine what a relief this would be to that part of the world which for some reason is called the Third World, even though it is the largest?. . .

I've only been president for two months and I haven't attended any schools for presidents. My only school was life itself. Therefore I don't want to burden you any longer with my political thoughts, but instead I will move on to an area that is more familiar to me, to what I would call the philosophical aspect of those changes that still concern everyone, although they are taking place in our corner of the world.

A New Vision

The failure of Marx's vision has created the need for another vision, not for a rejection of all visions. I do not speak of 'socialism with a human face', for that belongs to the past. I speak instead about a concern with society, civilization and humanity in a period when the nineteenth-century idea of progress has died out and a related idea, communist revolution, has disintegrated. What remains today is the idea of responsibility, which works against the loneliness and indifference of an individual living in the belly of a whale. Together with historical memory, the belief in personal responsibility has contributed to the Solidarity movement in Poland, the national fronts in the Baltic States, the Civic Forum in Czechoslovakia.

Czeslaw Milosz, *Granta*, Winter 1990.

As long as people are people, democracy in the full sense of the word will always be no more than an ideal; one may approach it as one would a horizon, in ways that may be better or worse, but it can never be fully attained. In this sense you too are merely approaching democracy. You have thousands of problems of all kinds, as other countries do. But you have one great advantage: you have been approaching democracy uninterruptedly for more than two hundred years, and your journey towards that horizon has never been disrupted by a totalitarian system. Czechs and Slovaks, despite their humanistic traditions that go back to the first millennium, have approached democracy for a mere twenty years, between the two world wars, and now for the three and a half months since the 17th of November 1989.

The advantage that you have over us is obvious at once.

The Communist type of totalitarian system has left both our nations, Czechs and Slovaks — as it has all the nations of the Soviet Union and the other countries the Soviet Union subjugated in its time — a legacy of countless dead, an infinite spectrum of human suffering, profound economic decline, and above all enormous human humiliation. It has brought us horrors that fortunately you have not known.

At the same time, however — unintentionally, of course — it has given us something positive: a special capacity to look, from time to time, somewhat further than someone who has not undergone this bitter experience. A person who cannot move and live a somewhat normal life because he is pinned under a boulder has more time to think about his hopes than someone who is not trapped in this way. . . .

The Importance of Human Responsibility

For this reason, the salvation of this human world lies nowhere else than in the human heart, in the human power to reflect, in human meekness and in human responsibility. . . .

We are still a long way from that "family of man"; in fact, we seem to be receding from the ideal rather than drawing closer to it. Interests of all kinds: personal, selfish, state, national, group and, if you like, company interests still considerably outweigh genuinely common and global interests. We are still under the sway of the destructive and vain belief that man is the pinnacle of creation, and not just a part of it, and that therefore everything is permitted. There are still many who say they are concerned not for themselves, but for the cause, while they are demonstrably out for themselves and not for the cause at all. We are still destroying the planet that was entrusted to us, and its environment. We still close our eyes to the growing social, ethnic and cultural conflicts in the world. . . . In other words, we still don't know how to put morality ahead of politics, science and economics. We are still incapable of understanding that the only genuine backbone of all our actions — if they are to be moral — is responsibility. Responsibility to something higher than my family, my country, my firm, my success.

Responsibility to the order of Being, where all our actions are indelibly recorded and where, and only where, they will be properly judged.

"Those who see democracy breaking out all over Eastern Europe should look more closely at what might hide under the democratic label."

Eastern Europe Will Not Be Able to Establish Democracy

Thomas Molnar

In the following viewpoint, Thomas Molnar disputes the belief that the nations of Eastern Europe will establish successful democracies. Molnar argues that these nations lack a political tradition of democracy and are too rent by ethnic discord to be able to establish true democracies. Molnar is a philosophy professor at the City University of New York and the author of *Twin Powers: Politics and the Sacred.*

As you read, consider the following questions:

1. What comparison does Molnar make between African nations in the 1960s and Eastern European nations in the 1990s?
2. What conditions are necessary for democracy to be established in a country, in the author's opinion?
3. What is Molnar's advice to U.S. political leaders?

Thomas Molnar, "Eastern Europe: History Resumed," *First Things,* April 1990. Reprinted with permission.

Eastern Europe in 1990 is not to be confused with Africa in 1960. African decolonization was a relatively peaceful affair. It was sponsored and financed by the former colonial powers, and the new regimes, with one or two exceptions, accepted either some semblance of democracy or a benevolent one-man rule. Later on, most of the new nations changed their minds and reverted to traditional tribal ways, though even then they still paid lip-service to western models. In contrast, Eastern Europe, while it knows what democracy is about, has hardly ever practiced it, at least its American variety. Czechoslovakia is an exception, although that nation's record with respect to its German and Hungarian minorities has not been a distinguished one.

Old Ways Will Reassert Themselves

A new chapter is now opening in Eastern Europe, but we should not be overly surprised if, as in Africa, the old ways soon reassert themselves. The things that people and governments say in the flush of sudden change may not correspond closely to the structures they elaborate with the passage of time. In the gray morning after the previous night's celebration old mental habits easily reappear, especially if vague but heady promises of better days are not soon realized.

The prospects for the region are thus rather different from those suggested in Francis Fukuyama's vision of an imagined western triumph over history. In a way, history may just be beginning in an Eastern Europe that has been excluded from it since the 1500s, when the Ottomans occupied a huge chunk of it. The Turks were followed by the Hapsburgs here, by the Muscovites there, and Eastern Europe was condemned to a political, cultural, and even linguistic somnolence for four centuries. And we know what happened when the hibernation seemed finally to be over: first Versailles, then Yalta.

The situation is, thus, quite unsettled, and the United States, a relative newcomer in the area, ought to be especially careful about stepping into a hornet's nest (which is not to be confused with a vacuum). The nations of Eastern Europe may be novices in democracy, but they know something about history and geopolitics. George Bush would do well to avoid prescribing for Eastern Europe in the manner adopted by Zbigniew Brzezinski toward the Soviet Union. Brzezinski has written (in *The Washington Post*) that we expect the new Russia to be democratic, adopt the free-market system, and dissolve itself in a confederacy. Such hubristic drawing up of blueprints for others can only wind up in mutual frustration and disappointment.

After all, Russia *is* a great power, and a jealous one at that, whether tsarist, Stalinist, or pan-Slavist or whether the president is Mikhail Gorbachev or, tomorrow perhaps, Alexander Solzhenitsyn. We are naive to be scandalized that Moscow still increases some branches of its weaponry, sends out spies, and practices disinformation. Tomorrow we will no doubt be similarly scandalized that Communist parties in Eastern Europe remain in the hastily set up parliaments and that they gather some old and many new votes as the economy does not improve overnight and the fragile social structures show signs of stress. For decades, the Communist vote in France and Italy was largely a protest vote; this could well become the case in Eastern Europe, where Marxist parties will no longer bear the burden of being associated with Soviet tanks.

Ed Gamble. Reprinted with permission.

Washington thus ought to remember that it cannot govern the planet, and that it is counter-productive to try to impose the same model of political economy on islands in the Pacific and on the Russian steppes. The sending of emergency aid accompanied by hectoring admonitions is not the equivalent of a sustained foreign policy. Those who see democracy breaking out all over Eastern Europe should look more closely at what might hide under the democratic label. There are strong possibilities, as in post-1960 Africa, that the new regimes will indeed opt for "democracy," not because they actually believe in it or mean to practice it but because it has become a universal, thus increasingly meaningless, term with a greatly varied bag of contents. The form it takes in Latvia will be quite different from that in Bulgaria.

Geopolitics commands the elements of political choice. Placed between a reunited Germany and a convalescent, hence temporarily weak, Russia, Eastern Europe can look forward to years of adjustment in the region's power equilibrium. In reality, the current situation favors Germany, the big winner in the present upheaval. A united Germany is likely to instill a new vigor to national feelings. Germany's Prussian half, although numerically in the minority, may become a pole of attraction for the rest of the country. Was East Germany not hardened by Marxism and by suffering, is it not exposed to the East, is it not more historically conscious than the West German consumer society? Will the reunited nation (its capital, Berlin) not repudiate the French connection? Will relations not cool with Washington?

These reflections serve as reminders that Washington cannot take for granted either Fukuyama's Hegelian rhapsody or its own blueprint of post-Soviet democracy in Eastern Europe. Nationalistic feelings aroused by recent developments already show signs of reigniting old controversies. Germans in Poland greeted Helmut Kohl as "our chancellor"; Hungarians claim parts of Transylvania; Rumania wants Bessarabia back; Yugoslavia may dissolve at any time; Bulgarians, remembering Ottoman suppression, attack their Turkish minority. For years Russian dominance froze inter-satellite hostilities. We may see them soon erupt.

The Conditions Needed for Democracy

Given all this, one must remain skeptical about Washington's hope of Eastern Europe choosing democracy and joining the western orbit. Nationalism, now intensified by its long forcible denial, is not a promoter of the democratic system, whether in Argentina or Rumania. Fukuyama and other enthusiasts of democracy have broken out the champagne bottles a little too early. Democracy seems to require for its success a bourgeois social consciousness based, as in the United States, in sustained prosperity, political moderation, and a liberal tradition. These factors do not exist in Eastern Europe, where the Communist regimes have left behind massive social dislocation, a tenacious *nomenklatura,* and a proletarianized mass of ideologically rootless and politically skeptical individuals. The dominant political creed is: everyone for himself. True, this leaderless population was able to storm the new Bastilles, the Berlin Wall and

Nicolae Ceausescu's luxury palace. But they did so not so much in the expectation of democracy as of a modicum of well-being and freedom of movement that almost any successor regime can satisfy.

Politically Underdeveloped

Nowhere in Eastern Europe is there "normal parliamentary democracy." How could there be? By Western standards, the region has always been politically underdeveloped. It industrialized late, and patchily. Its middle classes never quite achieved critical mass. On the eve of World War II the largest segment of the population of Eastern Europe was still the peasantry—historically, a class with deep suspicion of politics as a preserve of the landed gentry. As a result, autonomous spheres of power such as unions grew slowly and stayed weak. Almost by default, writes George Schöpflin of the London School of Economics in *Daedalus*, "the state exercised a paramountcy over society that the latter could do little to modify." When the Communists swept into power in the late 1940s, they inherited a culture congenial to one-party rule.

Peter McGrath, *Newsweek*, May 21, 1990.

Washington would be well advised not to put all its political hopes in one basket, thereby contributing to the blockage of Eastern European evolution. The tremendous significance of 1989 was precisely to open up a whole bundle of historical possibilities the outcome of which it would be folly prematurely to attempt to prescribe.

"With the erosion of communism, ethnic problems are bursting out all over Eastern Europe."

Eastern European Nationalism Will Prevent European Unification

Robert D. Kaplan

In the following viewpoint, Robert D. Kaplan points out alarming parallels between Europe at the turn of the century and Europe today. Kaplan discusses nationalism, an ideology that encourages strong loyalty to one's nation and culture. It was nationalism that promoted instability in southeastern Europe in the early 1900s and eventually drew all the great powers into World War I. These nationalist grievances have never been settled, Kaplan maintains. He predicts that ethnic hatreds in today's Eastern Europe will prevent unification and peace in Europe. Kaplan is a journalist living in Portugal and the author of *Surrender or Starve: The Wars Behind the Famine.*

As you read, consider the following questions:

1. What does Kaplan mean when he writes that communism "stopped the clock" in Eastern Europe?
2. Describe three examples of ethnic hatreds that Kaplan discusses.
3. What are the ethnic rivalries in Yugoslavia, according to Kaplan?

Robert D. Kaplan, "The Balkans: Europe's Third World," *The Atlantic Monthly,* July 1989. Reprinted with permission.

The violence of the twentieth century has derived in large measure from the ethnic hatreds of the Balkans. Bucharest, Belgrade, Sofia, and Adrianople: these were once the datelines of choice for ambitious journalists—the Kabul, Saigon, and Managua of a younger world. Ernest Hemingway filed his most famous dispatch from Adrianople (now Edirne, in Turkish Thrace) in 1922, describing Greek refugees "walking blindly along in the rain," with all their worldly possessions piled on oxcarts beside them. Lawrence Durrell, Eric Ambler, and Rebecca West all found the Balkans to be fertile terrain. As late as 1938 the President of Czechoslovakia, Edvard Beneš, advised the future *New York Times* columnist C.L. Sulzberger, "Go to the the the Balkans, Cyrus. . . . That will be the most interesting place."

The Collapse of Empires

The curtain rose in 1912, when Bulgaria, Greece, Montenegro, and Serbia declared war on the waning Ottoman Empire and stripped it of most of its remaining European possessions. A second war on the Balkan Peninsula was fought in 1913, over boundaries. Bulgaria attacked Serbia and Greece, leading to an invasion and a partial dismemberment of Bulgaria by its former Balkan allies and Turkey. The following year the assassination of Archduke Francis Ferdinand of Austria, by a Serbian nationalist, Gavrilo Princip, brought on the First World War. The war was won and lost on a grand scale. The Austro-Hungarian Empire collapsed, and a sprawling new nation, Yugoslavia, was formed. It was tenuously dominated by Serbs, and the aspirations of Croats and other minorities were harshly suppressed. Romania was enlarged; Hungary and Bulgaria were reduced and envious. Large numbers of ethnic Hungarians found themselves trapped inside Romania. Meanwhile, the collapse of the Ottoman Empire left many ethnic Turks subject to the Bulgarians, and the first attempts at forging a new, homogeneous Turkish state in Anatolia resulted in the slaughter of around a million Armenians.

Following the First World War, democracy sank shallow roots in the countries of southeastern Europe, where the peasantry was illiterate and the middle class underdeveloped or, in certain areas, virtually nonexistent. Parliamentary governments rose and fell, undermined by corrupt and meddling monarchs and by ethnic passions that refused to subside. During the 1930s the British and French policy of appeasement placed the Balkans at the mercy of the Nazis and the Russians. It was Hitler's step-by-step subversion of Romanian independence, helped along by the Romanians' fear of the Russians, which

236

was greater than their fear of the Germans, that attracted Sulzberger and other journalists to Bucharest in 1939.

The Russians eventually triumphed, and for four decades after the Second World War, communism virtually stopped the clock in Europe's poorest corner. Economies remained plundered and backward. Hungry peasantries exist today in Romania and Albania. . . . National disputes remained unresolved. Stalin, writes Milovan Djilas, a former Vice-President of Yugoslavia and that country's leading dissident, "was far more interested in Balkan hatreds than in Balkan reconciliations."

What Happens When Legitimate Interests Collide

As the tragic history of 1919-39 shows, the collapse of imperial systems does not in itself solve the successor-state problem and may vastly complicate it. Americans, moreover, are still attached to the Wilsonian doctrine of "self-determination," and believe that ethnic-linguistic nationalism, freely expressed, is the sovereign test of political legitimacy.

Have we considered what happens when two nationalisms qualify for legitimacy under the same test of abstract justice, but also collide? . . .

The great revolution of 1989-90 has whipped nationalist passions into a froth, but those passions cut both ways. At the end of the day, when the cheering stops, East European nationalism will have to be subdued to larger interests, as it has been in the West, and old rivalries will have to yield to new forms of cooperation. It is the only way.

Edwin M. Yoder Jr., *Los Angeles Times*, March 11, 1990.

Today, as the Soviet Union finally relaxes its grip on Eastern Europe, that attitude has come back to haunt Stalin's successors in the Kremlin. "With the erosion of communism, ethnic problems are bursting out all over Eastern Europe," says Rudolph Joo, a leader of the Hungarian opposition. "While borders are coming down throughout Western Europe, here they're going up." For years it was NATO [North Atlantic Treaty Organization] that had to deal with a Balkan dispute within its ranks—the one between the Greeks and the Turks. Now, as the tiresome bickering of Athens and Ankara grows desultory, similar disputes threaten to fracture the communist world. George Konrad, another Hungarian dissident, suggests that the old fault line dividing East and West is changing in character: it now divides the East and the West not of the Cold War but of Byzantium and Rome—of Orthodox Serbs and Catholic Croats, of Orthodox Romanians and Catholic Hungarians.

In 1941, in her travel book about Yugoslavia, *Black Lamb and Grey Falcon,* Rebecca West stated flatly that "the Turks ruined the Balkans." When Turkish power in the region disintegrated at the beginning of this century, all the other national emotions exploded. Something similar is happening now. And once again refugees are marching in the rain and mud.

Hungary and Romania

"Our child is Magyar [ethnic Hungarian], and he has no future in Romania—that is the main reason why we fled," a thirty-year-old Magyar ironworker from Transylvania, a region that has been part of Romania since the end of the First World War, explained to me recently. The man insisted on anonymity in order not to endanger family members left behind. He and his wife and baby had crossed the border into Hungary at night on foot, evading Romanian soldiers, after being pressured by the Romanian authorities to christen their son with a Romanian name. All Hungarian-language secondary schools in Transylvania have been closed, he said, and Hungarian villages that have existed for centuries are being demolished, as part of President Nicolae Ceausescu's brutal scheme of rural reorganization. . . .

This family was among the more than 12,000 refugees who escaped across the Romanian border in 1988, after the Hungarian government, under public pressure initiated by dissidents, abandoned its policy of returning such refugees to Romania. Hungary thus became the first Warsaw Pact state to grant an official status to escapees from an allied communist state. There are between 2 million and 2.5 million Magyars in Romania, making them the largest ethnic minority in Europe. (They are equal in number to the Palestinian refugees throughout the Middle East.) A Western diplomat I spoke with in Budapest described the treatment of Magyars and others in Romania as "outrageous and horrific," and observed that the villages being destroyed were being replaced by unlivable apartment blocks, many with communal kitchens and outdoor latrines. . . .

Yugoslavia's Divisions

Ethnic divisions that date back to the breakup of the Hapsburg Empire not only threaten relations between Hungary and Romania but also threaten to tear up another Balkan state, Yugoslavia, from within.

The Yugoslavia that emerged from the First World War was dominated by the Serbian royal house of Karadjordjevic. In 1934 an assassin linked to the Ustashi, a Croatian terrorist group, killed King Alexander, aggravating a climate of communal hate between the Orthodox Serbs and the Catholic Croats which Hitler proved quick to take advantage of. During the Second World War, Ustashi gangs, which had been granted legitimacy by the Nazi puppet state of Croatia, massacred whole villages of Serbs (as well as villages of Jews and gypsies). The Serbs were not particularly enamored of Josip Broz Tito, the half-Croat, half-Slovene resistance leader who ruled Yugoslavia during most of its postwar existence. The miracle of a cohesive Yugoslavia under Tito was due in no small measure to repression. Purges were harsh and frequent. The most famous of the victims was Milovan Djilas, a Montenegrin and therefore a close kinsman of the Serbs, who was expelled from the Communist Party's Central Committee in 1954 and jailed in 1956. With Tito's death, in 1980, a gradual process of liberalization ensued in Yugoslavia. Djilas himself has been partly "rehabilitated" and allowed to travel abroad and speak publicly. At the same time, the very process of liberalization has resulted in a resurgence of the Serbian nationalism that Tito had managed to contain.

Profound Problems

Nationalism, ethnic identity and religion played crucial roles in shattering the communist domination of Eastern Europe. As the extraordinary forces of an extraordinary 1989, they were more powerful than the Moscow brand of Marxism-Leninism imposed four decades ago. . . .

Yet nationalism, ethnicity and religion may also create problems no less profound in post-communist Eastern Europe—antagonisms between countries and within them. Positive forces can become negative forces, undermining the effort to build democracies, reconstruct economies and assure reasonable social harmony.

Tad Szulc, *Los Angeles Times*, December 17, 1989.

A photograph of Slobodan Milosevic, a Serbian nationalist, adorns a wall in many a Serbian household. Milosevic, a plump, baby-faced man in his mid-forties, is the first charismatic figure to emerge in post-Tito Yugoslavia. Like Tito, he is considered by many in Belgrade to be a ruthless strong man. Observers believe that Milosevic is attempting to use his position as the leader of the Communist Party in Serbia to take over the national Yugoslav Communist Party, headed by a Croat, Stipe Suvar.

Although Milosevic's aims have brought Yugoslavia's 8.6 million Orthodox Serbs into head-on conflict with its 4.6 million Catholic Croats, a situation that could lead to widespread civil disorder, the most immediate consequences of his rise to power involve the 1.7 million Muslim Albanians in the southern province of Kosovo, within Serbia. Serious Serbian-Croatian political enmity goes back, after all, only to the First World War; the conflict between the Serbs and the Albanians has its roots in the Battle of Kosovo Polje, in 1389, when the Serbian hero Lazar lost his kingdom to the Ottoman Turks, a circumstance that would eventually encourage the settlement of large numbers of Albanians in what had been Orthodox Christian territory. The 600th anniversary of the most tragic day in Serbian history was marked in June 1989.

The first ethnic Albanian riots in Kosovo since Tito's death occurred in 1981, with protesters demanding that Kosovo, an autonomous province within Serbia, be made a full republic. Since then tens of thousands of the province's 200,000 Serbs and Montenegrins have fled to other parts of the country, alleging ill treatment at the hands of the more numerous Albanians.

The birthrate among Albanians in Kosovo is the highest in Yugoslavia, and the Serbs are clearly afraid of being engulfed. Miroslav Markovic, a high-ranking Serbian official in the federal government, said to me in an interview, "The Albanians have seven children per family and they demand we give them aid. The Constitution says you have the right to have only as many children as you can feed. This [the high Albanian birthrate] is an Asiatic mentality that the most well-heeled of Western governments couldn't cope with.". . .

Bulgarians and Turks

More so even than the Serbs, the Bulgarians shoulder a morose sense of lost national destiny. Since its re-emergence as an independent nation, Bulgaria has failed to realize its historical claim to Macedonia (now a Yugoslav republic), and almost all of its outlying territories were annexed as a result of unlucky alliances in the two world wars.

At points in its early history Bulgaria was among the most powerful and advanced kingdoms in all of Europe. In the ninth century, and again in the thirteenth, Bulgaria stretched from present-day Albania in the west to the Black Sea in the east, and from the Carpathian Mountains in the north to the Aegean Sea in the south. Unlike nations whose empires faded gradually into oblivion, Bulgaria was cut down summarily by a series of invasions that culminated in a 500-year-long Ottoman Turkish occupation. 'The Turkish slavery is still our biggest national obsession, in relation to which the struggle of the superpowers is a mere passing phenomenon," a Bulgarian official once said to me. One of the most important dates on the Bulgarian calendar is the holiday, celebrated on February 19, that commemorates the execution, in 1873, of the Bulgarian guerrilla leader Vasil Levski by the Turks.

With respect to the Turks, the Soviet Union has served Bulgaria like a weight-lifting older brother. In its dealings with Bulgaria, the Turkish government must be cautious. The Bulgarian regime of Todor Zhivkov was able to act with virtual impunity when, in 1984, it stepped up a campaign to require the country's 900,000 ethnic Turks—who make up nearly 10 percent of the Bulgarian population—to Bulgarize their names. Eyewitness accounts told of people being forced at gunpoint to sign documents. Entire villages were sealed off, and reportedly, scores of executions occurred. Bulgarians claim that Bulgarization has been a voluntary program. When I last visited Bulgaria, in late 1986, Nikolai Todorov, the vice-president of the Bulgarian Academy of Sciences, told me, "The state has to protect the interests of the nation, and in the Balkans a nation means one particular ethnic group." He went on: "Keeping the peace in the region means every minority has to be completely assimilated into the majority. It's a pity to say, but it's true." Another Bulgarian was more blunt: "If it weren't for the Turkish invasion in the fourteenth century, we would be eighty million now. The Turks still have an invoice to pay.". . .

The Old World Strikes Back

In his address in 1987 commemorating the seventieth anniversary of the Bolshevik Revolution, Mikhail Gorbachev boasted that in 1917 "mankind crossed the threshold of real history . . . we departed from the old world and irreversibly rejected it." As Djilas and others have pointed out, the "old world" is now striking back with a vengeance. The economic underdevelopment engendered by what Djilas calls Moscow's "industrial feudalism" simply aggravated ethnic hatreds and postponed the day of reckoning.

In the 1970s and 1980s the world witnessed the limits of superpower influence in places like Vietnam and Afghanistan. In the 1990s those limits may well become visible in a Third World region within Europe itself. The Balkans could shape the end of the century, just as they did the beginning.

"The drastic redrawing of the ethnic map in Eastern Europe might explain . . . why peoples of the region recently seemed capable of solidarity beyond petty nationalism."

Eastern Europe May Renounce Nationalism

István Deák

Eastern Europe's boundaries have changed frequently over the past century, as diplomats tried to draw the borders to satisfy (or sometimes frustrate) the national aspirations of various ethnic groups. István Deák, the author of the following viewpoint, argues that Eastern Europe may at last have achieved some stability. He states that Poles, Hungarians, and many other Eastern Europeans look to the West as their role model, and thus may have a more international than national outlook. Deák is a history professor at Columbia University in New York City and the author of *Beyond Nationalism*.

As you read, consider the following questions:

1. What are the differences between the history of Eastern Europe and the history of other parts of Europe, in the author's view?
2. Why does the author believe the predictions of nineteenth-century advocates of nationalism were proven wrong?
3. What signs does Deák find that suggest Eastern Europe may be able to avoid nationalist turmoil?

István Deák, "Uncovering Eastern Europe's Dark History," *Orbis*, Winter 1990. This paper was originally prepared for a 1989 conference on foreign policy at the Washington Institute for Values in Public Policy. Reprinted with permission.

Scarcely linked, if at all, by language, religion, culture, or earlier social and economic developments, the East European peoples have never been able to coordinate their actions against great power encroachments or against social and economic ills. Soviet-imposed slogans of ideological affinity and friendship among peoples have not succeeded in veiling the reality of divergent interests and popular enmities. Economic and other forms of cooperation among the communist states has been unsuccessful and is viewed by the public there as an unwanted burden.

At most, the peoples of Eastern Europe are bound together by their backwardness relative to Western and, increasingly, even Southern Europe. Agriculture and industry experience great difficulty adjusting to the dynamic world market, and environmental pollution has become uncontrollable.

This gap between Eastern Europe and the rest of the continent is not due solely to the Soviet military presence in the region or to the worldwide crisis of Marxist-Leninist systems. After all, the crisis of the Soviet system cannot account for the near-collapse of Yugoslavia, which has been free of Soviet influence for over forty years. What, then, does explain the common, unifying backwardness of Eastern Europe?

Social Turmoil

For many centuries before the Iron Curtain descended, the countries of Eastern Europe partook of experiences very different from those of Western and Southern Europe. Here, as opposed to other parts of the continent, the migration of peoples has never ceased. Political boundaries have shifted often and dramatically. Great wars and invasions have ravaged the cultural heritage of past generations. Feudal social relations, particularly the institution of serfdom, lasted longer than in the West. And parliamentary politics, although not unknown, has been thwarted again and again by war and social turmoil.

Worse still for the cooperation of East European peoples, the area has been divided by culture and history. The Catholic Church predominates in Poland, Bohemia, and Hungary; Orthodox Christianity holds sway in Russia and Southeast Europe. Muslims predominate in Albania and constitute sizeable minorities in Yugoslavia and Bulgaria. Up to 1939, Eastern Europe held about 5 million Jews and up to 13 million Germans. Russian, Prussian, Habsburg, or Swedish rule forms the tradition in the Baltic countries and Poland; Habsburg, Venetian, or Ottoman domination in the Danube region and the Balkans. Noble-dominated Polish, Russian, Lithuanian, Hungarian, Romanian, and Croatian society developed differently from the essentially peasant societies of Serbia and Bulgaria, and from the Czech lands, which became increasingly middle-class, industrial, and commercial. As for the provinces that make up the German Democratic Republic (GDR, or East Germany), they shared a mixed tradition of East European noble hegemony, Prussian bureaucratic state power, and West European modernization and industry.

Dick Locher. Reprinted by permission: Tribune Media Services.

But perhaps the most harrowing aspect of East European development in modern times was the introduction in the nineteenth century of the West European ideology of nationalism. This ideology was born of the Romantic era's repudiation of the Enlightenment, and specifically of the Enlightenment's attempt to organize society scientifically and rationally. Nationalist ideology professed the goal of ethnic self-determination: the creation of polities in which each ethnic group would be free to exercise its natural right to national sovereignty and to determine the laws by which it is governed. Even in Western Europe, it was responsible for many bloody conflicts. But there it did allow for the creation of powerful and prosperous nation-states, sufficiently self-confident to cooperate, and now even to consider surrendering part of their sovereignty to a supranational authority, the European Community.

In Eastern Europe, nationalism was adopted in conscious imitation of the West European model, and like its archetype led to terrible conflict. But the Eastern model also gave rise to a plethora of states, none truly national and none secure enough to cooperate voluntarily in a regional grouping. Thus, while Western and even the long-backward countries of Mediterranean Europe now seem to be entering a post-nationalist stage, Eastern Europe still suffers the hatreds and conflicts—and stagnation—of fervent nationalism.

Establishing the East European states was in itself an impressive achievement. Indeed, it may be the most spectacular political change on the European continent in the last one hundred and fifty years, and the only one to prove lasting.

Consider that in 1848 no truly independent nation-state existed in the region, and that even in 1914 only a handful of minor ones existed, all in the Balkans. Since then, East European states have multiplied rapidly. Only three, the small Baltic lands of Estonia, Latvia, and Lithuania, have been reabsorbed by a great power, and even this reabsorption is forcefully being challenged today. The other states have endured, albeit within shifting political boundaries and with ever-changing ethnic compositions. Unfortunately, these states have been a source of infinite political trouble for the countries that created them, for their ethnic minorities, and for one other. Why?

Nationalism in Theory and Practice

Nineteenth-century apostles of nationalism assumed that the nation-state would bring happiness to its citizens and harmony among sovereign nations. Ethnic minorities, these Romantic ideologues believed (if they acknowledged the existence of such minorities), would willingly be incorporated into the new and progressive nation-states, which would guarantee the legal equality of all citizens and the right of minorities to speak their own languages—although preferably only in the privacy of their own homes. The assimilation of minorities into the state-building nation was expected to be merely a question of time, something to be achieved not by force but by shining example. This development was thought to be inevitable.

As it turned out, however, every East European nation-state was a multinational construct, created with little or no regard for the rights and aspirations of the substantial ethnic groups inside its borders. This had not happened in the West. In France, for example, ethnic minorities such as the Bretons were a small portion of the population and economically weak, allowing the Jacobins and every French regime thereafter to transform that country with relatively little violence into a genuine nation-state.

In Eastern Europe, the ethnic situation was infinitely more complex, with the result that every purported nation-state negated the principle of self-determination, even while basing its legitimacy on that principle. Only during and after World War II, as we shall see, did East European countries succeed in becoming genuine nation-states. This, however, was at the price either of drastically redrawn political boundaries, as in the case of Poland; or of previously unimaginable violence, in the form of forced assimilation and mass expulsion, as in Czechoslovakia.

Bitter Memories

The multinational composition of East European nation-states, and the brutality characterizing the transformation of some into genuine nation-states, have together prevented these countries from engaging in concerted action to resist the encroachments of neighboring great powers. The bitter memory of past persecution and some very real present-day injustices toward surviving ethnic minorities still remain the chief obstacle to united action. In fact, some minorities, such as the two million Hungarians in Romania, perceive a Soviet military presence, and even Soviet armed intervention, as a lesser threat to their cultural survival than the oppressive policies of the Romanian government. On the other hand, fear of Hungarian (and Bulgarian) territorial revisionism may be the major reason why Romanians endured the nearly unendurable tyranny of the Ceausescu regime for so long.

Conditions Are Less Volatile

The restlessness of nationalities in Eastern Europe may resemble that of a century ago, but conditions now are less volatile. In 1914, there was no Poland, Czechoslovakia, independent Hungary or Yugoslavia as such. Bulgaria and Romania existed, but with boundaries in flux. Today boundaries are relatively stable and nations, although dominated until 1989 by communism, have a long record of existence.

Gaddis Smith, *Los Angeles Times*, December 10, 1989.

East European nationalists have tended to promote extremes of intolerance and violence, in part because they were forced to create their nation-states against overwhelming odds, combatting multinational empires as well as neighbors and ethnic minorities. In part too, ideologists of nationalism analyzed their nation's history in terms of spectacular upheavals, cruel defeats, and great national victories, rather than in terms of patient effort and gradual development. East European historians tended to present the past of their respective nations as alternating between lengthy periods of sterile stagnation and brief outbursts of concerted national action. It was as if the nation had leapfrogged from one great upheaval to the next, and between these heroic events there was either nothing or, at best, a conscious preparation for the next manifestation of national vitality. . . .

These Romantic views of history (including the Marxist-Leninist view) ignored much: for example, that national revolutions were aggravating national tensions rather than lessening them, resulting in increased oppression of ethnic minorities, rather than liberation. Nationalists also ignored the grave setbacks to cultural achievement that often resulted from their revolutions. Yet this was a striking aspect of nationalist victories: the more radical the upheaval, the more conservative, and even reactionary, the final outcome. The reason is that cities in Eastern Europe, had traditionally been inhabited by alien elements. So, with only some exaggeration, it may be said that nationalist revolutions were marked by xenophobia and a revolt of the countryside against an alien, Westernized, culturally more developed city. In consequence, 100 to 150 years ago, most inhabitants of East European cities spoke languages and represented cultures other than those of the rural population; today no such differences exist between country and city. . . .

The Persistence of Nationalism

Over the last 150 years, liberal, conservative, democratic, authoritarian, fascist, and Bolshevik regimes have held sway in Eastern Europe. But all of these East European regimes as well as their professed ideologies have proven ephemeral. What has been permanent is nationalism. Not one of these regimes, except perhaps the outright fascist governments, advocated the annihilation or even the oppression of ethnic minorities, but every regime consistently pursued a policy of assimilating such minorities and, when given the opportunity, of oppressing them as well. These policies have wrought an irreversible change in Eastern Europe.

It is difficult to tell whether East European national animosities are as grave today as they were in earlier times. The conflict between Hungary and Romania over the question of the Magyar minority in Transylvania is so acute that Hungarian leaders have been hinting at a direct Romanian military threat. Relations between Turkey and Bulgaria over the Bulgarian Turks are equally bad, and both Bulgarians and Yugoslavs talk openly of the "unresolved Macedonian question." The Albanian government directs an unrelenting propaganda campaign against Yugoslavia for its alleged oppression of the Albanians in the Kosovo region. Romanians have not forgotten the Soviet seizure of Northern Bukovina and Bessarabia, and in the latter province, Moldavian (i.e. Romanian) nationalism is about to reassert itself most forcefully.

Yet, in some respects the situation is better. It may be cruel, but twentieth-century changes in Eastern Europe's ethnic mosaic could hold the key to better relations among the East European states. Though achieved at the price of incredible suffering, these changes have drastically diminished the number of ethnic minorities, and thus also the number of potential conflicts.

Important Differences

The world just before World War I was multipolar, reverberating with demands of ethnic and nationality groups, politically fluid, unpredictable and heavily armed. The Untied States was not a world power. Russia was in decline. Japan was ascending. In Europe all eyes were on Germany—strong, assertive, ready to pursue national interest at the expense of others.

These conditions erupted in August, 1914, into the hideous European war from which, in turn, flowed the Bolshevik Revolution, the rise of Hitler, World War II and so much of the Death, suffering and waste of the 20th Century. If one believes that history repeats itself and that conditions similar to pre-1914 are about to reappear, then the outlook for the 21st Century is hardly happy.

But the differences between two eras are greater than the similarities. We have cause for hope—though not for euphoria.

Gaddis Smith, *Los Angeles Times*, December 10, 1989.

There have also been other, much more positive developments. In recent decades, the peoples of Eastern Europe have proven repeatedly that their hearts and minds are with the West and Western liberalism. Polish Solidarity, now more or less in power, has categorically condemned any form of nationalist bias and has offered a friendly hand to the country's remaining if minuscule Ukrainian, German, and Jewish minorities. Solidarity preaches only as much patriotism as is indispensable for asserting national independence and for resisting potential Soviet/Russian imperialism.

The same can be said about the political groupings in Hungary, including the reform Communists who have brought about a revolution from above. The Transylvanian dilemma remains, of course, but no matter what the Romanian government has been saying, no political party in Hungary has, as yet, advocated territorial revisionism. All East European reformers regard Western Europe and the United States as their political and economic model.

Solidarity

The drastic redrawing of the ethnic map in Eastern Europe might explain, along with the fading memory of past injustices and the collapse of the Marxist-Leninist experiment, why peoples of the region recently seemed capable of solidarity beyond petty nationalism. It may just be possible that the peoples of Eastern Europe can transcend historical patterns and find harmony among themselves. If so, they may come to form, at last, a happier region.

"The Alliance has . . . major roles to play in the emerging European and world orders."

European Unification Requires NATO's Assistance

Manfred Wörner

In 1949 the United States, Canada, and several Western European countries created the North Atlantic Treaty Organization (NATO) to counter Soviet influence in Europe. Now that the Soviet Union no longer dominates its former Eastern European satellites, many people debate NATO's future role. In the following viewpoint, Manfred Wörner, the secretary general of NATO and chairman of the North Atlantic council, argues that NATO should take on the political role of working toward a united, stable Europe. Before becoming NATO secretary general in 1988, Wörner was the West German minister of defense. He also served in the West German parliament, the Bundestag, for more than twenty years.

As you read, consider the following questions:

1. What is the Allies' vision for Europe that the author outlines?
2. How should NATO help the economies of Eastern Europe, according to Wörner?
3. What role does the author believe the United States and Canada should have in NATO?

Manfred Wörner, "A Time of Accelerating Change," *NATO Review*, no. 6, December 1989. Reprinted with permission.

The values that will shape world affairs in the coming decade will be our Western democratic values. To the extent that we can strengthen the Atlantic partnership—based on a firm North American and a firm European pillar—we will be better able to be a force for democracy, cooperation and prosperity throughout the world. . . .

Two Major Roles

Clearly the Alliance has two major roles to play in the emerging European and world orders that will result from the historic move to democracy and freedom.

It must continue to function as the guarantor of stability, which the dynamic acceleration of events makes all the more necessary. Change requires security: otherwise it can prove fragile and can suddenly be reversed. The developments we have seen thus far in Central and Eastern Europe have been dramatic, and up to now peaceful—with the exception of Romania. Yet we cannot exclude the possibility of setbacks and reversals when we stop to consider the pressures that long-overdue reform has released. A mutually reassuring East-West security structure, of which NATO [North Atlantic Treaty Organization] is the foundation, helps to ensure that change remains peaceful and there is no temptation to resort to force to resolve domestic problems. A secure Alliance defence is consequently not an impediment to necessary change. Indeed, it is a precondition for it. Naturally, in the new European environment that is unfolding, arms control, cooperation and interdependence will play a prominent role in ensuring security and defusing tensions. Nevertheless, a secure defence is, in the final analysis, the only watertight insurance policy.

That said, the scope and pace of recent developments in Central and Eastern Europe give NATO a much greater opportunity to give expression to its political role as a motor and promoter of peaceful change. The upheavals that we see throughout this region have been caused by the failure of Communism. As time has passed, it has created only mounting disillusionment at its incapacity to address, let alone solve, the problems of modern, post-industrial societies. The peoples of Central and Eastern Europe are no longer prepared to be second-class citizens when they know that it is the system, not they, which is to blame for their difficulties.

They are calling and organizing for change with a force that has made it only too clear to Communist regimes that freedom, democracy and real economic opportunities can no longer be suppressed. Moreover, these peoples are considerably assisted in their reformist efforts by the fact that there is an alternative socioeconomic model close by: our successful and dynamic

Western system. It is the success of the Alliance that has created the stable basis for our economic prosperity. It is our political culture and economic market system that are now inspiring the peoples of Central and Eastern Europe and fuelling the acceleration of history.

Vision for Europe

For forty years, the Allies have never wavered in their vision for a future Europe. The onward march of events has now brought the realisation of this vision immeasurably closer:

• a Europe of open borders with all peoples exercising their inherent right of self-determination, including for Germany;

• a Europe of democratic states, respecting human rights, the rule of law, and holding free elections at regular intervals;

• a European security system with less weapons, forces that are structured only for defensive purposes and where military affairs would increasingly be subject to monitoring, transparency and cooperation;

• a new transatlantic partnership based on a strong, prosperous North America and a strong, prosperous Europe;

• a new global order of cooperation in which East and West would work increasingly together to address the global problems—hunger, drugs, the environment and terrorism—that are now decisive for stability and world peace in this new decade.

An Important Security Mission

The political strategy for NATO that we agreed upon in May 1989 makes the promotion of greater freedom in the East a basic element of Alliance policy. Accordingly, NATO should promote human rights, democracy, and reform within Eastern countries as the best means of encouraging reconciliation among the countries of Eastern and Western Europe.

Although this is a time of great hope—and it is—we must not blur the distinction between promising expectations and present realities. We must remain constant with NATO's traditional security mission. I pledge today that the United States will maintain significant military forces in Europe as long as our allies desire our presence as part of a common defense effort. The U.S. will remain a European power. And that means that the United States will stay engaged in the future of Europe and in our common defense.

George Bush, News Conference at NATO Headquarters, December 4, 1989.

This changing international landscape defines the future tasks of our Alliance. . . .

First, we must do our utmost to help ensure the success of

democratic reform and economic restructuring in Central and Eastern Europe. The reforming states have come far indeed in such a short space of time, but they lack at the moment both a solid, experienced leadership and a coherent political concept. It is hardly surprising that they look to us not only for a model to guide their efforts but also for concrete assistance. If it is true that the hard decisions to break with the past can only be taken by these governments themselves, it is also true that even the boldest reform stands little chance of success without our support. During 1989, Alliance governments have followed the overarching policy guidelines set out in our Summit Declaration of May, 1989 and put together a variety of initiatives both to reward and to stimulate reform. Hungary and Poland have been the main beneficiaries so far, but the Allies have stated unambiguously that such help will be extended to all those other nations that follow the Polish and Hungarian example.

A Future of Instability

Naturally, success or failure in the East is not for us to preordain. We can prime the pump with such things as food aid or debt rescheduling; we can use arms control to create a more stable international environment, and we can give—as indeed we are giving—all kinds of technical assistance and trade facilitation. Yet we must not allow our hopes to cloud the real facts of the situation. Economic conditions throughout the old Communist world are extremely serious. Popular expectations of the new governments are rising, but not unfortunately the ability of the governments throughout this region to fulfil those expectations. We are in for a long period of political instability.

Yet reform will not fail through a lack of Western responsiveness. Short-term aid will help to win a breathing space for reform to take root, but the Alliance is also aware that it cannot be a substitute for a long-term effort to build a political architecture in Europe that will establish new structures of cooperation. Thus the Foreign Ministers committed themselves to build on the Conference on Cooperation and Security in Europe (CSCE), not only to ensure that the Helsinki commitments on human rights are universally observed, which unfortunately is still far from being the case, but also to activate certain provisions of the Helsinki Final Act, such as Basket Two on economic cooperation, which have been relatively underused. . . .

The Alliance is not, of course, trying to impose our Western model on the states of Central and Eastern Europe. They must decide on their own route to democracy and the form of their association with their neighbours. The Alliance equally will not be the only institution involved. The European Community is playing an important political role, as its aid to Poland and

Hungary, its economic agreements with several Warsaw Pact countries, and its coordination of the relief programme of the Group of 24 industrial countries, abundantly testify. The Alliance has welcomed the results of the European Community's Strasbourg Summit which gave great impetus to the process of European integration. This process is strengthening NATO through the establishment of a genuinely self-standing European pillar; and it is enabling the Community to shoulder its full share of common alliance responsibilities. The European Community will need to balance two essential goals: to further deepen the cooperation among its members while extending a hand towards the newly emerging democracies in the East. Rather than attempt to settle on a fixed mould now for our concept of a future European architecture, we would no doubt be better served by a flexible form of East-West cooperation that can be adapted to changing circumstances.

A Period of Historic Change

There have been increasingly dramatic advances towards greater democracy and freedom in most Eastern European countries. Through the long dreamt-of opening of borders, the free flow of people and ideas between the countries of East and West has accelerated. There has been widening recognition of the need for reform towards more market-oriented economies and individual choice. . . .

These events challenge us to look at our own responsibilities as Allies. The Atlantic Alliance serves as the essential basis for the security of our peoples. By keeping the peace for the past four decades it has enabled our peoples to prosper in freedom, and democratic values to serve as an inspiration for other societies. In the midst of change and uncertainty, the Alliance remains a reliable guarantor of peace. It will provide an indispensable foundation of stability, security and co-operation for the Europe of the future.

North Atlantic Council Ministerial Communique, December 1989.

The second future role of the Alliance will be to create a new European security system to ensure that military power can no longer perpetuate unjust political divisions and intimidate neighbouring states. A major element of such a system will be an agreement on Conventional Forces in Europe resulting from the Vienna negotiations. . . .

A CFE agreement will lead to a situation of much greater military balance in Europe that will enable both sides to move closer to a central Alliance objective: maximum deterrence with minimum weapons. That is the very definition of stability. The way will thus be more open for the Warsaw Pact to be restructured so as to be more like NATO: an organisation that is no longer an instrument of ideology, that fully respects national sovereignty, that allows its members to participate equally in collective decision-making, and that is entirely defensive both in overt intention and in structural capabilities. NATO is ultimately seeking to convert a confrontational relationship into a cooperative one. . . .

To eyes conditioned by long years of Cold War, all this may well appear a dream, but I have good reason to be optimistic. The Soviet Union has expressed an interest in changing the Warsaw Pact into a more political organisation; and, in any case, is being pushed more and more in this direction by its Warsaw Pact allies. Moreover, the Soviet Union has changed its attitude towards NATO. Instead of arguing for its dismantlement, the recent statements from Moscow welcome NATO as a crucial element of stability.

Sharing the Defense Burden

A key related task of the Alliance in the next decade will be to conduct the build-down of forces that will hopefully result from a CFE agreement, in an orderly fashion. We will need to take burden-sharing into account, so that there is an equitable shouldering of the roles, risks and responsibilities of our common defence. This will require the continued presence of Canadian and US forces in Europe, even though there is nothing sacrosanct about precise figures. Their number can be reduced as arms control and political developments permit. Yet all allies have emphasized that force reductions must be within the context of arms control and subject to prior consultation within the Alliance. Security and stability will not be served by overhasty and unilateral force reductions that might impair our defences before arms control agreements have been concluded.

It is important that Canada and the US are firmly committed politically to Europe. Any other formula could lead to instability. The Soviet Union under any future scenario will remain a considerable nuclear and conventional power which Western Europeans cannot balance by themselves. Both President George Bush and Prime Minister Brian Mulroney made unambiguously clear at our NATO Summit in December 1988 that their nations will remain committed to NATO and to European security. This is also, I believe, in the interest of the Soviet Union, as the Soviets themselves are increasingly acknowledging.

The third and final task of the Alliance will be to enhance the Atlantic role, as the success of our Western democratic values urges us to do. The achievement of this Alliance in securing democracy and economic prosperity within post-war Europe is not a formula that we either can or should reserve jealously for ourselves. In the 1990s, not simply Central and Eastern Europe but indeed all nations of the world will be looking to us for inspiration and practical solutions to their pressing problems. In forty years, our Alliance has not only given us security. It has equally created among its members a common political culture that rules out serious friction between them and allows for differences of interest to be resolved smoothly. . . .

An Appealing Model

NATO may have its greatest and most lasting effect on the pattern of change by demonstrating to the nations of the East a fundamentally different approach to security. NATO's four decades offer a vision of cooperation, not coercion; of open borders, not iron curtains. The reconciliation of ancient enemies, which has taken place under the umbrella of NATO's collective security, offers the nations of Eastern Europe an appealing model of international relations.

Whatever security relationships the governments of Eastern Europe choose. NATO will continue to provide Western governments the optimal instrument to coordinate their efforts at defense and arms control and to build a durable European order of peace. The interests of Eastern Europe and, indeed, the interests of the Soviet Union will be served by the maintenance of a vigorous North Atlantic Treaty Organization.

James A. Baker III, Speech to the Berlin Press Club, December 12, 1989.

An enhanced Atlantic relationship will thus be a vital extension of an Alliance that has already been for forty years the major policy-making instrument bringing Europe and North America together in a union of destiny. Their combined ingenuity and resources certainly enable both continents to achieve a power of influence and attraction that neither, working in isolation, could command. An ultimate goal will be gradually to draw the Soviet Union into this new global order of cooperation—both because it shares many of the problems of the West in its own society as well as legitimate security concerns that lie beyond its borders.

The Alliance has not merely responded to change, it has done much to stimulate it. It thus remains, as we fast approach the 21st century, not only the best means of preserving democratic values but also of promoting them.

"The 'threat' that created NATO and sustained it for 40 years has disappeared."

European Unification Makes NATO Obsolete

Malcolm Chalmers

In the following viewpoint, Malcolm Chalmers argues that the North Atlantic Treaty Organization (NATO) is preventing European unification. Chalmers contends that NATO has out-lived its role of containing Soviet influence. He suggests replacing NATO and the Warsaw Pact with a new organization that would include both Western and Eastern European countries. Chalmers is a research fellow at Stanford University's Center for International Security and Arms Control. He also lectures in the Department of Peace Studies at Bradford University in Great Britain.

As you read, consider the following questions:

1. How has the issue of German unification affected the question of NATO's future, according to the author?
2. While Chalmers advocates dismantling NATO, he believes some sort of a European security organization is necessary. Why?
3. What steps does Chalmers argue are leading to European unification?

Malcolm Chalmers, "Beyond the Alliance System," *World Policy Journal*, vol. vii, no. 2, Spring 1990. Reprinted with permission.

The North Atlantic Treaty Organization (NATO) was formed in 1949 because the nations of Western Europe feared that, without a counterweight to Soviet military power, they would soon suffer the fate of their East European neighbors. More than 40 years later, the tables have turned. The countries of Eastern Europe are dismantling the structures of one-party rule and central planning and replacing them with Western-style political and economic institutions.

These changes have been accompanied by a transformation in the security policies of the Warsaw Pact countries. Until recently, the main role of the armed forces of Eastern Europe was to defend Soviet-style socialism against internal and external (i.e. Western) threats. Now this role has ended. Despite the apparent continuation of the communist monopoly on organized violence, democratic governments are being elected throughout the region, and the likelihood of a reassertion of communist control is diminishing rapidly as a result of structural reforms and personnel changes. The "threat" that created NATO and sustained it for 40 years has disappeared.

In their initial reactions to events in Eastern Europe, Western governments have hastened to reaffirm their belief that NATO should continue in existence. After centuries of intermittent warfare and mutual mistrust, the nations of Western Europe have enjoyed 45 years of peace and increasing prosperity, in large part because of their willingness to bury their differences and join in collective organizations. Thus, many West Europeans argue that NATO should not be abandoned unless something better is found to take its place.

An Untenable Position

As the consequences of the democratization of Eastern Europe unfold, however, this position will face a mounting problem of credibility. It is already evident that accelerated progress in arms control negotiations, while necessary and welcome, will not be enough to ensure Europe's security in the new conditions. Rather, the most basic questions about the organization and role of military force in a post-Cold War Europe will need to be addressed. Such a fundamental reassessment will be difficult for many in the West. While there have been lively debates on security policy within NATO's "expert" community and in the public arena, the focus of these debates has generally been limited to military-technical questions such as the role of nuclear weapons, the viability of defensive defense, and the desirability of particular arms control proposals. The most basic feature of the European security system—the bipolar division of Europe—has been largely taken as a given.

Military-technical questions should continue, of course, to be the focus of sustained analysis and debate. Yet if such discussions rest on the assumption of bipolarity, they are likely to become quickly irrelevant. In the 1980s, it was reasonable to assume that the two opposing blocs would continue to exist for the foreseeable future. Today, those concerned with the formulation of European security policy can no longer afford the certainty of that assumption. . . .

Matt Wuerker. Reprinted with permission.

The countries of Europe have been grappling with the problems posed by the imminent prospect of German unification. It is already apparent that it would be completely artificial for a united Germany to have two armies, each belonging to a different alliance; one government implies one army. What is far less clear is how a single German army could be accommodated within the existing bipolar alliance system. Each of the main proposals for solving the "German question" on its own—unity within NATO and neutrality—risks triggering a series of new tensions and conflicts, something Europe can ill afford at this time.

As a consequence, many European leaders have come to accept the need for an entirely new approach, in which German unity would be a catalyst for the creation of a wider European peace order. An all-European security organization, which would replace NATO and the Warsaw Pact and function within the framework already established by the CSCE (Conference on Security and Cooperation in Europe) process, could be an important component of that order.

German Unity: The Security Implications

By January 1990, it was clear that the opening of the intra-German border was making German unity a fait accompli faster than anybody—including the Germans themselves—had thought possible. . . . West German Foreign Minister Hans-Dietrich Genscher argued that "anybody who wants to extend NATO's borders to the Oder and Neisse shuts the door on a united Germany." Shortly thereafter, he obtained U.S. agreement to a proposal that would combine NATO membership for the new German state with a special status for the area that is now the GDR [German Democratic Republic]. . . . The Genscher plan . . . cannot be considered a permanent solution. Essentially, the plan is an attempt to freeze, as far as possible, the military status quo in Central Europe. . . .

Given the current preoccupation of its leadership with internal problems, the Soviet Union may well decide it does not have the ability to prevent Germany from joining NATO. The lack of a veto, however, should not be equated with lack of interest, since the Soviet Union is clearly concerned that such a development could be detrimental to its security. If NATO expands while the Warsaw Pact collapses, the result will be a continuation of the bloc system on terms much less favorable to the Soviet Union. A NATO commitment not to deploy its forces in the eastern part of Germany will be of little military value once there are no Soviet forces left in the GDR to block them if NATO leaders change their mind. Soviet leaders continue to have considerable apprehension about the future role of a united Germany. Such concerns will hardly be assuaged if the Soviet Union is left alone facing a powerful and cohesive NATO.

Yet this is just what seems likely to happen once German unity within NATO is achieved. It is still conceivable that Poland and Czechoslovakia will breathe new life into the Warsaw Pact in order to deter Germany from pressing long-standing territorial claims. But if Germany is willing to accept a lasting settlement of these claims, it seems much more likely that unification will also bring about, in rather short order, the breakup of the Warsaw Pact. With East European political and economic aspirations so clearly focused on Western Europe, and with the Soviet Union preoccupied internally, one country after another is likely to leave the Pact altogether.

If no new pan-European security arrangements are available

when this occurs, each country will seek whatever combination of permanent and ad hoc arrangements it feels can best protect its security. In recognition of the diminishing cohesion of the Warsaw Pact, there has already been discussion of Austrian-Hungarian, Greek-Bulgarian, and Polish-Czech alignments. The possibility of a revival of the Austro-Hungarian empire in a new guise—perhaps even including parts of Yugoslavia—has also been raised. The potential for instability under such a patchwork of alliances and security arrangements would be considerable. For discontented nationalities might seize the opportunity presented by the disintegration of old security structures (and perhaps even of some of the existing states) to press longstanding territorial claims. . . .

Getting the Soviets Out of Eastern Europe

In 1947 critics like diplomat George F. Kennan and commentator Walter Lippmann questioned both the necessity and desirability of a formal alliance between the United States and Western Europe. . . . They believed the proposed North Atlantic Treaty would militarize containment and result (in Kennan's words) in an "irrevocable congealment of the division of Europe" into Soviet and American spheres of influence. If the Soviets were in Eastern Europe because of concerns about national security, the way to get them out, Kennan and Lippmann believed, was to alleviate those fears by negotiating a simultaneous withdrawal of U.S. and Soviet forces from Central Europe. . . .

The realist critique of NATO advanced by the Kennan-Lippmann school retains its intellectual freshness forty years later.

Christopher Layne, in *NATO at 40: Confronting a Changing World*, 1990.

The preservation of NATO as envisioned by the Genscher plan will affect more than Europe's military security. It will also pose a threat to the political and economic integration of the two halves of Europe, the success of which is probably more important than the security structures themselves in determining whether or not Europe can live at peace in the future.

The Efforts of the European Community

The main vehicle for European integration today is the European Community. The passage of the Single European Act in 1987 ushered in a series of measures designed to deepen the process of economic and political integration within the Community. As a result, decisions in more and more areas of economic and social policy are taken at a European level, usually by majority vote.

Many steps along the road to West European unity have already been taken. Free movement of labor is allowed, and the last obstacles to the free movement of capital are now being dismantled. Soon all border controls among France, Germany and the Benelux countries (Belgium, the Netherlands, and Luxembourg) are to be removed. Plans for a single European currency, and with it a European central bank and a harmonization of fiscal and monetary policy, are far advanced. And, perhaps most important for the durability of the whole exercise, power is to be increasingly transferred to the directly elected European Parliament. This will lend the Community's decisions a democratic legitimacy entirely separate from that of individual national governments.

The very dynamism of the European Community, which stands in stark contrast to the impending collapse of Comecon (the Council for Mutual Economic Assistance), its twin in the East, is not only making membership increasingly attractive to nonaligned European countries such as Austria and Sweden. It is also encouraging the new democracies in Eastern Europe to seek membership. Even the Soviet Union is aware that it is only through close links with the Community that it can achieve its goal of entering the "common European home."

Obstacles to the East Bloc

A continued division of Europe into NATO and non-NATO countries would inhibit such an expansion of the European Community. Already it is clear that one of the main objections to the enlargement of the Community relates to its implications for security policy. The Single European Act called upon Community members to "jointly implement a European foreign policy," and some members see cooperation on defense and security issues as the logical extension of this mandate. They have argued for strengthening West European military cooperation within NATO (the "European pillar"), perhaps by giving the EC a more direct say in security policy. Their case is likely to be strengthened by the withdrawal of most of the U.S. forces now on the continent, as well as by the perceived need to bind the German army firmly into European structures.

Yet increased cooperation on security policy only makes sense if membership in the European Community is limited to countries that are also members of the same alliance. In current circumstances, it would act to cement the division of Europe at a time when the Iron Curtain is dissolving before our very eyes. Requiring West European institutions, and perhaps the Community itself, to take on a more prominent role in formulating NATO policy would effectively exclude such countries as Austria, Hungary, and Poland from membership in those institutions. . . .

Increasingly, Europeans are coming to realize that a satisfactory solution to the "German problem" must go beyond the proposals for German neutrality or NATO membership. Each of these models of German unity is flawed by posing the problem in a purely national, rather than European, framework. Instead, it is now being argued, German unification should be linked to a wider European settlement, in which NATO and the Warsaw Pact would be replaced by an entirely new all-European security system. By creating an organization that I shall christen the European Security Organization (ESO), the division of Europe could be ended in a way that would preserve those aspects of current collective security arrangements that remain useful. . . .

Challenges to the Alliances

Careful though many East-bloc activists have been not to explicitly repudiate the Warsaw Pact, the USSR faces mounting de facto challenges to its domination of Eastern Europe. As the vision of an independent Eastern Europe takes on flesh, the role of NATO necessarily comes into question. In fact, the end of the Cold War division of Europe into competing military blocs suddenly seems like a possibility that must be seriously considered.

Joanne Landy, *Peace & Democracy News*, Winter/Spring 1990.

One possibility would be simply to expand NATO to include all the members of the Warsaw Pact and all of Europe's nonaligned countries. Yet an expanded NATO would not only be difficult for the Soviet Union to accept, but would also be less likely to fit easily into existing patterns of pan-European cooperation. Thus, while the new European security organization may take over many of NATO's roles, methods, and assets, it should preferably be an entirely new entity in order to emphasize the substantial differences that would exist between the old and new security regimes.

The most likely institutional framework for a new pan-European security organization is the 35-nation Conference on Security and Cooperation in Europe (CSCE), which includes all the European states except Albania, together with the United States and Canada. Created by the Helsinki Final Act of 1975, CSCE has embodied the Western view that issues of human rights are closely related to security issues, while providing the Soviet Union with guarantees that postwar European borders would not be changed. Many in the United States have viewed CSCE, especially in the early years of its existence, largely as a forum for exposing the bankruptcy of the Soviet system. Yet for European governments, CSCE has always had a larger significance, since it symbolized the hope that one day the division of Europe could be ended. . . .

One of the lessons drawn, on both sides, from 40 years of Cold War is that East and West now have many security interests in common. In the 1960s and 1970s, the two alliances were already aware that they were doomed to "peaceful coexistence" even as they pursued conflicting ideological objectives. Now the area of agreement—on human rights, on economic policy, on the resolution of disputes—is widening, while the possibilities for discord are dwindling. Increasingly, the two alliances are viewed by both sides as "partners" rather than rivals. By creating an all-European security organization, it will be possible to extend the principle of collective security, as it has been practiced within NATO, to all of Europe. As U.S. Secretary of State James Baker has argued, "NATO may have its greatest and most lasting effect on the pattern of change by demonstrating to the nations of the East a fundamentally different approach to security. . . . The reconciliation of ancient enemies, which has taken place under the umbrella of NATO's collective security, offers the nations of Eastern Europe an appealing model of international relations.". . .

A Realistic Goal

Because of the transformation of the political situation in Europe, what [once] seemed absurd and unthinkable has become possible and even necessary. Today, the creation of an all-European security organization is not only a realistic goal, but also the best way to ensure a secure and prosperous future for Europe as the bipolar division of the continent comes to an end.

The potential benefits of such an organization are great indeed. ESO would institutionalize common security, and thus help prevent a new division of Europe into two or three opposing blocs. It would safeguard the new democracies of Eastern Europe against Soviet intervention, and thus formalize the end of the Brezhnev Doctrine. And it would address the concern, felt perhaps most strongly in the Soviet Union, that German unity could lead, in time, to military expansionism. The creation of ESO would also remove one of the major obstacles to the full political and economic integration of Eastern Europe—and possibly even portions of the Soviet Union—into the European Community. It would thus help to accelerate a process that is at least as crucial to a lasting European peace as the security structures themselves.

Recognizing Deceptive Arguments

People who feel strongly about an issue use many techniques to persuade others to agree with them. Some of these techniques appeal to the intellect, some to the emotions. Many of them distract the reader or listener from the real issues.

A few common examples of argumentation tactics are listed below. Most of them can be used either to advance an argument in an honest, reasonable way or to deceive or distract from the real issues. It is important for a critical reader to recognize these tactics in order to rationally evaluate an author's ideas.

   a. *bandwagon*—the idea that "everybody" does this or believes this

   b. *categorical statements*—stating something in a way that implies there can be no argument or disagreement on the issue

   c. *deductive reasoning*—the idea that since *a* and *b* are true, *c* is also true, although there may be no connection between *a* and *c*

   d. *patriotic appeal*—using national pride to sway the reader into favoring a position which flatters one's own culture

   e. *personal attack*—criticizing an opponent *personally* instead of rationally debating his or her ideas

   f. *slanter*—trying to persuade through inflammatory and exaggerated language instead of through reason

   g. *testimonial*—quoting or paraphrasing an authority or celebrity to support one's own viewpoint

The following activity can help you sharpen your skills in recognizing deceptive reasoning. The statements below are derived from the viewpoints in this chapter. *Beside each one, mark the letter of the type of deceptive appeal being used. More than one type of tactic may be applicable. If you believe the statement is not any of the listed appeals, write N.*

1. I lived in a country ruled by the most conservative Communist government in Europe. Our society slumbered beneath the pall of a totalitarian system.

2. Although African decolonization was relatively peaceful, later, the Africans changed and the continent erupted in violence. We should not be surprised if the same thing happens in Eastern Europe.

3. The West has a long tradition of democracy. Compare this to politically backwards Eastern Europe. No wonder the Communists easily took over in the late 1940s.

4. Slobodan Milosevic, the Serbian nationalist, is a plump, baby-faced man who has shown himself to be ruthless, cruel, and out for power, no matter what the cost.

5. All East European reformers regard Western Europe and the United States as their political model.

6. The intense hatred between ethnic groups in Hungary, Romania, Bulgaria, and Yugoslavia will consume Eastern Europe.

7. Esteemed people like George Kennan and Walter Lippmann criticized NATO when it was first formed. Their critique is still relevant—NATO should be disbanded.

8. The values that will shape world affairs in the coming decade will be our Western democratic values.

9. All political scientists agree that Eastern Europeans will not bond with their Western European counterparts and form a stable Europe.

10. The ego and hubris of Zbigniew Brzezinski is evident in his drawing up of blueprints for other nations' economies.

11. Most esteemed American economists are leery of a cohesive, economically coordinated Europe.

12. Not simply Central and Eastern Europe, but in fact all nations of the world will be looking to us for inspiration and solutions to their problems.

13. The Philippines suffered from totalitarian rule. Eastern Europe also suffered from totalitarian rule. Since the Philippines were able to establish democracy, so the nations of Eastern Europe will become democratic.

14. Europeans, like our great American forefathers, will toss off the yoke of tyranny and create a united, democratic Europe.

15. The fact that the former Warsaw Pact nations have made much progress is proven by the fact that even conservative politicians like Margaret Thatcher and George Bush applaud their policies.

Periodical Bibliography

The following articles have been selected to supplement the diverse views presented in this chapter.

Alex Alexiev — "Tale of Two Emerging Eastern Europes," *Los Angeles Times*, July 8, 1990.

Timothy Garton Ash — "Entering the 'Age of Deals,'" *World Press Review*, March 1990.

James A. Baker III — "A New Europe, A New Atlanticism," *Vital Speeches of the Day*, January 15, 1990.

Zbigniew Brzezinski — "Post-Communist Nationalism," *Foreign Affairs*, Winter 1989/1990.

R.V. Burks — "Eastern Europe: Two Case Studies in Nationalism," *The World & I*, December 1989.

George Bush — "President's Remarks to Residents, Leiden," *Department of State Bulletin*, September 1989.

Milovan Djilas — "National Identity/Individual Integrity," *Society*, May/June 1990.

Mikhail Gorbachev — "The International Community and Change: A Common European Home," *Vital Speeches of the Day*, September 15, 1989.

Otto von Habsburg, interviewed by George Urban — "After Communism, What?" *Crisis*, April 1990.

Vaclav Havel — "The Great Moral Stake of the Moment," *Newsweek*, January 15, 1990.

International Affairs — "The Future of Europe: A Debate," April 1990.

George F. Kennan — "On the Soviet Union and Eastern Europe," *New York Review of Books*, March 3, 1990.

Lucy Komisar — "East Erupts, NATO Squirms," *Bulletin of the Atomic Scientists*, January/February 1990.

Adam Michnik — "After the Revolution," *The New Republic*, July 2, 1990.

Czeslaw Milosz — "From the East: A Sense of Responsibility," *New Perspective Quarterly*, Spring 1990.

Radek Sikorski — "Nobody Here but Us Democrats," *National Review*, September 29, 1989.

Jill Smolowe — "This New House," *Time*, May 14, 1990.

Milan Svec — "East European Divides," *Foreign Policy*, Winter 1989/1990.

Chronology of Events

1848	Karl Marx and Friedrich Engels publish the *Communist Manifesto*.
1908	Austria-Hungary annexes the Balkan state Bosnia-Herzegovina, breeding discontent among Serbian nationalists.
1914	Hostile to Austrian rule in Bosnia-Herzegovina, members of the Serbian Black Hand Society assassinate Austrian Archduke Francis Ferdinand, precipitating World War I. The conflict is waged primarily between the "Central Powers," Germany and Austria-Hungary, and the "Allies," France, Britain, and Russia.
1917	Communism is established in Russia when the Bolsheviks, led by Vladimir Lenin, depose Czar Nicholas II. One year later, they rename themselves Communists.
1918	World War I ends when the Allies impose the Treaty of Versailles on Germany. Under the treaty, Germany loses its colonies and is forced to reduce its armed forces and pay heavy reparations. The treaty also establishes the League of Nations, an international organization to resolve conflicts peacefully.
1921	Amidst economic impoverishment and social chaos after the war, the National Socialist Germany Worker's (Nazi) Party forms in Germany. Nazi Party leader Adolf Hitler wins mass public support by promising to restore the greatness of the German state.
1933	Adolf Hitler becomes chancellor of Germany.
1933-1945	Exploiting anti-Semitic feeling under the pretext of preserving German nationalism, Hitler begins passing discriminatory measures against Jews. The persecution culminates in the killing of six million Jews during the Holocaust.
1938	Hitler forcibly annexes Austria. At the Munich Conference in September, an agreement is signed by Germany, Britain, France, and Italy. The pact forces Czechoslovakia to cede its Sudetenland (western border) to Nazi Germany in an effort to avert war. The treaty proves ineffectual when Hitler takes over the rest of Czechoslovakia the following March.
1939	In August, Soviet leader Josef Stalin and Hitler sign a non-aggression pact. On September 1, Germany invades Poland. Britain and France demand that Germany withdraw. World War II begins two days later when both nations declare war on Germany.
1940	The USSR invades Poland. The same year, the USSR invades the Baltic states of Latvia, Estonia, and

Lithuania, absorbing the states as Russian republics.

1941 Hitler negates the non-aggression pact and orders his troops to invade the USSR.

1942-1943 Germany loses initiative when troops are severely defeated by the Russians at Stalingrad.

1944-1945 Soviet troops overthrow the pro-Nazi regime in Romania.

After routing German troops, the Soviets occupy Poland, Hungary, and most of Czechoslovakia. Poland's borders are shifted westward.

1945 As Russian troops move into Berlin, Hitler commits suicide. Nazi Germany surrenders unconditionally.

U.S. President Franklin Roosevelt, British Prime Minister Winston Churchill, and Soviet leader Stalin participate in the Yalta Conference. The conference plans for treatment of post-war Germany, including its division into four zones of occupation. The former capital of Berlin is similarly divided.

Potsdam Conference makes plans for disarming and fostering democratic government in defeated Germany. U.S. President Harry Truman, Churchill, and Stalin participate.

United Nations is established to create peace and international cooperation between the nations of the world.

Yugoslavian president Josip Tito proclaims Yugoslavia a federal republic of six states and establishes a Communist government.

1946 Churchill denounces the self-imposed isolation and aggression of Communist countries in his Iron Curtain speech in Fulton, Missouri.

Bulgaria, which had entered World War II on Germany's side, is defeated by the Soviet Union. Soviet-type Communist rule is established.

1947 U.S. announces containment doctrine, pledging aid to countries resisting Communist takeover.

Communists gain control of Hungary's government.

In Romania, King Michael is forced to give up the throne, and Communists proclaim Romania a people's republic.

Soviets announce the formation of Cominform, an organization to create unity among the Communist parties of the USSR, its Eastern European satellites, and France and Italy.

U.S. initiates Marshall Plan to aid war-ravaged Europe. The Soviet bloc nations refuse assistance.

1948 Czechoslovakia is integrated fully into the Soviet bloc after Communists seize control of the government.

Yugoslavian President Tito, pursuing an independent national communism, defects from the Soviet bloc.

Yugoslavia is expelled from the Cominform.

Soviets set up land blockade of West Berlin (the American, British, and French zones of occupation) to force Western garrisons out of the city. Allies respond by flying crucial supplies into West Berlin. Blockade is lifted after six months.

1949 North Atlantic Treaty Organization (NATO) is founded to establish military cooperation between the U.S., Canada, and ten West European nations.

The German zones occupied by the three Western powers merge into the Federal Republic of Germany (West Germany). The Russian zone emerges as the German Democratic Republic (East Germany). The former capital, Berlin, is similarly divided between East and West.

With Russian troops occupying Hungary, the Hungarian government adopts a Soviet-type constitution. The same year, Roman Catholic Cardinal Joseph Mindszenty is accused of treason for his opposition to communism. He is sentenced to life imprisonment.

Russia establishes the Council for Mutual Economic Assistance (COMECON) to promote cooperation be tween the countries of Communist Europe.

1953 Polish Cardinal Stefan Wyszynski is arrested for denouncing the persecution of the Church by the Communist government.

East Berlin workers demonstrate against austere living conditions. Soviet tanks suppress the uprising.

Imre Nagy becomes premier of Hungary.

1955 Warsaw Pact, a military alliance between the USSR and Eastern Europe, is established.

1956 Opposition to Soviet domination leads to uprising in Poznan, Poland. Communist leader Wladyslaw Gomulka, who is opposed to heavy Russian domination, becomes first secretary of the Polish Communist Party. Cardinal Wyszynski is released.

Hungarians revolt against Soviet domination and President Nagy criticizes Soviet presence. Cardinal Mindszenty is freed. Soviet troops suppress the uprising, killing at least seven thousand demonstrators. Nagy is deposed and the Russians set up a government headed by Janos Kadar, secretary of the Hungarian Communist Party.

Soviet leader Nikita Khrushchev disbands Cominform.

At the twentieth Congress of the Soviet Communist Party, Khrushchev denounces Stalin for establishing a cult of personality and for creating a reign of terror.

1958 Khrushchev becomes premier of the USSR. He plans a series of economic reforms to improve the Soviet economy.

The Soviets secretly try and execute Nagy.

1961	East Germany builds a wall between East and West Berlin to stem the flow of refugees to the West.
	Opposed to Khrushchev's policies of de--Stalinization, Albania breaks diplomatic relations with the USSR and aligns itself with Communist China.
1962	Khrushchev authorizes the placement of missiles in Cuba, precipitating the Cuban missile crisis. The crisis is defused when U.S. president John Kennedy orders a naval blockade of Cuba.
1964	Khrushchev is ousted from Soviet leadership. Leonid Brezhnev becomes first secretary of the Party.
1965	Nicolae Ceausescu becomes head of Romania's Communist Party.
1968	Invading Soviet and other Warsaw Pact troops crush an uprising in Czechoslovakia. Reformist Party leader Alexander Dubcek, who attempted to liberalize and democratize communism during the "Prague Spring," is ousted. The pro-Soviet Gustav Husak is put in power. The uprising prompts massive purges of dissidents in the Communist Party.
1969	Willy Brandt is elected chancellor by the parliament of West Germany. His *Ostpolitik* (Eastern policy) marks a major step toward improved relations with East Europe.
1972	U.S. president Richard Nixon and Premier Brezhnev meet in Moscow and agree to a period of "detente," a policy of easing tensions between the U.S. and the USSR.
1974	U.S. Congress passes Jackson-Vanik amendment, barring trade with communist countries not permitting free emigration.
	Ceausescu becomes president of Romania.
1975	The U.S., Canada, the USSR, and thirty-five European countries sign the Helsinki accords, a document outlining a policy of peaceful relations in Europe. Its provisions call for nations to respect human rights and recognize European borders.
1976-1977	Playwright Vaclav Havel helps publish the declaration of Charter 77, an association of citizens monitoring human rights in Czechoslovakia. Havel and others who signed the Charter are arrested.
1979	East-West detente ends when Soviets invade Afghanistan to support Marxist regime.
1980	In Poland, a mass strike at the shipyards in Gdansk gives rise to the independent labor union Solidarity. Led by Lech Walesa, the union demands more workers' control of industry.
1981	Polish leader Wojciech Jaruzelski imposes martial law, suspends Solidarity, and arrests many of its leaders, including Walesa.
1985	Mikhail Gorbachev becomes general secretary of the Soviet Communist Party. Concerned with the stagna-

tion of the Soviet economy, he initiates policies of *glasnost* (openness) and *perestroika* (change).

1987   In Romania, an austerity program to pay off foreign debt results in strikes, protests, and an economic slide.

East German leader Erich Honecker rejects Gorbachev's reform program.

1989

January   In Hungary, party leaders promise the creation of independent political parties. The 1956 rebellion is commemorated.

In Poland, the Communist Party agrees to the gradual legalization of the banned trade union Solidarity.

February   Polish government and Solidarity begin roundtable discussions to plan Poland's future. Violence erupts when police attempt to subdue anticommunist demonstrations in Warsaw and other cities.

Ethnic unrest between Albanians and Serbians results in riots throughout Kosova, Yugoslavia. Over thirty demonstrators are killed when armed forces subdue the rioting.

Hungarian Communist Party sanctions creation of independent political parties.

March   Ceausescu's policies stir opposition. Romania is marked with shortages in food, fuel, and other consumer goods. Ethnic Hungarians in Romania accuse Ceausescu of "cultural genocide" when he announces plans to demolish ethnic Hungarian villages to make room for modern housing. Petitioners circulate a letter stating that Romania's political and economic ills are a direct result of Ceausescu's mismanagement.

In Budapest, 75,000 demonstrators listen to speeches calling for free elections and the removal of Soviet troops from Hungary. Authorities do not interfere.

April   Roundtable discussions in Poland result in the legalization of Solidarity.

May   Hungary becomes the first Soviet bloc nation to open a border with the West when it demolishes a barbed-wire barrier on the Austrian border. On May 8, Hungarians oust Communist leader Janos Kadar from office, replacing him with centrist Karoly Grosz. Politburo members Imre Pozsgay and Reszo Nyers and other reformist Communists urge radical economic change and talks with opposition groups.

Bulgarian leader Todor Zhivkov admits that problems exist with collective farming and plans alternative means of food production.

Poland becomes the first Soviet bloc nation to grant legal status to the Roman Catholic Church.

June   Over 250,000 Hungarians attend a reburial ceremony honoring Imre Nagy, hero of the 1956 uprising. Regime and opposition groups begin talks, and on

June 24, reformist Reszo Nyers is chosen to lead new four-party collective presidency.

In the first free election in over forty years, Solidarity candidates win decisively in Poland's parliamentary elections.

British and Soviets protest the erection of a barbed-wire fence in Romania. The fence, built by the government to contain fleeing Romanians, is dismantled.

July

U.S. president George Bush visits Eastern Europe to encourage democratic reforms and the adoption of free-market principles.

In a speech to the Council of Europe, Gorbachev tells reporters that he will not intervene in the political affairs of Hungary and Poland.

August

Agreement reached in Poland for Solidarity to take control of social and economic policy, while Communists will be in control of the military. Senior Solidarity leader Tadeusz Mazowiecki becomes the new non-communist prime minister.

In West Germany, hundreds of East German refugees seek political asylum.

In Prague, three thousand demonstrate on anniversary of the 1968 invasion of Czechoslovakia by the Soviet Union. Turkey closes its border with Bulgaria to stem the exodus of over 300,000 Turks fleeing political and economic unrest.

September

Hungary opens its borders with Austria. Diplomatic crisis is created when thousands of East Germans travel to Hungary and head for West Germany via Austria. In Leipzig, East Germany, over ten thousand demonstrators march for democracy. Pro-democracy group New Forum holds founding conference.

In Poland, Parliament announces a new coalition cabinet that includes only four Communists.

October

Talks between Bonn and East Berlin result in over 17,000 East Germans fleeing to West Germany from Poland and Czechoslovakia. Street protests break out when the East German government tries to stem the exodus by closing its border with Czechoslovakia. More than 100,000 demonstrate for reform in Leipzig. As political unrest escalates, Honecker is forced to resign and is replaced by Communist Politburo member Egon Krenz, who promises sweeping political changes. Plans are announced to ease travel restrictions.

Communist Party in Hungary renounces Leninism and changes its name to the Socialist Party. Constitution is rewritten to allow for a multi-party political system and free elections. Hungarians proclaim a new Hungarian Republic.

Pro-democracy demonstrations break out in Czechoslovakia, as ten thousand protest the arrest of playwright Vaclav Havel and other dissidents.

273

After public protests in Bulgaria, Communist leader Todor Zhivkov promises reforms.

November

Over 500,000 participate in pro-democracy demonstrations in East Berlin. As more East German refugees flee to the West, the Politburo resigns. On November 9, the East German government allows free travel and the Berlin Wall is opened.

West German Chancellor Helmut Kohl outlines steps towards the unification of East and West Germany.

In Bulgaria, Zhivkov is removed after thirty-five years in power. His replacement, Petar T. Mladenov, appears more open to reform. A week later, over fifty thousand Bulgarians demonstrate for democracy.

Discontent grows in Czechoslovakia as demonstrations escalate. Opposition groups coalesce into the Civic Forum, led by dissident Vaclav Havel. When over 350,000 demonstrate in Prague, party leaders resign. Karel Urbanek replaces Milos Jakes. On November 27, a two-hour general strike brings the nation to standstill. The party pledges to give up absolute power absolute power and travel restrictions are eased.

Communist Party in Romania rejects reforms and unanimously reelects Ceausescu.

Hungarians hold first free vote for Parliament since 1945 and delay presidential election until Spring 1990.

December

In East Germany, Parliament ends Communist Party's constitutional monopoly on power. Communist Party Chairman Krenz quits, along with other members of the Politburo. Non-communist reformer Manfred Gerlach is named acting head of state. Former leader Honecker is arrested on corruption charges. Communist Party agrees to free elections in 1990.

In Czechoslovakia, 150,000 rally to protest new cabinet of sixteen Communists and five non-communists. After talks held on forming new government, Communist president Gustav Husak quits. Dubcek is elected speaker of parliament. Havel is elected president.

Romanian troops fire on and kill thousands of people protesting in Timisoara. In Bucharest, when security forces open fire on demonstrators, the army joins the rebellion to overthrow the government. On December 24, secret trial and execution of Ceausescu and his wife is announced. Ion Iliescu is named interim president, and free elections are set for 1990.

1990

January

Government in Poland implements plan to restructure economy into a market-oriented one. Walesa demands the removal of Soviet troops by the end of 1990.

Hungarian officials call for removal of fifty thousand

Soviet troops by the end of 1991.

In Bulgaria, deposed Communist leader Zhivkov undergoes house arrest.

February

The Communist government resigns in Bulgaria. Reformer Andrei Lukanov becomes premier.

Gorbachev tells Soviet citizens that it is time to end the dogmatism of Communist ideology and recognize the validity of other political parties.

Czechoslovak government and Moscow officials agree to withdraw Soviet troops from Czechoslovakia.

March

The Baltic Republic of Lithuania declares independence from the Soviet Union on the grounds that secession is a constitutional right. Gorbachev threatens to impose economic blockades if the republic does not rescind its declaration.

East German elections result in the victory of a three-party alliance headed by the Christian Democratic Union. The CDU, led by Lothar de Maiziere, is the sister party of the conservative West German Christian Democratic Party.

Polish government says that it will demand financial reparations from Germany to atone for the poor treatment of Poles during World War II.

In the first free elections in forty-five years, Hungarians vote for anticommunist opposition parties.

April

In East Germany, thousands of demonstrators demand investigations to verify whether any members of the new Parliament ever worked for the secret police.

A vote in Prague results in the renaming of Czechoslovakia to The Czech and Slovak Federative Republic. The new name is intended to ease ethnic tensions.

May

Latvia declares independence from the Soviet Union. The three Baltic republics of Lithuania, Estonia, and Latvia forge a political alliance and proclaim solidarity in their quest for independence.

Albanian government announces a series of liberalizing laws, such as freedom to travel abroad and the right to practice religion.

In Romania, former Communist Party official Ion Iliescu and the National Salvation Front win in national elections.

July

The economies of East and West Germany merge into one. East Germany adopts the deutsch mark and a free market.

Gorbachev reverses his opposition to a unified Germany becoming a member of NATO. The path is cleared for free elections by the end of 1990.

Organizations to Contact

The editors have compiled the following list of organizations that are concerned with the issues debated in this book. All of them have publications or information available for interested readers. The descriptions are derived from materials provided by the organizations. This list was compiled upon the date of publication. Names and phone numbers of organizations are subject to change.

American Committee on U.S.-Soviet Relations
109 11th St. SE
Washington, DC 20003
(202) 546-1700

The Committee includes members of the academic and business communities, former ambassadors, labor leaders, and public interest spokespersons. It believes tensions between East and West can be reduced by strategic arms agreements, trade, and scientific and cultural exchanges. The Committee publishes *Soviet Outlook*, as well as books and occasional papers, including, "Abstract, Stability, and Change in International Relations," "Gorbachev and the Ghost of Stalin: History and the Politics of Reform," and "The Nineteenth Conference of the CPSU: Politics and Policy."

American Enterprise Institute for Public Policy Research (AEI)
1150 17th St. NW
Washington, DC 20036
(202) 862-5800

AEI is a conservative research and education organization which aims to provide an analysis of national and international issues. It promotes the spread of democracy and a strong military to protect against the spread of totalitarianism. It publishes the monthly *AEI Economist,* the bimonthly *Public Opinion*, and various books on topics concerning Eastern Europe and the Soviet Union.

American Friends Service Committee
1501 Cherry St.
Philadelphia, PA 19102-1479
(215) 241-7000

The Committee is a Quaker organization that seeks to apply its religious beliefs in peace and pacifism to better international relations. Its purpose is to relieve human suffering and to find new approaches to world peace through nonviolent social change. The Committee's publications include *The Dialogue Continues with the Soviets, Sorting Out the Soviets,* and *Beyond Detente: Soviet Foreign Policy and U.S. Options.*

American Jewish Committee
2027 Massachusetts Ave. NW
Washington, DC 20036
(202) 265-2000

The Committee serves as a distribution center for materials that concern the American Jewish community. It publishes the monthly journal *Commentary*, the bimonthly *Present Tense*, and has published a statement on German unification that counsels caution and asks that East Germans recognize their responsibility for the Holocaust. The Committee also publishes a booklet entitled *The Jewish Stake in German Unification.*

Amnesty International (AI)
322 Eighth Ave.
New York, NY 10001
(212) 807-8400

Amnesty International monitors human rights throughout the world, including Eastern Europe. AI is independent of any government, political faction, ideology, economic interest, or religious creed. It publishes an annual report on human rights conditions worldwide and is closely watching the evolving conditions in Eastern Europe.

The Brookings Institution
1775 Massachusetts Ave. NW
Washington, DC 20036-2188
(202) 797-6000

The Institution, founded in 1927, is a liberal think tank that conducts research and education in economics, government, and foreign policy. It publishes the quarterly *Brookings Review*, the biannual *Brookings Papers on Economic Activity*, and various books, including *Eroding Empire: Western Relations with Eastern Europe* and *War and Peace in the Nuclear Age*.

Cardinal Mindszenty Foundation
PO Box 11321
St. Louis, MO 63105
(314) 991-9490

This anticommunist organization was founded in 1958 to conduct education and research activities concerning Communist objectives, tactics, and propaganda. The Foundation publishes the monthly *Mindszenty Report*.

CATO Institute
224 Second St. SE
Washington, DC 20003
(202) 546-0200

The Institute is a libertarian public policy research foundation dedicated to increasing foreign policy debate. Several of its publications have addressed superpower relations and Eastern Europe. It publishes the bimonthly *Policy Report* and the triennial *CATO Journal*.

Christian Anti-Communism Crusade (CACC)
PO Box 890
Long Beach, CA 90801
(213) 437-0941

The Crusade, founded in 1953, sponsors anti-subversive seminars "to inform Americans of the philosophy, morality, organization, techniques, and strategy of communism and associated forces." CACC publishes a free, semimonthly newsletter called the *Christian Anti-Communism Crusade*. Its brochures include *Why I Am Against Communism, Why Communism Kills*, and *You Can't Trust the Communists*.

Communist Party of the U.S.A.
235 W. 23rd St., 7th Floor
New York, NY 10011
(212) 989-4994

The Communist Party works to create a socialist society. While it supports perestroika and glasnost in the Soviet Union, the Party views the changes in Eastern

Europe with apprehension. It publishes the *People's Daily World* newspaper and the monthly *Political Affairs.*

The Conservative Caucus Foundation, Inc.
450 Maple Ave. E
Vienna, VA 22180
(703) 281-4108

The Caucus conducts research and analysis on foreign policy and promotes a conservative view of international relations. It publishes *The Howard Phillips Issues and Strategies Bulletin* weekly, as well as speeches on Soviet-American relations and Eastern Europe, such as the *Statement of Howard Phillips Before the Advisory Committee of the Export-Import Bank of the United States.*

Council for the Defense of Freedom
1275 K St. NW, Suite 1160
Washington, DC 20005
(202) 789-4294

The Council opposes communism and argues that the U.S. must actively support the democratic movements in Eastern Europe. Its weekly paper, *The Washington Inquirer*, covers international relations and the Soviets' role in European affairs. It also publishes a monthly *Bulletin* and numerous monographs.

The Council on Foreign Relations
58 E. 68th St.
New York, NY 10021
(212) 734-0400

The Council is a group of individuals with specialized knowledge of and interest in foreign affairs. It was formed to study the international aspects of American political, economic, and strategic problems. It publishes *Foreign Affairs*, a renowned foreign policy journal which covers a broad range of topics, including the political upheaval in Eastern Europe.

Czechoslovak National Council of America
2137 S. Lombard Ave., Room 202
Cicero, IL 60650
(312) 656-1117

The Council, founded in 1918, seeks to promote assistance to Czechoslovakia and advance the interests of Americans of Czech and Slovak descent. It publishes *The American Bulletin* bimonthly.

Embassy of the People's Republic of Bulgaria
1621 22nd St. NW
Washington, DC 20008
(202) 387-7969

The Embassy publishes the booklets *Party Renewal for Building a Democratic Socialist Society in Bulgaria* and *The Change.* It also makes available the books *Bulgaria: A Brief Historical Outline* and *Developing Countries: Disarmament and Development.*

Embassy of the Polish People's Republic
2640 16th St. NW
Washington, DC 20009
(202) 234-3800

The Embassy produces booklets, press releases, and position papers on current political topics concerning Poland, including *President Richard von Weizsäcker's Visit to Poland.*

The Fellowship of Reconciliation
Box 271
Nyack, NY 10960
(914) 358-4601

The Fellowship was founded during World War I by one German and one British citizen who wished to promote the Christian values of peace and avoidance of conflict. Its monthly magazine, *Fellowship,* has covered the changes in Eastern Europe.

Foreign Policy Association
729 Seventh Ave.
New York, NY 10019
(212) 764-4050

The Association, founded in 1918, provides information designed to help citizens participate in foreign policy decisions. It does not take sides. It publishes pamphlets entitled *Headline Series* and the annual report *Great Decisions,* the 1990 edition of which discusses the changes in Eastern Europe.

German American National Congress
4740 N. Western Ave.
Chicago, IL 60625-2097
(312) 275-1100

The Congress represents the interests of Americans of German heritage. It supports German reunification. Its monthly newsletter, *Der Deutsch-Amerikaner,* often deals with topics concerning Eastern Europe, especially the reunification of Germany.

German Information Center
950 Third Ave.
New York, NY 10022
(212) 888-9840

The Center serves as the information branch of the German Embassy. It provides information about German unification, politics, and economics to students, teachers, politicians, and journalists. The Center publishes the newsletter *This Week in Germany* and the periodic *Statements & Speeches.*

Human Rights Watch
1522 K St. NW, Suite 910
Washington, DC 20005
(202) 371-6592

The Watch monitors human rights abuses in nations around the world and identifies those responsible for repression, torture, and terror. It is composed of five committees, including Helsinki Watch, which publishes the newsletter *News from Helsinki Watch.* It also publishes various books, including *From Below: Independent Peace and Environmental Movements in Eastern Europe and the USSR, Toward Civil Society: Independent Initiatives in Czechoslovakia,* and *Violation of the Helsinki Accords: Poland.*

Institute for Democracy in Eastern Europe (IDEE)
48 E. 21st St.
New York, NY 10010
(212) 677-5801

IDEE works to promote independent social movements in Eastern Europe. It publishes a bimonthly magazine, *Uncaptive Minds,* which often contains articles by leading anticommunist dissidents.

Institute for Democratic Socialism
15 Dutch St., Suite 500
New York, NY 10038-3705
(212) 962-0390

The Institute works for social justice and a socialist society. It publishes the pamphlets *Toward a Democratic Socialism: Theory, Strategy, and Vision* and *The Question of Socialism.*

Institute for Policy Studies (IPS)
1601 Connecticut Ave. NW, Suite 500
Washington, DC 20009
(202) 234-9382

The Institute's program on national security provides both factual analysis and critiques of foreign and military policy. Its goal has been to unravel the myths of the Cold War and provide a more balanced view of international relations. The Institute publishes several books relating to the Soviets' role in Eastern Europe, including *The Rise and Fall of the Soviet Threat* and *Soviet Policy in the Arc of Crisis.*

NSDAP Ausland—und Aufbauorganisation
PO Box 6414
Lincoln, NE 68506

NSDAP is the American branch of the underground National Socialist ("Nazi") movement in Germany. Its goals are to legalize the Nazi party in Germany, reunify Germany under Nazi leadership, and encourage the alliance of white nations to promote the survival and advancement of the white race. It supplies propaganda materials and publishes the bimonthly newspaper *The New Order.*

Pilsudski Institute of America
381 Park Ave. S
New York, NY 10016
(212) 683-4342

The Institute researches the modern history of Poland from 1865 to the present. It maintains a library of over fourteen thousand books. The Institute has published press releases on the reunification of Germany. It also publishes the yearly *Independence* and *Bulletin.*

The Revolutionary Communist Party USA
3449 N. Sheffield Ave.
Chicago, IL 60657
(312) 528-5353

The Party advocates the overthrow of capitalism in favor of a new economic system that does not exploit workers. It believes that the revolutions in Eastern Europe mark an end to Stalinism, not communism. The Party publishes the newspaper *Revolutionary Worker.*

Soviet Embassy
Information Department
1706 18th St. NW
Washington, DC 20009
(202) 232-6020

The Soviet Embassy distributes speeches by Mikhail Gorbachev and other Soviet leaders on many topics, including Eastern Europe, German unification, Soviet reforms, and the Soviet economy. Among the publications available are *Yearbook USSR*, a review of events; *Soviet Life*, a monthly photo-feature magazine; *USSR, 100 Questions and Answers*; and *News and Views from the Soviet Union*, its series of press releases.

The Spartacist League

PO Box 1377 GPO
New York, NY 10116
(212) 732-7860

The League follows the teachings of Leon Trotsky. It opposes the trend toward capitalism in Eastern Europe and the Soviet Union. The League publishes the biweekly, working-class newspaper, *Workers Vanguard*, the semiannual theoretical journal *Spartacist*, and the annual *Women in Revolution*.

World Policy Institute (WPI)

777 United Nations Plaza
New York, NY 10017
(212) 490-0010

Founded in 1948, the Institute formulates alternatives to war, social injustice, and ecological damage. WPI has followed the changes in Eastern Europe through its publications, which include *Alternatives: A Journal of World Policy*, the quarterly *Bulletin of Peace Proposals*, and *World Policy Journal*, as well as various books and position papers.

World Socialist Party

295 Huntington Ave.
Boston, MA 02115
(617) 535-2510

The Party fights for common ownership and democratic control of industry, free access to all goods and services, and abolishing the monetary system. It publishes the monthly *Socialist Standard* and the quarterly *World Socialist Review*.

Bibliography of Books

John Ardagh — *Germany and the Germans.* New York: Harper & Row, 1987.

Timothy Garton Ash — *The Magic Lantern: The Revolution of '89.* New York: Random House, 1990.

Colin Barker — *Festival of the Oppressed: Solidarity, Reform, and Revolution in Poland.* Chicago: Bookmarks, 1982.

Dan Bar-On — *Legacy of Silence: Encounters with Children of the Third Reich.* Cambridge, MA: Harvard University Press, 1989.

Willy Brandt — *The Ordeal of Coexistence.* Cambridge, MA: Harvard University Press, 1963.

Zbigniew Brzezinski — *The Grand Failure: The Birth and Death of Communism in the Twentieth Century.* New York: Charles Scribner's Sons, 1989.

James F. Byrnes — *Speaking Frankly.* New York: Harper & Brothers, 1947.

David Cannadine, ed. — *Blood, Toil, Tears, and Sweat: The Speeches of Winston Churchill.* Boston: Houghton Mifflin Company, 1989.

Ted Galen Carpenter, ed. — *Collective Defense or Strategic Independence?* Lexington, MA: Lexington Books, 1989.

Ted Galen Carpenter, ed. — *NATO at 40: Confronting a Changing World.* Lexington, MA: Lexington Books, 1990.

Lucius D. Clay — *Decision in Germany.* Garden City, NY: Doubleday & Company, 1950.

Tony Cliff — *State Capitalism in Russia*, 5th ed. Chicago: Bookmarks, 1990.

David S. Collier and Kurt Glaser, eds. — *Berlin and the Future of Eastern Europe.* Chicago: Henry Regnery Company, 1963.

Bogdan Denitch — *The End of the Cold War.* Minneapolis: University of Minnesota Press, 1990.

John Feffer — *Beyond Detente.* New York: Hill and Wang, 1990.

G.E.R. Gedye — *Betrayal in Central Europe.* New York: Harper & Brothers, 1939.

German Democratic Republic — *Documentation on the Question of West Berlin.* Berlin: Ministry of Foreign Affairs, 1964.

Trond Gilberg — *Nationalism and Communism in Romania.* Boulder, CO: Westview Press, 1990.

Chris Harman — *Class Struggles in Eastern Europe 1945-1983.* Chicago: Bookmarks, 1984.

Vaclav Havel — *Disturbing the Peace.* New York: Alfred A. Knopf, 1990.

Vaclav Havel — *The Power of the Powerless.* Armonk, NY: M.E. Sharpe, 1985.

Michael T. Kaufman — *Mad Dreams, Saving Graces.* New York: Random House, 1989.

Gerhard Kirchhoff, ed. — *Views of Berlin.* Boston: Birkhauser, 1989.

Jeane J. Kirkpatrick   *The Withering Away of the Totalitarian State . . . and Other Surprises.* Washington, DC: American Enterprise Institute, 1990.

Walter Lafeber   *America, Russia, and the Cold War 1945-1975,* 3rd ed. New York: John Wiley and Sons, 1976.

Maciej Lopinski, Marcin Moskit, and Mariusz Wilk   *Konspira: Solidarity Underground.* Berkeley: University of California Press, 1990.

Arno J. Mayer   *Why Did the Heavens Not Darken? The "Final Solution" in History.* New York: Pantheon Books, 1988.

Roy Medvedev   *Let History Judge: The Origins and Consequences of Stalinism,* rev. ed. New York: Columbia University Press, 1989.

Judith Miller   *One by One: Facing the Holocaust.* New York: Simon & Schuster, 1990.

Victor Nee and David Stark   *Remaking the Economic Institutions of Socialism.* Stanford, CA: Stanford University Press, 1989.

Ellen Frankel Paul, ed.   *Totalitarianism at the Crossroads.* New Brunswick, NJ: Transaction Books, 1990.

Stevan K. Pavlowitch   *The Improbable Survivor: Yugoslavia and Its Problems.* Columbus: Ohio State University Press, 1988.

Xavier Richet   *The Hungarian Model: Markets and Planning in a Socialist Economy.* Cambridge, UK: Cambridge University Press, 1989.

Jacques Rupnik   *The Other Europe.* New York: Pantheon Books, 1988.

Paul S. Sharp, ed.   *Problems of Balkan Security: Southeastern Europe in the 1990s.* Washington, DC: The Wilson Center Press, 1990.

Peter Sichrovsky   *Born Guilty: Children of Nazi Families.* New York: Basic Books, 1988.

Soviet Ministry of Foreign Affairs   *Stalin's Correspondence with Churchill, Attlee, Roosevelt, and Truman.* New York: E.P. Dutton & Co., 1958.

Jan Stransky   *East Wind over Prague.* New York: Random House, 1950.

Peter Van Ness, ed.   *Market Reforms in Socialist Societies.* London: Lynne Rienmer, 1989.

Lech Walesa   *A Path of Hope.* London: Collins Harvill, 1987.

Richard von Weizsäcker   *A Voice from Germany.* New York: Weidenfeld and Nicholson, 1985.

Thomas P. Whitney, ed.   *Khrushchev Speaks: Selected Speeches, Articles, and Press Conferences.* Ann Arbor: University of Michigan Press, 1963.

Peter Wyden   *Wall: The Inside Story of Divided Berlin.* New York: Simon & Schuster, 1989.

Daniel Yergin   *Shattered Peace: The Origins of the Cold War,* rev. ed. New York: Penguin Books, 1990.

Index

284